A GRIM ALMANAC OF

SOMERSET

A GRIM ALMANAC OF

SOMERSET

NICOLA SLY

ALSO BY THE AUTHOR

A Ghostly Almanac of Devon & Cornwall
A Grim Almanac of Dorset
Bristol Murders
Cornish Murders (with John Van der Kiste)
Dorset Murders
Hampshire Murders
Herefordshire Murders
More Bristol Murders
More Cornish Murders (with John Van der Kiste)
More Hampshire Murders
More Somerset Murders
Murder by Poison: A Casebook of Historic British Murders
Oxfordshire Murders
Shropshire Murders
Somerset Murders (with John Van der Kiste)
West Country Murders (with John Van der Kiste)
Wiltshire Murders
Worcestershire Murders

First published 2010

The History Press
The Mill, Brimscombe Port
Stroud, Gloucestershire, GL5 2QG
www.thehistorypress.co.uk

British Library Cataloguing in Publication Data.
A catalogue record for this book is available from the British Library.

ISBN 978 0 7524 5814 4

Typesetting and origination by The History Press
Printed in Great Britain

CONTENTS

INTRODUCTION & ACKNOWLEDGEMENTS

Having previously written about historical murders in Somerset, my research at the time unearthed dozens of accidents and incidents, strange or macabre deaths, assaults, manslaughters and other dreadful deeds, which are collected here in a day-by-day catalogue of ghastly tales from the county.

They are sourced entirely from the contemporary newspapers listed in the bibliography at the rear of the book, the study of which has proved a fascinating exercise. However, much as today, not everything was reported accurately and there were often discrepancies between publications – one particular crime featured was apparently committed on five different dates and there are frequent variations in names and spelling.

As always, there are a number of people to be thanked for their help in compiling this book, not least my husband, Richard, whose input was invaluable, as ever. I would also like to thank Matilda Richards, Beth Amphlett and Jennifer Briancourt, my editors at The History Press, for allowing me to delve into the darker side of Somerset's history and for their assistance in bringing the results to print.

Every effort has been made to clear copyright; however, my apologies to anyone I may have inadvertently missed. I can assure you that it was not deliberate but an oversight on my part.

Nicola Sly, 2010

JANUARY

The Market Place, Wells. (Author's collection)

1 JANUARY

1831 Hugh Callow and Richard Judd were watchmen, forerunners of the modern police constable. Although officially on duty in the city of Wells, both had been celebrating the New Year and they had each drunk a quart of ale and a large glass of gin.

At about two o'clock in the morning they spotted Mr Frankland, one of the vicars attached to Wells Cathedral, and asked him for a Christmas box. Frankland gave both Judd and Callow a shilling and suggested that they might like to join him at his home for a drink. Once at Frankland's house, Callow and Judd each drank a further five glasses of gin. As they were leaving, a companion of Frankland's gave Judd a shilling to buy yet another drink.

Judd went home, leaving Callow still on duty. He had not walked more than a few yards when Callow called him back and asked for the shilling that he had just been given. Judd replied that it had been intended to buy them both a drink, which he would do the next day. He then continued walking but, almost immediately, something hit him hard on the back of the head. He remembered nothing more until he woke up in bed the next day.

Wondering why he had not arrived home, Judd's wife had gone to look for him and found him lying insensible on the pavement, covered in blood. Callow lay on the ground about twenty yards away, also insensible, and the bloodstained watchman's staff lay midway between them. Mrs Judd called for help and both men were taken home and put to bed.

Charged with having maliciously wounded Judd with intent to murder him, Callow stood trial before Mr Justice Park at the Somerset Assizes. Having listened to the evidence, Park directed the jury to acquit Callow, stating that although there was little doubt that Callow had struck Judd, both men had been in such a state of 'beastly intoxication' that they had knocked each other about until they had little sense remaining. The judge then went on to censure them for drinking on duty, saving his most damning comments for Mr

Vicar's Close,
Wells. (Author's
collection)

Frankland, who, according to the judge, had given them such large quantities of spirituous liquor as to render them unfit for the duty for which they had been appointed.

2 JANUARY

1889 Nine-year-old Emma Jane Davies went to collect milk from the farm at Yeobridge where her father worked as a labourer. When she didn't return, her mother and brother set out to look for her and tragically, at one o'clock in the afternoon, they found her body lying in a roadside field. Emma was covered in cuts and gashes. There was a cord tied around her neck and her throat had been cut, almost decapitating her. The metal milk-can that she was carrying had evidently been used as a weapon to beat her about the head and a bloody razor was found nearby.

Twenty-three-year-old farm labourer Samuel Reylands (or Rylands) was arrested two days later and charged with her murder. Tried before Mr Justice Wills at the Somerset Assizes, he protested his innocence but, although much of the evidence against him was circumstantial, after deliberating for an hour and a half, the jury returned to pronounce him 'Guilty'.

Before his execution on 13 March 1889, Reylands made a full confession to the murder in a letter to his parents.

3 JANUARY

1913 Frank Atyeo shot his estranged wife, Alice, and the couple's twenty-month-old daughter, Frances, at North Petherton, before turning the gun he had purchased earlier that morning on himself.

The couple had separated in November 1912, after Atyeo was convicted for drunkenness and assaulting a police officer. He was fined for both offences but stubbornly refused to pay and was sentenced to twenty-one days' imprisonment. As a result, he lost his job as a farm labourer and the tied cottage that went with it, forcing Alice to live with her mother and stepfather.

The scene of the tragedy in North Petherton, 1913. (Mike Clapperton)

Frank Atyeo.

While in prison, Atyeo fretted constantly about Alice. He falsely believed that information she had given to the police had led to his imprisonment, and he also thought that she had been unfaithful to him and was carrying another man's child. On his release from prison, he soon found another job, although it did not come with accommodation. Thus Alice and Frances remained with Alice's mother, although Atyeo visited them regularly and gave Alice money for maintenance. Alice's family believed that the couple were considering reconciliation at the time of her death.

At the inquest into the three deaths, the jury returned a verdict of wilful murder against Frank Atyeo for the seemingly motiveless killings of his wife and daughter. They could find no evidence that he was of unsound mind at the time and so recorded a verdict of *felo de se* – malicious self-murder – on Frank Atyeo.

4 JANUARY   **1868**   In the early hours of the morning, Taunton and the surrounding villages were shaken by an earthquake. The tremor started with a loud bang, followed by several seconds of trembling and undulation, which shook beds and rattled crockery. The sentry on guard at the barracks in Taunton was later to say that he found it difficult to keep his feet during the quake, which was felt for a radius of several miles. The noise was variously described as sounding like 'an express train passing at full speed', 'an explosion' and 'somebody throwing down an iron chest'.

5 JANUARY   **1885**   Eighty-year-old Mrs Sarah Gregory attended an 'old folks' tea' at Yeovil. When she didn't return home as expected, her family began to search her anticipated route. She was found dead early the following morning in a roadside ditch near Yeovil. It was later determined that she had frozen to death.

6 JANUARY   **1865**   Shoemaker Henry Fisher and his wife, Mary, had always lived happily together during their fourteen years of marriage. Henry was known as a sober, hard-working man but he became severely depressed, convinced that the introduction of machine sewing to shoemaking would lead to his poverty and destitution. He communicated his fears to his wife and the couple decided that they would rather die than live in want.

On 6 January, Fisher's stepdaughter called at their house in Northampton Street, Bath, but there was no reply to her knocks at the door. She returned three times that day but it wasn't until the evening that Fisher finally opened the door, looking weak and ill. He told his stepdaughter that he and Mary had each taken eleven spoonfuls of laudanum by mutual consent and that Mary was dying.

Mary lingered until the following morning before succumbing to the poison, while Henry, who had vomited up most of the laudanum, recovered to be charged with the wilful murder of his wife. He appeared at the Spring Assizes in Taunton before Mr Justice Crompton.

His defence counsel, Mr Prideaux, made much of the fact that Henry was always very submissive to his wife and did everything that she told him to do. Before his marriage, Henry had spent some time in the lunatic ward of the workhouse. According to Prideaux, Mary Fisher's death was due to love and 'this poor man', who had once been a lunatic, was simply acting under the control of his strong-minded wife. In summing up the case, the judge commented to the jury that it was regrettable that there were not different punishments for different degrees of murder but the law was quite clear. If two parties agreed to commit suicide and only one died, then the survivor was guilty of murder.

The jury found Henry Fisher guilty of wilful murder, although they tempered their verdict with a strong recommendation for mercy. Mr Justice Crompton agreed with their verdict and promised to pass on their recommendations to the proper authorities, although, as demanded by the law, he then sentenced Henry Fisher to be executed. Fisher was later reprieved due to his weak mind.

7 JANUARY

1826 Eighteen-year-old Mary Anne Gane called at a house near Shepton Mallet asking for assistance and saying that she was very ill. When questioned by the lady of the house, she admitted that she had just given birth to a baby, which her father had delivered in a nearby shed. Her father had then wrapped the baby in a handkerchief and taken it away and, as soon as she was alone, Mary Anne had left the shed to find help. She alleged that her own father had sired her baby.

John Gane was arrested and taken to Shepton Mallet Prison, where he admitted everything, directing searchers to a pond where he had hidden the baby's body. At the request of the coroner a post-mortem examination was conducted, but it was impossible to establish whether or not the infant was born alive and the inquest jury recorded a verdict of 'stillborn'.

Even so, Mary Anne was tried at the Somerset Assizes for the wilful murder of her baby while John Gane was tried at the same court for concealment of the body of his bastard child. Both were acquitted.

8 JANUARY

1923 Percy Chiswell was a persistent offender with a string of convictions behind him and, by the time he was twelve years old, he was confined in a reformatory school. Percy didn't take his imprisonment lightly and made persistent attempts to escape.

On the morning of 8 January, Percy succeeded in escaping for the third time in just a few weeks. While free, he broke into a hut at Claverton near Bath and stole an axe, which he used to cut four stout pieces of timber from a footbridge. He then laid the wood across the railway line and sat back to await the arrival of the Great Western Railway express train from Cardiff to Brighton.

Fortunately, the driver of a train travelling in the opposite direction spotted the obstruction and blew his brake whistle in time to warn the driver of the oncoming express train. By the time the express reached the timber on the line, its driver had slowed the train to a speed of seven miles an hour and certain disaster was averted.

It was thought that Percy wanted to recreate a scene of a train wreck that he had recently watched on film at the cinema. Appearing before magistrates at Bath County Police Court, Percy told them that he wanted to go to sea. His wish was partially granted, as he was sent to a reformatory ship, where he was to remain until he reached the age of eighteen. He was also ordered to receive six strokes of the birch.

9 JANUARY

1897 Charles Tucker Roach of North Petherton took advantage of his railway employee's privilege ticket and went to Exeter, where he married his partner Elizabeth at the Registry Office. Just two days later, Roach killed both his wife and their ten-month-old baby, Jessy, then cut his own throat.

The dreadful deed was discovered by Roach's married sister, Jessie, who called at the couple's home to find out why Elizabeth hadn't arrived at her house for her customary morning cup of tea. Unable to rouse anyone, she was about to go back home when her brother opened the door, his shirt drenched with blood. Jessie called the neighbours for assistance and, on entering the house, they found Roach in bed, cradling the body of his dead daughter in his arms. Elizabeth, who was pregnant, lay lifeless beside him, her throat cut.

Roach survived his attempted suicide to stand trial at Wells in June 1897 for the wilful murder of his wife and daughter. He appeared in court sporting a full beard, having vowed never to touch a razor again.

It emerged that Roach was an epileptic with a family history of insanity, who had suffered several accidental head injuries in the years prior to the murder. He was apparently very happy with his wife, devoted to his baby daughter and eagerly looking forward to the arrival of the new baby. He continuously maintained that he couldn't think what had made him do it, professing to love every hair on his wife's head and to not know what had come over him.

The jury debated the case for around fifty minutes before returning a verdict of guilty, but insane, at which Roach was sentenced to be detained during Her Majesty's pleasure.

North Petherton. (Author's collection)

Fore Street, North Petherton.

1838   When a young boy went to light the fire at the watch-house in Yeovil, he found a stiffened corpse lying on the floor. The deceased was a pauper, who was believed to have come from Sherborne to Yeovil in search of work. On the evening of 8 January, he applied to relieving officer Mr Porter for parish relief but, at the time, Porter believed that the man was drunk and turned him away. Shortly afterwards, the man was found lying insensible on a lane by Borough Constable Slade.

10 JANUARY

Slade took the man to the Yeovil watch-house – the forerunner of the modern police station – and left him lying on a bench there. He instructed his fellow watchmen, George Theodore Butler Hill and Thomas Beare (or Bear), to release the man when he had sobered up.

Hill and Beare then apparently forgot all about their 'guest' and left him lying in the dark, cold watch-house without food, water or a fire. Over the next couple of days, groans were heard coming from within but nobody thought to investigate until the man's body was found on the evening of 10 January.

At the subsequent inquest, Hill and Beare were charged with the manslaughter of the unnamed pauper. (The jury were equally divided seven to seven on the culpability of Constable Slade, who was consequently discharged.) Thus only Hill and Beare appeared before Mr Justice Denman at the next Somerset Assizes, charged with manslaughter by gross neglect. Both were found guilty, but it was such an unusual case that Denman deferred sentencing the two men until he could consult with a panel of judges.

Hill and Beare were later released on bail, to appear at the assizes if called upon in future. Neither appears to have faced any legal penalty for their part in the death of the anonymous beggar.

1876   An inquest was held at Williton by coroner Mr W. Munckton on the death of Samuel Henry Gayton.

11 JANUARY

On 8 January, Gayton had helped to put out a fire in Escott, leaving there at about seven o'clock at night. Three hours later, Isaac Langdon was walking home to the hamlet of Woolston Moor and stumbled across Gayton lying in the road. Langdon asked if he was all right. Gayton claimed to be almost frozen, asking Langdon to put his hand on his chest. Langdon did and found it to be 'cold as stone'. Gayton was unable to stand, so Langdon went to some nearby cottages to ask for some tea or hot water. The occupants, Mr and Mrs William Routley, came out to look at Gayton. They refused to get him a hot drink, saying that they had none to give. Gayton asked if he might lie down in their cottage, or even in their pigsty, but was refused. Instead, Routley hauled Gayton to his feet, gave him a kick and told him to go home.

Langdon then left Gayton in the care of the Routleys and continued his journey. Meanwhile, Routley tried for a little longer to get Gayton to go home and, when he wouldn't, Routley decided that he was simply being contrary and went to bed, leaving Gayton in the road, where he subsequently died.

The inquest jury returned a verdict of 'died through exposure to the inclement weather' and donated their fees to Gayton's widow. They handed a rider to the coroner condemning Isaac Langdon and the Routleys for their brutal and inhuman conduct. (Another man, George Parsons, was similarly censured, although the cotemporary newspapers do not go into any detail about the extent of his involvement in Gayton's death.) The coroner gave his opinion that Isaac Langdon and William Routley were morally responsible for Gayton's death.

12 JANUARY   **1858**   The inhabitants of South Hill Farm at Withycombe were awakened in the middle of the night by the sound of a gunshot. When they went to investigate, they found that the house was on fire; the sound had come from the farm gun, which was normally kept hanging over the mantelpiece and had exploded in the heat.

The Hayes family, and most of their servants, succeeded in reaching the front door of the farmhouse but it was locked and the key was not in the lock where it was normally kept. One son jumped out of a window and managed to break down the door from the outside, dragging his badly burned wife to safety. Seeing the door open, the farm labourer rushed through the flames and thus saved himself.

Meanwhile, Mr Hayes senior and his youngest son had gone to the room of the servant girl whose job it was to lock the door each night, on the assumption that she had accidentally put the key in her pocket. All three perished in the flames.

The house and its entire contents were completely consumed by the fire, as were several adjoining corn ricks. The three survivors lost everything but their nightclothes, and the property was not insured.

13 JANUARY   **1930**   In the early morning, a former police constable was walking along the seafront in Weston-super-Mare when he spotted the faint orange glow of flames licking around the pavilion at the end of the Grand Pier. The alarm was raised and, together with another passer-by, the policeman ran onto the pier to see if the fire could be extinguished before it took hold. Unfortunately, the two men found that the water supply had been cut off.

Although the fire brigade were on the scene very quickly, they were hampered by the fact that they could not access the pier with their fire engines, which had to be parked on the foreshore, with the firemen running their hoses nearly a quarter of a mile along the pier before they could reach the heart of the blaze. Even with the hoses in place, a gale blew the jets of water away from the fire, which was soon raging out of control.

The flames rose to a great height, lighting up the sky and sending up noxious smoke, which billowed across the bay, joined by great clouds of steam as parts of the building collapsed into the sea. Just a couple of weeks earlier, the building had played host to the town's Christmas pantomime but fortunately, at the time of the fire, the pavilion was closed to the public until the following month. At full capacity, the pavilion could seat 2,500 people.

As well as damage to the buildings, the fire wrecked the funfair with its thousands of pounds' worth of slot machines and the children of Weston-super-Mare scrambled in the sand for pennies from the machines at the next low tide.

The fire was thought to have started in the boiler house. The pier was erected in 1904 at a cost of £120,000 and the entire pavilion was totally consumed in a matter of minutes, causing damage estimated to be in excess of £200,000

The Grand Pier, Weston-super-Mare, in 1913. (Author's collection)

and leaving nothing remaining of the far end of the pier but a few steel support girders.

1854 A bread riot took place in Taunton as an angry and determined mob attempted to reduce the price of provisions being sold in the town. Following similar riots in Devon, a 'few low fellows from the neighbourhood beer-house' vowed to follow the Devonshire lads in protesting against high food prices. Armed with sticks and stones, they were soon joined by a gaggle of women and gathered around a farmer, who had brought his wheat to market. Appalled at the price of 8s 6d being demanded for a sack of what they believed to be wheat of inferior quality, the mob remonstrated with the famer and, when he refused to reduce his asking price, they emptied the sacks and scattered the contents around the market.

14 JANUARY

The police were called but the rioters had moved to the butter market, where they upset tables until the besieged butter sellers agreed to reduce their prices from 1s 4d a pound to 1s. From there the mob went to butcher's row, where they pelted the unfortunate tradesmen with stones, and to the bakers' shops, where they 'assailed the proprietors with threatening language'.

A number of special constables and magistrates were hastily summoned to the area and eventually the mob was dispersed.

15 JANUARY   **1898**   Ann and Charles Banwell spent the evening drinking at the Anchor Inn at Bleadon. They left to walk home together but somehow became separated and Charles arrived home alone.

Rather than going to look for his wife, Charles went straight to bed. When Ann still hadn't arrived the following morning, a search was instigated and she was found dead in a ditch, close to her expected route home. Marks on the sides of the ditch indicated that she had tried desperately to extricate herself before drowning.

At an inquest held two days later, the coroner surmised that, it being a very dark night, Ann had simply wandered off the path and into the ditch. The jury returned an open verdict of 'found drowned', adding a rider to condemn Charles Banwell for his uncaring behaviour in not escorting his wife safely home or going to look for her when she failed to arrive.

16 JANUARY   **1880**   Left unsupervised by her mother for just a few minutes, four-year-old Hester Bond from Dundry took a candle from the mantelpiece and tried to light it. The little girl's pinafore caught fire and she ran from the house screaming. Her mother extinguished the flames and called for surgeon Dr E.T. Hale of Chew Magna. Sadly, Hester was so badly burned that she died within hours.

17 JANUARY   **1848**   Walsingham Hazell, a sixty-four-year-old farmer from Dundry, ate lunch with his nephews Benjamin and James at one o'clock. As he always did after lunch, he sat down briefly to enjoy his pipe and a mug of cider, before going out to resume his work on the farm. At about half-past three, he was seen heading towards the stables, where his nephews were at work. That was the last time he was ever seen alive.

When he didn't return for supper, a search was initiated. However, it wasn't until a few days later that someone thought to check the farm well and Hazell's body was found. He had fatal head wounds and had obviously been murdered before being dumped in the well. A number of hay seeds were stuck to his clothes, suggesting that he had been killed in a stable.

A minute examination of the farm buildings revealed traces of blood in the stable, along with a bloody stick, which had been thrust into a dung heap. Hazell's umbrella was also found concealed in the hayloft. James and Benjamin Hazell were arrested on suspicion of having murdered their uncle. On his arrest, blood was found on James's clothing – but he was known to have recently cut his finger and also to have slaughtered a pig.

Although eighteen-year-old James and his fifteen-year-old brother were tried at the Somerset Assizes for Hazell's murder, the evidence against them was scant and purely circumstantial. They were not known to have quarrelled with their uncle, nor did they have any apparent motive for killing him. Both boys were eventually acquitted.

However, the strangest thing about Walsingham Hazell's murder was the finding of his body. No-one had even considered searching the old well; it had a wooden cover, topped by a very heavy stone which did not appear to have been moved. Allegedly, the well was only searched after an old man had a dream that Hazell's body would be found there.

1896   As Mr Bishop took an early-morning stroll along the sands at Weston-super-Mare, he was shocked to find the body of a man on the beach close to the Royal West of England Sanatorium. The police were summoned and the body was taken to the mortuary for a closer examination. 18 JANUARY

The man had the appearance of a high-class seafarer who, judging by his advanced decomposition, had been in the water for several weeks. Aged between forty and fifty years old, he was about 5ft 10in tall and had black hair. Several of his back teeth were missing. He wore no coat but was dressed in striped grey trousers, a white shirt with a linen stand-up collar, black waistcoat, brown worsted socks and black lace-up boots. There was a silver watch and chain in his pocket, along with a tortoiseshell-handled knife. The inside of his shirt was marked either 'E. Milton' or 'E. Milsom' and the initials EM were embroidered in black wool on his underpants.

Dr Reginald Earle made a post-mortem examination of the body and could find no marks of violence. Although the body was badly decomposed, Earle believed that the man had drowned at least four weeks earlier.

Deputy coroner Dr Wallace held an inquest at the Three Queens Hotel and the jury returned a verdict of 'found drowned' on the man, who was never positively identified.

1856   James Howell and his heavily pregnant wife Eliza were drinking in the Seven Dials public house in Bath when Eliza said something that displeased James, who promptly slapped her face, making her mouth bleed. The quarrel was soon forgotten and the couple continued drinking together for several hours. However, when they returned to their home in Avon Street, the row flared up again and Howell kicked his wife to death. Surgeons made a valiant attempt to deliver her baby by Caesarean section after her death, but the child was also deceased. 19 JANUARY

'It was a drop of drink. I meant no harm,' insisted Howell at his trial at Taunton Assizes for Eliza's murder.

Mr Justice Crowder instructed the jury that, since Howell had used no weapon and had not intended to kill his wife, he thought that they should consider the lesser charge of manslaughter. The jury duly found Howell guilty of that charge and he was sentenced to six years' imprisonment.

By 1864, Howell had been released from prison and was living in Bath with a woman named Susan Cleverley. On 21 February 1864, cries of 'Murder!' were heard coming from their lodgings and a policeman was summoned. Susan begged the policeman to take James into custody, alleging that he had been beating her and jumping on her. She had a large lump over her right eye and, when the constable asked Howell if he had done that, he admitted that he had. Inexplicably, the policeman then left Susan to her fate.

Although Susan left Howell the next morning, she was so badly beaten that she died within a couple of days. A post-mortem examination noted two black eyes, numerous scratches, an internal wound and a grossly swollen abdomen, and attributed her death to injuries received from being recently beaten.

Once again, Howell was tried for wilful murder, this time before Mr Baron Martin. And, once again, the judge suggested to the jury that the offence was actually manslaughter, although as near to murder as was possible. Howell had blackened both of Susan's eyes, knocked her down and then jumped on her, all because she accidentally tore his shirt.

When the jury found Howell guilty of manslaughter, the judge sentenced him to penal servitude for life, on the grounds that he had previously killed another woman.

20 JANUARY   **1823**   Nine-year-old William Bartlett, who was apprenticed to chimney sweep William Hunt, died in Bridgwater. When surgeon Mr J. Haviland conducted a post-mortem examination on the boy's body, he found that his intestines and lungs were very inflamed. In addition, the body bore numerous marks of violence, as a consequence of which Hunt and his wife, Mary, were charged with the child's wilful murder by ill-usage.

The couple were tried before the Honourable Sir James Burrough at the Somerset Assizes in Taunton. The principal witness against them was another of their apprentices, thirteen-year-old John Clarke, who could only be persuaded to testify by a promise that he would never have to work for the Hunts again.

Clarke told the court that he and William Bartlett had slept together on a chaff mattress, their only cover a thin soot cloth. William had frequently soiled his bedding and clothes – something which infuriated Hunt, who threatened to cut the boy into pieces if he continued.

The Hunts tried several different punishments in an effort to train their young apprentice. He was beaten on several occasions and was once tied naked to the stair banisters for a whole day. At other times, he was plunged into the horse trough in the yard – often in near freezing temperatures – and forced to remain there for long periods of time. Clarke told the court that William Hunt had once picked up William Bartlett by his feet and slammed him headfirst onto a brick floor.

On the day before his death, William had refused to eat his supper and was severely beaten by Mary Hunt. William crawled off to his bed, where he died later that night. Initially, Mary moved his body to her children's bed, before deciding that the child was so dirty that he would be better kept in the coal hole.

Whereas surgeon Mr Haviland had stated at the inquest that he believed William Bartlett had died as a result of physical abuse at the hands of his master and mistress, and a lack of proper nutrition, at the Hunts' trial he had modified his opinion somewhat and now believed that the boy's death had resulted from inflammation of his lungs and intestines. In other words, the boy had died from natural causes rather than as a result of ill-treatment.

With the prosecution's chief witness now vacillating on the cause of William Bartlett's death, the jury had little alternative but to find William and Mary Hunt 'Not Guilty' of the wilful murder of their apprentice.

21 JANUARY   **1811**   Almost everyone who knew Betty Townsend of Taunton believed her to be a witch. Thus, when she approached a thirteen-year-old girl who was taking apples to market for her father and demanded money from her, the frightened child gave her 2s – Betty threatened to kill her if she didn't.

Betty's demands on the child continued for weeks and her extortion went undiscovered until the girl's father, Jacob Poole, went to pay a bill at a druggist's shop and found that he owed more money than he thought. On questioning the druggist, Poole discovered that his daughter had been borrowing money in his name. Poole confronted his daughter, who tearfully related Betty Townsend's demands and threats. Poole, his wife and the little girl, promptly went to Betty's house. Betty admitted to knowing the child, and threatened to kill the whole family by inches if they accused her of taking money. Mrs Poole quickly whipped out a pin from her sleeve, scratching Betty's arm and drawing blood, thus supposedly removing her supernatural powers. The family then went to the police.

Seventy-seven-year-old Betty was tried at the Somerset Assizes, charged with obtaining monies from a child. The jury found her guilty and the judge told her that, if it weren't for her age, he would have awarded her the severest sentence that the law would allow. He settled for six months' imprisonment with hard labour.

1927   At the Somerset Assizes, thirty-five-year-old Reuben Doidge was sent to prison for twelve months with hard labour for stealing and slaughtering a lamb in a field near Taunton. Doidge, an unemployed ex-army gunner and professional boxer, told the court that he had been unable to obtain work and that, as a consequence, his family were starving. The judge showed very little sympathy, telling Doidge that farming would become impossible if sheep could not be left to graze in the fields with perfect security.

22 JANUARY

1886   John Jones and Sydney John Butler were walking together at Catherine Hill, Frome, when they happened upon a snowball fight. Jones was hit by a snowball and immediately accused Butler of having thrown it. Butler denied having done so, at which Jones called him a liar.

The two men squared up to each other and Jones took a swing at Butler, who threw up his hand to protect himself. The blow thrown by Jones landed on Butler's wrist, which immediately began to spurt blood. Jones ran away but, when apprehended later, was found to be carrying a knife, which doctors believed had caused the serious injury to Butler's wrist. Several of the major blood vessels were severed, including the main artery and, by the time the case appeared before magistrates in April, Butler was still unable to move two of his fingers.

Charged with malicious wounding, Jones insisted that he had been provoked. Nevertheless, he was found guilty and sentenced to three months' imprisonment with hard labour.

23 JANUARY

1831   Joshua (or James) Haslam, a member of a well-known gang of criminals, was arrested in Taunton on suspicion of having committed a recent jewellery robbery. Since the robbery had occurred in Bristol, Haslam was escorted back to the city in a coach by PC Long. Even though he was securely handcuffed, during the journey Haslam tried to pick the pockets of a female passenger on the coach.

24 JANUARY

He was tried for burglary at the Gloucester Assizes in April 1831 but found 'Not Guilty'.

25 JANUARY   **1830**   As a thirteen-year-old boy named Carpenter from Bleadon was walking to his school in Lympsham, he slipped on a footbridge over the river Axe and plunged into the freezing cold water. His companion, a fifteen-year-old boy named Rich, immediately dived in to try and rescue him. He managed to reach Carpenter, who grasped him so tightly that Rich was unable to swim. A third youth spotted the two boys struggling and he too dived into the river but was quickly taken by the current.

Fortunately, a local farmer was drawn to the river by the boys' terrified shouts. He pulled one boy to the safety of the river bank, then went back into the water and rescued a second. Sadly, by the time he reached the third, the boy had drowned. The victim was Master Rich – and the man who failed to rescue him was his own father. When Mr Rich had arrived at the river, all three boys were still alive.

26 JANUARY   **1823**   In the winter of 1823, much of Somerset suffered from unusually cold weather that was so severe that water pipes lying nearly 3ft beneath ground level froze solid.

On the morning of Sunday 26 January, three men from Crowcombe were found frozen to death in the deep snow near to the village. They had spent the previous night drinking at the Gore Inn, 'whether intemperately or not, we are not informed,' related *The Times*, somewhat pompously. Between them, the men left nineteen children to mourn their deaths.

Crowcombe Combe.
(Author's collection)

27 JANUARY   **1921**   It was reported in *The Times* that seventy-four-year-old Frederick Bates had been sentenced at the Somerset Assizes to nine months' imprisonment with hard labour for burglary. In passing sentence, Mr Justice Bailhachie told Bates that, since he had been in prison on and off for the past sixty years, he personally believed that he was now too old to reform.

1860 Benjamin Hobbs of Charlinch had long suspected that someone was
stealing his cider. Eventually he reported his suspicions to the police and it
was arranged that a constable would hide in his cider house to try and catch
the thief red-handed.

As the policeman lay in wait, William Hurley crept in and siphoned off a
quantity of cider using a tube. Hurley then left, returning shortly afterwards
with another man, at which time the policeman revealed himself and Hurley
was arrested.

He appeared at the Somerset Assizes in March, charged with stealing one
hogshead of cider, worth 30s. His thirst cost him one month's imprisonment
with hard labour.

1877 Hannah Hawkins and Hugh Clark were walking from Donyatt to
Ilminster, when they came across a group of young boys making 'rough music'
in the street with a motley collection of homemade instruments. As the couple
passed the boys, a man staggered drunkenly out of a nearby house, raised a
gun to his shoulder and fired. The only person injured was Mrs Hawkins, who
was hit by shotgun pellets on her cheek and ear. Mrs Hawkins remonstrated
with the shooter, who immediately turned on her and threatened to shoot her
again.

Edward Challice of Donyatt was brought to trial at the Somerset Assizes,
charged with maliciously wounding Hannah Hawkins. His defence counsel, Mr
T.W. Saunders, maintained that Challice had no prior intention of wounding
Mrs Hawkins and therefore the incident could not be described as 'malicious',
only 'unlawful wounding'. It was Challice's wedding day – his third marriage
– and the boys were deliberately provoking him by derisively celebrating the
occasion, making an unpleasant noise in the street outside his house. His only
desire in firing his gun was to get them to desist.

The judge pointed out that people could not just fire weapons in the street
at will and, even after hearing several witnesses give Challice an excellent
character witness, the jury concurred, finding Challice guilty of the lesser
charge of unlawful wounding.

Rather sympathetically, Lord Chief Justice Cockburn bound Challice over
for the sum of £50, to be paid should he misconduct himself in the future.
He then discharged eighty-four-year-old Challice, who was described in the
contemporary newspapers as a 'frail, asthmatical and decrepid man' [sic], to
enjoy his married life with his seventy-year-old bride.

1878 Emma King, a pauper from Keynsham Union Workhouse, was brought
before magistrates charged with being 'refractory' (resistant to authority).
Magistrates ordered her to be sent to Shepton Mallet Prison for fourteen days.

It was normal practice for prisoners to walk to the gaol, a distance of some
fourteen miles, which Emma did, in spite of the fact that she had to carry her
eighteen-month-old baby all the way. However, when she reached the gaol, the
governor refused to admit the baby, since it was not included on the warrant.
PC Baker, who had escorted Emma to gaol, was ordered to return the child to
Keynsham Union Workhouse.

By the time he got back, the workhouse master told him that it was too late to admit the child that night, leaving Baker literally holding the baby. The next morning, having sorted out the necessary paperwork, he was forced to walk to Shepton Mallet to reunite the baby with his mother.

31 JANUARY   **1823** The inhabitants of Crewkerne were startled by a deafening crash at about seven o'clock in the evening. Residents of East Street rushed outside to find that a house had completely collapsed. A woman and three children escaped but one little boy remained buried in the rubble. People dug frantically with their bare hands to try and extricate him but, after fifteen minutes, he was pulled from the ruins dead.

At the subsequent inquest, the coroner's jury returned a verdict of 'accidental death' on Master Reader. The house was a very old building and it was believed that recent heavy rains had affected its foundations. At the time of the collapse, the three other children of the family were actually on the stairs, on their way up to join their brother in bed. Had the building fallen just minutes later, it is probable that all four children would have been killed.

FEBRUARY

Aerial view of Bath. (Author's collection)

1 FEBRUARY

1881 Twenty-four-year-old Rhoda Day was tried at the Somerset Assizes for the murder of her new-born daughter at Spaxton in November 1880.

The child was Rhoda's second illegitimate baby, the first having supposedly been stillborn. When it was rumoured that she had given birth again, Rhoda denied having ever been pregnant. The rumours reached the local police, who visited Rhoda at her father's home and conducted a search of the premises, finding the infant buried in an old sack in the garden, a piece of tape tied tightly around her neck. A post-mortem confirmed that the baby had been strangled and Rhoda admitted, 'I done it, but I hope I shan't have the rope for it.'

In spite of her confession, Rhoda was found guilty only of concealment of the birth of her child and was sentenced to nine months' imprisonment with hard labour.

2 FEBRUARY

1884 Charles Kite, a twenty-one-year-old hawker, was tried before Mr Justice Cave at the Somerset Assizes in Taunton for the wilful murder of Albert Miles on 2 January.

The two men had argued in a public house in Bath; Kite had then taken a knife from his pocket and threatened to stab Miles. The latter tried to make peace, holding his left hand out to Kite and saying, 'Well, Charley, we won't be bad friends; let us shake hands.' Kite shook Miles's hand with his left hand, at the same time stabbing Miles in the breast with his right.

The jury found Kite guilty of murder but recommended him to mercy. The recommendation was not taken up, since Kite was hanged on 25 February.

3 FEBRUARY

1862 James George Wyatt was a butcher, with a shop on the corner of Westgate Street and Parsonage Lane, Bath. For twelve months, he had employed a young man named William Weaver but had recently sacked him after a dispute. Soon afterwards, Wyatt received a tip-off that Weaver was planning revenge for his dismissal that night, so the butcher hid in his shop, waiting for whatever Weaver had in mind.

There was a heavy iron trapdoor in Parsonage Lane, which opened into the cellar of Wyatt's shop. At twenty past four in the morning, Wyatt heard someone entering through the trapdoor, striking matches and opening the shop till. Wyatt shouted and the intruder fled, with Wyatt in hot pursuit.

By pure chance, PC Hiscox was outside the shop at the time and saw a man exiting via the trapdoor. Both Wyatt and Hiscox pursued the intruder for some distance until he gave them the slip. However, Hiscox thought he had recognised Weaver and, on hearing from Wyatt that he suspected his former employee, Hiscox arrested Weaver and he was charged with burglary – the sum of 13*d* had been taken from the shop till.

Weaver appeared at the Somerset Assizes and, although the evidence against him was circumstantial, he was found guilty. Having a previous conviction, he was sentenced to three years' penal servitude.

4 FEBRUARY

1850 Mr A.H. English, the coroner for Bath, held an inquest into the deaths of thirty-seven-year-old Edmund Francis Hunt and his two-year-old daughter, Dora. Their bodies had been found in the river Avon two days earlier, Hunt's almost directly outside the door of his Bath home and Dora's eighteen miles downriver.

Hunt was a steady and industrious man, who had four sons and a daughter. His wife was addicted to stealing and had several convictions, the last of which was in late 1849. At that time, Hunt told his wife that if she ever disgraced the family again, he would 'do away with himself' and, on 2 February, he arrived home from work to find that she had been arrested for shoplifting and taken to the police station.

Hunt said goodbye to his oldest child, thirteen-year-old Edmund, and sent him to bed, after asking him to bring Dora downstairs. From his bedroom, Edmund heard his father go out and close the door behind him and, when he woke up the next morning, his father and Dora were gone.

Edmund told the inquest that Dora was his father's favourite and added that, whenever his mother was 'taken up' for stealing, his father was almost out of his mind with worry. The jury obviously appreciated Hunt's despair since they concluded that he had murdered his daughter and then killed himself while temporarily insane.

1946 An inquest was held by the coroner for North Somerset on two elderly sisters found dead in the kitchen of their home in Southside, Weston-super-Mare. 5 FEBRUARY

The coroner surmised that seventy-five-year-old Edith Deborah Wolton had suffered a fatal heart attack in the kitchen as she was turning on her gas cooker to make a cup of tea. Shortly afterwards, she was found by her sister, seventy-three-year-old Eva Maude Wolton, who promptly fainted from the shock and was quickly overcome by the gas escaping from the unlit cooker.

Verdicts of 'accidental death' were recorded on both women.

1895 An explosion rocked Timsbury Colliery near Radstock, killing seven of the miners working the night shift, along with several horses. 6 FEBRUARY

The colliery had two working pits, Upper and Lower Congyre. Upper Congyre, the site of the disaster, employed eighty-seven men, although fortunately the explosion occurred when only nine were underground. George Flower and John Fear were rescued and related that forty-one-year-old James Carter had fired a shot to widen the main underground 'road' through the pit, causing a build-up of coal dust in the vicinity to ignite and explode.

The dead men were James Carter, George Harding, Joseph Bridges, James Edwin Durham, John Gage, John Keeling and George Sperring. (Keeling was so mutilated that his son could only identify him by his boots.) James Carter left eleven children and George Sperring was seventy-eight years old.

1899 Charles Purnell of Bristol fell ill with what he believed was a cold. As his illness gradually worsened, his doctor diagnosed acute rheumatism but, by 17 February, Charles was displaying all the characteristic symptoms of lead poisoning. He died on 23 February. 7 FEBRUARY

Charles had worked for twenty-four years in the white lead works at Avon Street, Bristol, owned by Messrs Hare. At the inquest into Purnell's death, the works manager stated that there had only been four cases of lead poisoning in the past two years, none of which had proved fatal. John Belsten outlined the strict safety procedures followed at the works, saying that the men worked only four-hour shifts, were provided with overalls, instructed to bathe and given aperient medicine.

The jury found that Purnell had died from acute rheumatism, accelerated by the effects of lead. They added that they saw nothing dangerous in the system employed at the works.

8 FEBRUARY   **1889**   The body of a baby was found in a stream at Westford, near Wellington. A surgeon who examined the child stated that it was so neglected that it would soon have starved to death, had it not drowned. The child's parents, Joseph and Elizabeth Jane Westcott, were arrested and charged with the child's murder. Elizabeth insisted that she had left the child asleep in bed while she went out to buy food. When she returned five minutes later, the baby was missing.

Elizabeth alone was tried at the Somerset Assizes for wilful murder and was acquitted.

9 FEBRUARY   **1888**   The inhabitants of Watchet were horrified to find two men lying at the bottom of the 50ft cliffs above the beach. One was dead and the other barely alive, dying before a doctor could be summoned to help him.

The two men were George Withers and George Payne from Kilne, who had driven a pony and cart to Watchet the previous day on business. On their journey home, they had apparently missed their road in the dark and driven across a ploughed field to the cliff edge. Scuff marks on the cliff top appeared to show that the pony's front feet had gone over the edge of the cliff but that it had somehow righted itself and managed to scramble backwards. However, in the process, the cart had tipped, precipitating the two men to their deaths.

10 FEBRUARY   **1857**   Josiah Parker, a butcher from Wells, had been married to his wife Ann for seventeen years and the couple had four children. At about five o'clock in the afternoon, Ann's thoughts turned to preparing supper and she popped her head round the door of her husband's shop to ask if he had any veal cutlets.

'I'll give thee veal cutlets,' Parker replied and, picking up his meat cleaver, he dealt his wife a fearsome blow. He continued to chop at her head until neighbours rushed in and pulled him away. Ann Parker survived until 16 February, when her husband was charged with her wilful murder.

Although the Parkers' marriage was happy and Josiah was described as a fond and affectionate husband, he had become convinced that his wife was being unfaithful. Unable to convince him otherwise, Ann had consulted a surgeon about her husband's mental state and, just the day before the attack on his wife, Josiah Parker had officially been pronounced sane! (The same surgeon was summoned after the attack to tend to Ann and then described Josiah as 'perfectly mad'.)

It emerged at his trial that Josiah's father, aunt and cousin had all been insane. Not only that but he had spent some time in a lunatic asylum himself and had recently become addicted to drink. He had also attempted suicide several times. On hearing this, the judge directed the jury to acquit Josiah Parker on the grounds of insanity and ordered him to be detained during Her Majesty's pleasure.

1859 Mrs Thorne, the landlady of the Black Horse Inn at Taunton, dressed her infant son, Henry, and left him safely in a bedroom while she went downstairs to help her husband, who was getting ready to go out. Minutes later, she heard the baby screaming. She rushed back upstairs to find Henry's clothes on fire. The baby was badly burned and died from his injuries the next morning.

Strangely, there was no fire, candle or any other flame in the baby's room. At the inquest, the coroner could only surmise that a spark must have fallen on the baby's clothes while they were being aired in the kitchen immediately before he was dressed.

1873 *The Times* published a letter from F. Simcox Lea, the vicar of Compton Dundon. The letter described Lea's detailed analysis of the Burial Register from his parish, covering the years between 1813 and 1873 inclusive.

According to Lea, the average age at death during this period was fractionally under thirty-eight years old. (Lea pointed out that this had risen slowly and for the last twenty years had been just over forty-one years old.) Throughout the entire period, nobody attained their hundredth birthday, although one person lived to the age of ninety-nine and a further nine lived past the age of ninety. This compares with a current life expectancy in Somerset of around seventy-nine years for men and eighty-two for women.

During the sixty years covered by the register, there were almost as many deaths of children under two years old as there were of those aged over seventy.

1850 Two sixteen-year-old boys, Alfred Bond and William Munday, attacked John Richards as he walked home from Wincanton Fair. Luckily for Richards, as the boys viciously beat him with a stick and tried to rob him, the assault was interrupted by passers-by and the boys fled.

They were soon apprehended and both made statements admitting the offence. However, by the time their case was tried at the Somerset Assizes, Bond had changed his story and now accused Munday of committing the offence alone.

The jury found both boys guilty and, in passing sentence, the judge told them that, had their attack on Richards not been cut short, they could have been facing a far worse fate. He sentenced each to be transported for fifteen years.

1823 Passengers on the Bristol to Bath Coach, driven by George Clerk, noted with some consternation that their driver appeared to be 'in liquor'. Clerk drove at a furious pace, frenziedly whipping his horses to gallop faster.

As the coach passed through the turnpike gate near Bristol, its speed was such that it nearly clipped the gate posts. The four inside and eight outside passengers clung on for dear life as Clerk ignored their pleas to slow down. Eventually the coach overturned, spilling all the passengers onto the road.

One, James Hamilton, sustained a fractured skull and later died from his injuries in Bath Hospital.

Clerk stood trial at the Somerset Assizes, charged with his manslaughter. The defence insisted that the coach had overturned when a spring accidentally broke, throwing it off balance and causing it to tip over. Although the coach was found to have a broken spring after the accident, it was shown that it had been broken some time previously and was inadequately repaired with a thin piece of metal.

Found guilty by the jury, Clerk was sentenced by Mr Justice Burrough, who commented that he didn't think it necessary to mete out the maximum penalty allowed by the law. Instead, he had decided to treat Clerk fairly leniently, in the hope that the incident would serve as a warning to other coachmen. Burrough felt that the coach proprietors were more to blame than the drivers, who were encouraged to complete their journeys in as short a time as possible so that more money could be made.

However, speeds of twelve to fourteen miles an hour in a coach laden with passengers were dangerous and illegal, and those who drove at such speeds must be aware that they did so at their peril. Burrough then sentenced Clerk to twelve months' imprisonment.

15 FEBRUARY **1861** At the hearing in Keynsham of a summons issued by Clara Jones on farmer Mr Parker, Clara swore that Parker was the father of her illegitimate child, born on Christmas Day 1860. Clara was asked by magistrates if she had 'had connexion' with any other men and swore an oath that she hadn't.

However, although Parker agreed that he was the child's father, thus making him liable to pay maintenance of 10s a month for the next thirteen years, after the hearing he accused Clara of lying. Clara was sent for trial at the Somerset Assizes charged with wilful and corrupt perjury. The prosecution questioned her about a man named Robert Tipney Williams, with whom she had been seen on 30 May at a fair at Penford. Clara admitted to having seen Williams but denied having slept with him.

The prosecution called several witnesses, including a police constable, who had seen Clara and Williams together. One witness, the owner of a lodging

High Street,
Keynsham.
(Author's collection)

house at Penford, even insisted that Clara and Williams had slept together as man and wife.

In Clara's defence, her counsel Mr Saunders told the court that, no matter what, Parker was obliged to pay maintenance for the child he had acknowledged as his own. Thus Parker's only motive for accusing Clara of perjury was revenge. He had seduced and debauched her and, out of spite, was now endeavouring to have her sent to gaol for a long time with her baby. The evidence by the prosecution witnesses was somewhat vague and utterly worthless to support such a charge as this, stated Saunders, adding that he couldn't understand why neither Parker nor Williams had been called as witnesses.

After a short deliberation, the jury acquitted Clara Jones, their verdict being greeted with spontaneous applause from the court.

1883 During a packed meeting of The Rising Sun Temperance Club in Wellington, the floor of the hall collapsed, plunging several people into a workshop below. Twelve-year-old Emma Shopland was killed instantly and several more people were seriously injured, although none of their injuries were thought to be life-threatening. At the subsequent inquest, a verdict of 'accidental death' was recorded on Emma, while the organisers of the meeting were exonerated from any blame for the tragedy.

16 FEBRUARY

1868 An unnamed bridegroom arrived at the church in Blagdon having celebrated his forthcoming wedding a little too enthusiastically. Throughout the service, he repeatedly slapped his intended wife's behind, the noise resonating through the church.

Every now and again he would kiss her cheek and, more than once, he extended his affectionate gestures to the bridesmaids. To the consternation of the presiding vicar, he accompanied his antics with a loud running commentary that was peppered with the sort of expletives that one wouldn't normally expect to hear in church.

Eventually the vicar refused to continue with the ceremony and, although the bridegroom pleaded with him to reconsider, he would not relent. It was reported that the marriage was finally solemnised the following day.

17 FEBRUARY

View of Blagdon. (Author's collection)

18 FEBRUARY

1880 Twenty-five-year-old Caroline Cottle had been a patient at the Bath Union Workhouse, where she was successfully treated for smallpox. Caroline, who was heavily pregnant, was overjoyed when she was finally told that she was fit for discharge.

Her husband organised a vehicle to convey her to their home in Swainswick but, as Caroline walked out of the workhouse, she suddenly dropped down dead. Robert Biggs, the workhouse medical officer, attributed her death to her intense excitement at going home, which had placed too much strain on a heart weakened by smallpox.

19 FEBRUARY

1868 William Hyde, the driver of the mail coach between Taunton and Ilchester, appeared at the Petty Sessions in the Shire Hall at Taunton charged with being drunk on duty and so endangering the safety of Her Majesty's mail bags. According to Taunton postmaster Mr Lucy, on 6 February Hyde had arrived three-quarters of an hour late at the Taunton office and, when asked for an explanation for his lateness, was so drunk that he couldn't offer one. He tossed the mail bags into the road and, when they were checked, two were found to be missing, although fortunately both were later found and handed in.

Shire Hall, Taunton. (Author's collection)

SHIRE HALL, TAUNTON

Hyde insisted that his horse had fallen and he had banged his head, leading the Post Office officials to believe that he was intoxicated. Mr Lucy asked the magistrates to fine Hyde £25, the maximum penalty allowed, to act as a warning against drunkenness to other Post Office workers. However, the magistrates agreed on a fine of £10 and, when Hyde stated that he could not afford to pay, he was sent to prison for three months.

20 FEBRUARY

1938 The fortieth case of typhoid fever was confirmed, in an epidemic exclusively affecting two areas of Somerset. All of the cases came from Huntspill or Highbridge, and the forty-bed hospital at Axbridge was commandeered for the reception and treatment of typhoid patients. Six people from Huntspill eventually died from the disease.

As soon as the first case was reported in January, Dr J.F. Davidson, the Medical Officer of Health for Somerset, began a detailed investigation into the source of the outbreak. This included examinations of the water and milk supplies, as well as the compilation of diaries that noted every single item of food eaten by all the members of the affected families in the previous few weeks. (This proved especially difficult since it encompassed Christmas, when many people had eaten more exotic or unusual food than usual.)

Various farms and food producers in the area were tested and the investigators also looked at social gatherings held in the two affected areas over the festive

Burnham Road,
Highbridge.
(Author's
collection)

period. All water and milk was boiled prior to consumption and the public were prohibited from eating duck eggs, since the ducks frequented the reens – specially constructed channels which diverted sewage into the river Parret, to be drained off to the sea.

It was eventually determined that the source of the outbreak was most probably Christmas foodstuffs.

21 FEBRUARY

1872 Twenty-one-year-old James Ashman reported for work on the four o'clock shift at the Huish Colliery near Radstock. He joined two other men waiting in the cage to be lowered into the pit. However, when the cage began its descent, Ashman's head became trapped between the wall of the cage and the pit mouth, and he was partially decapitated.

22 FEBRUARY

1850 Sixty-year-old Robert Best was seen coming out of the flax shed on a farm at Shepton Beauchamp, owned by John Naish. Moments later, the shed burst into flames. It seemed obvious that Best had started the fire and he was immediately apprehended. Asked why he had set fire to the shed, Best could offer no explanation apart from saying that the Devil had tempted him to do it.

When he stood trial for arson at the Somerset Assizes in April, Best still blamed the Devil and begged the court for mercy. The jury found him guilty but they too recommended mercy for the prisoner and Mr Justice Erle deferred sentence, saying that he wanted enquiries made in order to determine whether or not the arson was a malicious act by the defendant. He obviously concluded that it was not, since he sentenced Best to one month's imprisonment.

23 FEBRUARY

1880 Fourteen-year-old John Carter appeared before magistrates charged with stealing a live fowl from his uncle at Midsomer Norton on 29 January. The magistrates heard that Carter already had a previous conviction for stealing potatoes and that, just before his arrest on this current charge, he had roasted a live cat and forced his friends to eat it. Carter was sentenced to one month's imprisonment with hard labour, followed by four years in a reformatory school.

24 FEBRUARY **1881** Reverend Benjamin Speke, the rector of Dowlish Wake, committed suicide. Speke was the brother of the famous explorer Captain John Hanning Speke, who was credited with the discoveries of Lake Victoria and the source of the Nile. Captain Speke himself died in suspicious circumstances, shooting himself in the chest while out with a party shooting partridges. Although his death was officially recorded as accidental, many people believed that he had committed suicide.

Reverend Speke married Caroline Fuller in 1869 and the couple went on to have eight or nine children. In 1868, he caused a national sensation by suddenly disappearing while attending a wedding in London. Only his hat was found and rumours abounded throughout the country that he had been murdered, kidnapped, met with a fatal accident or had committed suicide. The £100 reward offered for news of his whereabouts went unclaimed.

Several weeks later, he was found masquerading as a cattle drover in Padstow, Cornwall. Police searching for a man who had absconded from Hull with a large amount of money became suspicious of Speke, who, when found, was carrying almost £200 in bank notes and gold. Initially detained on suspicion of being the refugee from Hull, Speke's true identity was soon discovered. His explanation for his disappearance was that he wished to labour and preach the gospel to his fellow working man in an area where he was not recognised.

Speke was distraught when his beloved wife Caroline died from congestion of the lungs. His friends feared that he would try to join her by committing suicide, so a close watch was kept on him. However, on the morning after his wife's death, he managed to momentarily evade the watchful eye of his butler, John Dunning, by climbing out through the window of his study. He was found drowned in the garden pond just minutes later.

25 FEBRUARY **1882** A donkey was turned out to graze on the withy beds at Creech St Michael. When the animal's owner went to collect it, he saw fourteen-year-old farm labourer William Verrier walking nearby with a long stick in his hand.

The owner asked William to drive the animal towards him but instead William brutally thrust his stick into the donkey's anus and pushed it as far into the animal as he possibly could. The animal later died in great agony from a ruptured intestine.

Tried at the Somerset Spring Sessions, Verrier vehemently denied having killed the donkey. The jury found him guilty as charged, although they made a recommendation for mercy. The magistrates sentenced him to three months' imprisonment with hard labour.

26 FEBRUARY **1876** An inquest was held at Watchet, by coroner William Munckton, on the body of Clara Webber, the six-week-old illegitimate daughter of Angelina Webber.

Clara had been ill for a couple of days before her death on 23 February and, according to Dr Frost, the baby had died from inanition from improper feeding – the exhausted state due to prolonged under-nutrition. Angelina had undoubtedly been a caring, loving mother but, at only sixteen years old, she had also been an inexperienced mother. As well as suckling her daughter, she had also fed it biscuits.

Describing Angelina as a 'poor girl', Munckton stated that, out of mistaken kindness, many mothers gave food other than the breast. Such young babies needed nothing more than their mother's milk and artificial food was a poison; nine out of every ten babies who were given it died.

1875 Samuel Webber, the lock keeper from Saltford, happened to glance into the river Avon and saw something floating gently past. He quickly realised that it was the body of a young woman and followed it downstream until he had the chance to retrieve it. Once the body drifted into shallower water, he slipped a rope around it, which he secured to a tree while he went to fetch the police. **27 FEBRUARY**

Doctors confirmed that the woman was about twenty-five years old and around three months pregnant. She appeared to have been hit several times on the head and had apparently been dead when she entered the water.

With no reports of any missing women in the area and no clues to the corpse's identity, the police published a description of the woman and her clothing in the local newspapers. Several people came forward to view the body, until it was finally positively identified as the daughter of a horse dealer from Devizes in Wiltshire. The police were delighted to have finally identified the dead woman but, just days later, found themselves back at square one when the woman from Devizes was located alive and well in Chippenham.

An inquest was opened and adjourned by deputy coroner Mr R. Biggs and, by the time it reopened in mid-March, the woman had been buried without a name. Given her rather coarse, working-class clothing, the coroner could only theorise that she was in some way connected to a boat or barge, an opinion that was strengthened by spots of pitch and tar staining her garments. The young woman was rather large and the coroner believed that, while it would have been relatively easy to throw her into the river from a boat, it would have proved very difficult to carry her to the water.

The police having reached a dead end with their investigations, the inquest jury eventually returned a verdict of 'wilful murder by person or persons unknown'.

1878 Letter carrier Charles Hale, aged nineteen, was bitten on the thigh by a dog at Swainswick. It was a painful bite, which bled heavily, and Hale consulted surgeon Mr T.W. Goss the next day. **28 FEBRUARY**

Goss treated the bite and Hale appeared to make a full recovery. However, early in April, he again called in Goss, now complaining of pain in the back of his neck and his chest, an inability to fully open his mouth and a raging thirst. Goss prescribed some medicine, which Hale immediately vomited up.

By the next morning, Hale's symptoms had worsened considerably and he was now suffering from crippling chest pains every few seconds. Goss called in another surgeon, Dr Fox, for a second opinion. Both doctors agreed that Hale was suffering from tetanus and, after giving him an injection of morphine for the pain, they arranged his admission to hospital, where he died within four hours.

Given that one of Hale's main symptoms had been an unquenchable thirst, there was some public concern that he might have died from rabies. None of the doctors treating him believed that his illness was anything more than tetanus resulting from the dog bite but, on the other hand, none had heard of a case of tetanus occurring so long after an injury.

At the subsequent inquest, coroner Mr English heard evidence from the dog's owner, Mrs Martha Pain, who had since had the dog destroyed. Mrs Pain testified that the dog was quiet and docile, with a playful, but harmless, nature. Her testimony was supported by several of her friends and neighbours but local tradesmen gave evidence to the contrary, saying that they too had been attacked by the animal.

The coroner pointed out to the jury that, if they believed that Mr and Mrs Pain had kept a dog knowing it to be ferocious, their verdict should be one of manslaughter. The jury deliberated for some time before returning to state that, in their opinion, the deceased died from tetanus resulting from the bite of a vicious dog. Although they pronounced themselves dissatisfied as to the character of the dog, after a lengthy debate with the coroner, the jury eventually agreed that Hale had died by misadventure, thus finding that the dog was not known to be vicious.

29 FEBRUARY   1896   The *Bristol Mercury* reported on a case heard by magistrates at Ilminster Police Court on 26 February, in which two women from South Petherton were accused of assaulting another woman from the village by sending her an ugly valentine. The Wells sisters indignantly denied the offence, with Phillis Wells insisting that she had never sent a valentine in her life. Nevertheless, the Bench found them guilty as charged and each woman was fined 4s 6d.

MARCH

Bishops Lydeard, 1905. (Author's collection)

1 MARCH

1864   Elizabeth Hembury worked as a maid for the Sully family at Wivelis-combe and slept in a bedroom shared with two of the family's children and a boy named Jim Webber. Soon after she had gone to sleep on 1 March, thirteen-year-old Elizabeth woke with a start to find her master Thomas Sully in bed with her.

Sully indecently assaulted Elizabeth, urging her to be quiet so that Jim didn't hear. Elizabeth submitted to Sully, until one of the children woke up crying. Sully got up and took the child to its mother, before returning to Elizabeth's bed.

Elizabeth tearfully complained to several of her fellow servants the next morning and her mother was summoned to take her home. She was taken to a doctor and, at the time of Sully's appearance at the Somerset Assizes nearly three weeks later, was still confined to bed.

At the trial, Sully's defence counsel called several character witnesses, all of whom gave the defendant glowing references. Surgeon Mr Legg was called to state that he had examined Elizabeth and, although there was some evidence that violence had been used against her, she was still a virgin. The defence implied that Elizabeth had made up the whole story but the jury found Sully guilty of assault and, still protesting his innocence, he was sentenced to twelve months' hard labour.

2 MARCH

1836   Twenty-three-year-old Sophia Edney of Compton Bishop was married to John, a poor watercress gatherer, who was many years her senior. When a much younger man took her fancy, Sophia purchased some arsenic, telling the druggist that she wanted it to kill rats. Instead, she fed the poison to John in some fried potatoes and he died on 2 March.

Tried for the wilful murder of her husband before Mr Justice Littledale at the Somerset Assizes, Sophia vehemently protested her innocence. However, the evidence against her was conclusive and Sophia was found guilty. She was executed at Ilchester on 14 April 1836.

3 MARCH

1852   Mary Amory gave birth to a healthy baby girl, her second illegitimate daughter. She had been living with her father at Bishops Lydeard but, when he realised that she was pregnant for the second time, Mr Amory threw her out and she was forced to live in the Taunton Workhouse.

Shortly before the birth, she left the workhouse, saying that she was going to meet her sister. She took a room in Bridgwater, passing herself off as a widow. Having given birth, Mary remained at Bridgwater for ten days before telling the landlady that she was going to Bishops Lydeard to have the infant christened. However, when she got back to her father's house, she did not have the baby with her and told people that it had been stillborn.

Some days later, a baby's body was found in a pit. It had been partially eaten by wild animals, hence it was impossible to determine the cause of death. The inquest jury returned a verdict of 'found dead' and the unidentified baby was buried, but gossip soon linked it to Mary Amory, who was arrested for wilful murder.

Mary insisted that she had handed her child over to gypsies on the road from Bridgwater. Tried at the Somerset Assizes in April 1852, the only real witness

View of Bishops Lydeard. (Author's collection)

Bishops Lydeard, 1908. (Author's collection)

against her was her six-year-old daughter, Sarah Jane, and the judge, Mr Baron Platt, did not feel that the little girl had received enough religious instruction to understand the concept of the oath. He therefore deferred the trial so that the child could be better educated.

Thus Mary Amory appeared before Mr Justice Erle at the assizes in March 1853. Sarah Jane still seemed to have little religious knowledge and eventually the judge took her to a private room, where he could question her personally. Having asked her about saying her prayers, the Son of God and the Holy Ghost, Erle returned to court saying that he was dissatisfied with Sarah Jane's answers and refused to allow her to be questioned.

With the only real witness against her prohibited from testifying, the jury acquitted Mary Amory and she was discharged from the court.

4 MARCH   **1871**   The *Bristol Mercury* reported the death of a railway porter employed at Bishops Lydeard station.

Mr Court had only worked at the station for a short while and was about to be married. As the train from Watchet slowed to enter the station, another porter jumped from the train onto the platform and accidentally bumped into Court, who was knocked onto the railway tracks, where the still moving train cut his body in two. Tragically, his fiancée was about to embark on a journey to Taunton and so happened to be within feet of the incident.

5 MARCH   **1879**   Returning from Chard to her home at Knowle St Giles, fifty-year-old Catherine Churchill found her husband lying on the fire. The back of his head was burned to a cinder and his shoulders were so badly burned that his arms were practically cooked and almost fell away from his body when touched.

At first glance, it seemed as though eighty-two-year-old Mr Churchill had suffered a fit. However, surgeons found a deep cut on his left hand and there was a bloodstained billhook under a chair. Catherine's dress bore spots of blood, as did the walls and floor of the room where Churchill was found and a pair of his bloodstained trousers were found hidden away in another room.

Although Churchill's head was too badly burned to identify any injuries it was determined that he had been murdered with the billhook before being dragged onto the fire, presumably to hide the evidence of the deadly assault.

Catherine Churchill was arrested on suspicion of the wilful murder of her husband – it was thought that she had killed him to prevent him from altering his will – and she was tried at the Taunton Assizes in May 1879.

The evidence against her was circumstantial but the prosecution's case rested largely on the testimony of a neighbour who had heard cries of 'Murder!' from the Churchills' home and had then seen Catherine through the window, pushing or dragging something towards the fireplace.

It took the jury one hour to deliberate the case and find Catherine Churchill guilty as charged. She was sentenced to death and executed on 26 May 1879.

6 MARCH   **1835**   Thomas Bevan, one of a gang of men arrested for an assault and burglary at Pill, made a daring escape from Taunton Prison while awaiting his trial. He was first missed from the prison infirmary at six o'clock in the morning. The police were immediately informed and eight constables were dispatched to search the surrounding area.

The landlord of the White Hart Inn at East Reach contacted the police to tell them that a near-naked man had called at the inn at about five o'clock that morning, demanding a suit of clothes. The landlord had threatened that he would send for the police and the man ran away.

Now that the police knew in which direction Bevan was heading, they were soon hot on his heels and he was found by PC Channing at half-past seven, hiding under a wagon of straw at Priory Farm near Taunton. When he finally stood trial in April, he was sentenced to be transported for twenty-five years.

7 MARCH   **1882**   Eighteen-year-old Caroline Bittinger and her sixteen-year-old sister, Charlotte, were members of a German band who were touring Somerset.

When the group left the inn at Williton on the morning of 8 March, a dead baby was found in the room shared by the two girls. The newly-born infant had a garter twisted tightly round its neck.

The girls were apprehended at the band's next stop in Watchet, where Caroline was charged with the wilful murder of her baby and Charlotte was charged as an accessory. The girls appeared before Mr Justice Hawkins at the Somerset Assizes in Taunton. The Grand Jury found 'no bill' against Charlotte and she was consequently discharged.

The doctor who had conducted the post-mortem on the baby had been unable to determine conclusively whether the baby had been born alive. Hence the jury baulked at finding Caroline guilty of murder, instead returning a verdict of guilty of concealment of birth. She was sentenced to one month's imprisonment without hard labour.

1868 As the parishioners of Wembdon enjoyed the morning service at St   **8 MARCH**
George's Church, a passer-by happened to notice smoke billowing from the roof. Mr Lynham alerted the congregation and, although no smoke or flames were visible inside the building, outside the roof was blazing. (The stove flue had apparently either overheated or malfunctioned, setting the rafters on fire.)

A messenger was sent for assistance, and Revd C.W. Alston and his flock rushed to rescue all the moveable items from within the church, while a group of young men managed to scramble onto the roof and create a firebreak around the tower. Their actions saved the tower and its peal of five bells as, by the time help arrived, a strong wind had fanned the flames and much of the building was burned to the ground.

When the blaze was finally extinguished, only the tower and the chancel remained. An almost-new organ was destroyed, as was the carved oak pulpit, and unfortunately the insurance on the building had recently lapsed.

The parishioners rebuilt the church at a cost of £1,300 and it opened again in November 1870.

1880 An inquest was opened into the death of eighty-year-old Ann Gillett of   **9 MARCH**
Ilchester. Paralysed for six years following a stroke, in the six weeks prior to her death on 8 March, she was treated by Dr Gibson, who repeatedly told her husband, Thomas, that Ann was dying from malnutrition.

Gillett employed Elizabeth Cox to nurse his wife, paying her 3s a week. Mrs Cox joined in the doctor's requests for Gillett to provide sustenance for Ann but Gillett insisted that he couldn't afford to buy the beef tea or meat extract that the doctor recommended. He fed Ann only bread with a scraping of butter and even then complained bitterly that she used too much butter.

In the last month of her life, Ann ate only a few biscuits and some soup sent to her by a neighbour. Two days before her death, her husband finally spent 1s on a pot of meat extract but it was too little, too late. Yet, even as his wife slowly died before his eyes, Thomas Gillett had £120 in an account at the Yeovil Savings Bank.

Dr Gibson refused to issue a death certificate and told the inquest that, although Ann obviously didn't have long to live when he started treating her, he was prepared to state that proper nourishment would have prolonged her life. At the same time, he admitted that the inadequate provision of food and comforts had merely hastened, rather than caused, her death. Nevertheless, Thomas Gillett was charged with Ann's manslaughter.

At his trial at the Somerset Assizes, the jury found Thomas Gillett guilty but, since he was seventy-six years old, he was given a fairly lenient sentence of one month's imprisonment with hard labour.

10 MARCH

1858   Thomas Pritchard of Middlezoy, a frail seventy-one-year-old shoemaker, who could only walk with the aid of two crutches, was beaten by his wife as he sat quietly by the fire. Mrs Pritchard then poured boiling water over her husband. Pritchard, who suffered terrible injuries, lived long enough to depose that his wife had suddenly attacked him with his crutches, knocking him to the ground and hitting his head and face several times. Mrs Pritchard was judged insane at the time of the attack.

Middlezoy village. (Author's collection)

11 MARCH

1849   An unnamed twelve-year-old boy was admitted to the Taunton and Somerset Hospital suffering from a baffling illness. For almost a year, he had complained of 'being helpless in all of his limbs' and, whenever he tried to stand up or exert himself in any way, he suffered from violent convulsions. Most unusually, he claimed to be completely incapable of swallowing and, given food or drink, would hold it in his mouth for long periods before eventually spitting it out.

He was an intelligent and articulate child and, after being observed in hospital for a few days, his condition was proving extremely puzzling to the doctors and all attempts at treatment had failed.

On Sunday, 11 March, all of the patients on the ward went to Divine Service, with the sole exception of the sick child. Unaware that a nurse had been left to look after him, the boy was seen to creep out of bed and help himself to ood from the lockers of all the other patients, which he devoured rapidly. When the nurse made a noise, the child raced back to his bed and resumed his former torpor.

Challenged by the doctors, the boy denied having left his bed but claimed that a lady had visited the ward while everyone was at worship and stolen food from the lockers. The doctors decided to play him at his own game. The next morning they told him that they had finally agreed on a cure for his maladies but warned him that it would be excruciatingly painful. They then prepared to administer the remedy.

As they did, the little boy said that he thought he might be able to stand up. He got out of bed but the doctors insisted that he still needed to be treated, at which he suggested that he might even be able to walk. Having demonstrated his new-found mobility, the doctors insisted that he must have the cure, since he still couldn't swallow. The little boy conceded that perhaps he should try, and he drank half a pint of tea and ate a large slice of bread and butter to prove that he didn't need the medication.

With the boy now miraculously cured, the doctors tried to find out what had started his deception almost twelve months earlier. The child was unable to offer any explanation and neither did he show any shame or remorse for his prolonged feigned illness.

1943 Twenty-one-year-old David Cobb became the first of eighteen US servicemen to be executed at Shepton Mallet Prison, having shot and killed 2nd Lieutenant Robert Cobner at Desborough Camp, Northamptonshire. During the Second World War, part of the prison was taken over by American forces as a place of execution for military personnel convicted of crimes while serving on British soil. Most of the executions were hangings, although two men – Alex Miranda and Benjamin Pyegate – faced a firing squad.   **12 MARCH**

Nearly all of the hangings were carried out by either Thomas or Albert Pierrepoint and took considerably longer than British judicial executions, since the death warrant was read out at the gallows and the condemned man was also permitted to make a last statement.

1828 An inquest was held by coroner Mr Caines on the death of fifteen-year-old Abraham Collins, who died the previous day at the ominously named Deadman's Cross in the parish of Pitminster. Collins was driving a cart loaded with elm saplings and, as he turned a corner, the wheel of his cart mounted the bank. The cart overturned and when it was righted, Collins was found dead, buried beneath the load.   **13 MARCH**

The jury returned a verdict of 'accidental death' and the coroner heavily censured one of the parish overseers, who had left the body lying on the road open to public view for some time while he went into Taunton to check the precise location of the parish boundaries. The spot where Collins met his death was on the border of two parishes and the zealous overseer was keen to ensure that the parish of Pitminster was not saddled with the cost of the funeral if the death had occurred outside parish boundaries.

14 MARCH

1869 James Hopes spent the evening drinking at Saltford with two men named Fletcher and Haynes. Both Fletcher and Haynes were employed by farmer John Rutter, as was Hopes before he was sacked six months earlier.

On leaving the pub, Hopes bought some tobacco and asked the landlord for matches, before walking home with his companions. When they reached Fletcher's home, Hopes asked to stay the night and, when Fletcher refused, Hopes threatened, 'If you don't give me a night's lodging, you shall be awoke tonight earlier than you think.'

The same process was repeated at Haynes's home and, sure enough, both men were woken soon afterwards by a fire on Rutter's farm. A shed and pigsty were completely destroyed, along with several pigs.

Hopes was suspected of starting the fire and was quickly arrested. While in custody, he remarked to PC Fry, 'If the old fellow [Rutter] presses this charge … I'll cook his goose for him if I live to come out of gaol.'

Rutter did press charges and, found guilty at his trial at the Somerset Assizes, Hopes was sentenced to seven years' penal servitude.

15 MARCH

1879 Thirty-seven-year-old farmer Lewis Franks visited Wells market. On his way home that evening he called at the Castle of Comfort Inn at East Harptree, leaving there at ten o'clock in the company of James Russell and George Palmer.

While Russell and Palmer were on foot, Franks was riding a rather frisky young horse and, almost a mile from the pub, the animal reared up, falling backwards onto Franks and crushing him. Russell ran to procure a cart and Franks, who was insensible and obviously badly injured, was taken back to the Castle of Comfort, where he lingered until the following evening.

An inquest held by Dr Craddock returned a verdict of 'accidental death' on Lewis Franks. By a strange coincidence, his father and father-in-law had both died in almost identical accidents and, at the time of his death, Franks had a son who had been badly injured in a similar fall from a donkey and was receiving treatment as an out-patient at the Bristol Infirmary.

16 MARCH

1878 Inquests were held on two unrelated accidental deaths by coroner Mr Munckton, at the West India House, Bridgwater.

By a strange coincidence, both of the victims – John Blackmore and William Upham – came from the small village of Spaxton. Both were killed in very similar accidents. Blackmore was trying to climb onto the shafts of his wagon when he slipped and fell under the wheels and was crushed, while Upham stumbled when jumping down from the shafts of his wagon to lead his horse uphill and was run over. The accidents occurred ten minutes apart, within yards of each other.

17 MARCH

1874 Eli Symes was driving bullocks in North Perrott, when the animals suddenly became restless. When Symes investigated the cause of their distress he found the battered body of a woman lying in a pond, her head stuck between the bank and a tree trunk and thus firmly lodged underwater. Her clothing was disturbed, she was barefoot and bare legged and there were splashes of fresh blood on the ground near the pond. A heavy, bloodstained stone lay nearby.

A search of the area revealed two places where a desperate struggle had apparently taken place. PC Joseph Williams noted the prints of small hobnailed boots and the imprint of a corduroy-clad knee, both in the mud and on the woman's clothes. He also saw a deep impression in the mud that looked as though a head had been forcibly pushed into the soft ground. Various items of women's clothing were scattered close by and a bonnet was found partially burnt.

When the body was removed from the pond, Constable Williams immediately recognised her. Ruth Butcher lived less than a quarter of a mile from the scene of her murder. In her early forties, she supported her two illegitimate children by working at home as a weaver for a manufacturer of hair netting and webbing and by taking in washing. She had the reputation of being 'of light character' and wasn't averse to making a little extra money by granting sexual favours. Her pockets were found to contain a piece of bacon weighing almost one pound, which had been neatly wrapped in paper and secured with a length of jute yarn.

Ruth's murder had probably occurred during the previous night, when a woman living nearby reported hearing screams. Bloodstains on gates and stiles led the police across the fields to Hardington, then back towards Haselbury Plucknett, until the trail eventually petered out close to the vicarage in Danes Field.

The killer was evidently a local man, since only someone familiar with the area would have known of the existence of the pond. Given that the murder took place in a small village, it seems inconceivable that the killer was never brought to justice, but in spite of an extensive search of the area, no trace was ever found of the murder weapon. With no real evidence, the inquest jury returned

Site of the murder of Ruth Butcher. (© N. Sly)

the verdict of 'wilful murder against some person or persons unknown', and the identity of Ruth Butcher's killer was never discovered.

18 MARCH   **1896**   The deputy coroner for West Somerset held an inquest on the death of six-year-old Olive Kate Northcombe, the daughter of the village schoolmaster from Winsham. Olive had just left school for the afternoon and was walking with her arm around the waist of another little girl when a pony and cart came towards them. The thirteen-year-old driver was galloping the pony at breakneck speed and had little control over the animal.

The girls separated, one moving to each side of the road, but the pony hit Olive and threw her under the wheel of the cart, crushing her chest and killing her almost instantly.

The inquest jury recorded a verdict of 'accidental death' and, although they felt that Master Brown's careless driving was the cause of the tragedy, because of his youth they stopped short of pronouncing him culpably negligent. He was reprimanded by the coroner, who told him that he had only narrowly escaped being charged with manslaughter.

19 MARCH   **1894**   Mervyn Nethercott stole a tame rabbit from George W. Sage in Bedminster, Bristol. Thirteen-year-old Mervyn had several previous convictions dating back two years and had twice been sentenced by magistrates to spend five years at a reformatory school. However, on each occasion, the Home Secretary had rescinded the sentence and now the only solution that the magistrates could see for Mervyn's persistent offending was to send him to take his chance at the assizes.

There the judge stated that he would not send the boy where the authorities did not want him to go. Instead, he sent Mervyn to prison for one month, additionally ordering him to receive twelve strokes with the birch rod.

20 MARCH   **1869**   Twelve-year-old Charlotte Seviour stood trial at the Somerset Assizes charged with setting fire to her father's house at Nunney on 17 December 1868.

Charlotte's father, Benjamin, told the court that he had gone out, leaving Charlotte in charge of her five younger siblings. When he returned at half-past five in the afternoon, his children were standing in the street, while his cottage burned down. The building was completely destroyed, as was the home of his next-door neighbour, Thomas Scammells.

A young boy claimed to have seen Charlotte jumping down from a wall at the back of the cottage and, immediately afterwards, the thatched roof burst into flames. Interviewed by the police, Charlotte initially denied having anything to do with the fire but eventually admitted to Superintendent Deggan of the Frome police that she had deliberately set the fire because her father beat and ill-treated her.

The jury found Charlotte guilty of arson but strongly recommended mercy on account of her age. Mr Justice Byles sentenced her to be imprisoned for fourteen days, with labour commensurate to her age and sex, after which she was to spend five years in a reformatory school.

1867 The trial of thirty-year-old James Thorne took place at the Somerset Assizes. At Stogursey almost two weeks earlier, Thorne had snatched a red-hot poker from the fire and flung it at his daughter, Charlotte, who was then about four years old. The poker hit Charlotte in the face, destroying the sight in one of her eyes and, for a while, her life hung in the balance. The trial judge debated whether to place Thorne on remand to see if the child lived or died, but eventually sentenced him to twenty years' penal servitude.

1895 Henry Dagger appeared at the police court in Bath, charged with assaulting fifteen-year-old Richard James Parr on 28 February and 1 March.

Parr was an inmate of the Somerset Industrial School and Dagger's father employed him as a farm labourer. Dagger had taken an instant dislike to Parr and seized every opportunity to bully him. The first charge related to Parr trying to escape from Dagger, who was about to horsewhip him for no reason. Parr hid behind a door and, finding him there, Dagger flung his weight against the door, crushing Parr between it and the wall. So violent was the act that the door was torn off its hinges. The second charge related to Dagger beating Parr with a large pebble. When Dagger's stepmother intervened, Parr was bleeding heavily from several cuts and had to be sent to hospital for treatment.

Dagger pleaded guilty and was fined 40s plus costs for the first assault and sentenced to ten days' imprisonment for the second.

1880 Henry William Wiltshire, aged nine, told his mother that he was going to Leigh Woods to cut some sticks to sell, to help pay for his sister to go on an outing. He called for his friend, William Thomas, and the two boys walked to the wood, a familiar place for both since they often played there.

After half an hour cutting sticks, the two boys reached the Portishead Tunnel and Henry suggested that they clamber down the rocks. As he tried to step off a rock onto the top of the tunnel, Henry slipped and plummeted 50ft onto the railway line below.

Bristol dock labourer Robert Bull saw Henry fall and rushed to help. He found the little boy unconscious and carried him to the New Inn but sadly Henry died in Bull's arms before they got there. At a later inquest, the jury returned a verdict of 'accidental death'.

1888 Fifty-four-year-old Martha Charles was found dead at a house belonging to George Lye in East Lambrook. Martha did housework for Lye and at half-past ten the previous evening, he woke her and demanded the return of some clothes she was laundering for him. Although Martha said she would return them first thing in the morning, Lye was adamant that he needed them urgently, as he was planning to go away.

Martha got up and finished ironing the clothes, then took them across the street to Lye's house. When she didn't return, her fifteen-year-old daughter Caroline went to ask where she was. Lye said that she was doing some mending for him, so Caroline went home to bed.

When her mother hadn't returned by daybreak, Caroline went back to Lye's house but there was no reply to her knocks. Caroline went for help and neighbours found her mother's body in a pool of blood in the sitting room. She had five major head wounds, inflicted with an axe. Police began an immediate search for Lye, issuing a description: 'George Lye, aged about thirty years, about 5ft 7in in height, light whiskers and moustache, brown hair, near sighted, large Roman nose; dressed in a speckled suit, nearly new, is wanted for murder.'

Lye was quickly apprehended and appeared before Mr Justice Day at the Somerset Assizes in July, charged with Martha's wilful murder. Since the death of his parents, Lye had lived off his inheritance. Described as a 'ne'er do well' and 'an idiot', he was known to be addicted to drink and, indeed, two empty gin bottles were found near Martha's body.

There was absolutely no motive for the brutal slaying and Lye was found guilty but insane. The judge ordered him to be detained until Her Majesty's pleasure be known.

25 MARCH **1784** At the Somerset Assizes in Taunton, four men were sentenced to death. John Jones was found guilty of highway robbery, while John Smith and John Channell were convicted for burglary. All three men were hanged at Gallows Field in Ilchester on 7 April. One day later, Richard Rendall was hanged at Totterdown in Bristol, after which he was left suspended in chains as an example to other would-be criminals. He was found guilty of highway robbery at the same assizes.

26 MARCH **1880** Edwin J. Richards walked from Bristol to Long Ashton, an area much frequented by city dwellers for recreation and fresh air. His leisurely lunchtime stroll ended at Bedminster police station, after he happened to glance into a ditch in Yandly Lane and spotted the dead body of a baby wrapped in a piece of red flannel.

Police retrieved the body and removed it to the Angel Inn, Long Ashton, where it was examined by a surgeon. Although the tiny body was in an advanced state of decomposition and had obviously been abandoned some time ago, it was thought that the child had died as a result of foul play. The police were amazed that none of the hundreds of people who had walked past the ditch in recent weeks had noticed the infant's bright red shroud.

In spite of exhaustive investigations, the mystery of the Long Ashton baby was never solved.

27 MARCH **1852** On 26 March, Ann Wilkins of Axbridge visited the town's fair, spending most of the evening dancing in a beer-house. By the time she left in the early hours of the next morning, she was very drunk. Although a hardened drinker himself, her husband, George, strongly disapproved of her intemperate ways and would frequently beat Ann when she got drunk. Thus she probably expected the beating she got when she returned home from the dance.

At nine o'clock on the morning of 27 March, George went to Ann's mother and asked her to make Ann a cup of tea. When she took the tea to Ann's bedroom, her mother found her daughter lying insensible in bed, her hair dishevelled and her clothes torn. She had wounds on her face and her thighs were dreadfully bruised. Ann died from her injuries later that evening and a post-mortem examination determined that she had been hit or kicked on the back of her head, which had caused her brain to swell. George Wilkins was distraught at his wife's death, kissing the corpse and saying, 'Oh, my dear wife, what shall I do?'

Charged with his wife's wilful murder, George Wilkins appeared before Mr Justice Erle at the Spring Assizes in Taunton. He alleged that both he and Ann had been extremely drunk at the time of the offence and that Ann had hit him over the head with a stick. Wilkins swore that he had taken the stick from her and had only hit her once or twice on the mouth.

Wilkins was found guilty of the lesser offence of manslaughter and sentenced to be transported for life. Remarkably, Ann Wilkins was killed during the early hours of 27 March. Her post-mortem took place on 27 March and she was buried on 28 March. Her husband was arrested on 27 March, appeared before the magistrates on 29 March and was then committed for trial. He was sent to Taunton Gaol on 30 March, the Grand Jury found a true bill against him on 31 March and his trial took place on 1 April. Thus, the whole proceedings, from the murder to sentencing the perpetrator, took less than one week.

1878 Forty-year-old Mary Ann Ford died at Henstridge. Mary Ann lived with her father, William, and, for many years prior to her death, she had shown signs of 'weakness of the mind'. Her symptoms worsened over the last nine months of her life and doctors suggested that she should be removed to the workhouse. However, the institution declined to accept her so, for her last months, she was confined to her bedroom, seen only by her father and an elderly neighbour, who occasionally came in to wash her. **28 MARCH**

When Mary Ann died, doctors found her to be in a shocking condition. She was filthy, covered with vermin and so emaciated that her body was little more than skin and bones. Doctors determined that she had starved to death and William was charged with her manslaughter.

He appeared at the Somerset Assizes, where his defence counsel Mr Odgers insisted that Mary Ann had died from 'softening of the brain' and that her father was in no way to blame for her death. The jury agreed and William Ford was found not guilty.

1855 Mary Ann Bryant was arrested in Bristol and charged with the attempted murder of her six-year-old illegitimate daughter, Hannah Selman. She told PC Bowden, 'It's no good to deny it. I did do so.' **29 MARCH**

On the evening of 28 March, John Coward heard a child screaming and, when he went to investigate, he found a little girl standing up to her armpits in water in the Floating Harbour at Bristol. Coward rescued the child and carried her to the police station at Clifton. When she was examined, Hannah had a distinct red mark around her neck and a stone weighing almost ten pounds was tied to the front of her dress.

Hannah told the police that her mother had tied the stone to her and thrown her into the water. She told officers that she lived in Wickwar and the police

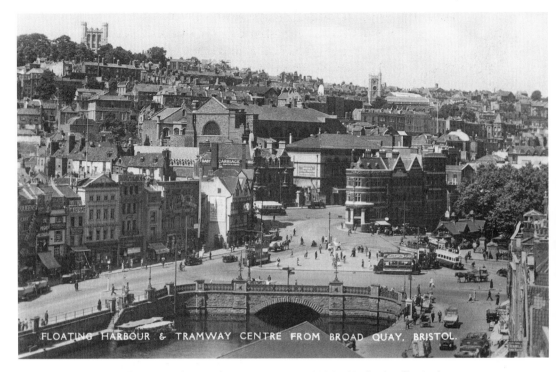

Floating Harbour and Tramways Centre, 1920s. (Author's collection)

went there the next day, and spoke to Mary Ann's mother, who directed them to her daughter's home in Bristol.

Hannah had lived with her grandmother since her birth but Mrs Selman's husband had recently died, leaving her with no means of financial support, and she asked Mary Ann to take her child. Mary Ann had married twelve months earlier, but although her husband knew of Hannah's existence he refused to have her in his home. When Mary Ann collected her daughter, she told her mother that she had arranged for Hannah to be fostered by a woman in Bristol.

Tried at the Gloucester Assizes just days later, Mary Ann Bryant pleaded guilty to the charge of attempted murder against her, leaving the judge no alternative but to sentence her to death. There is no evidence that the sentence was ever carried out.

30 MARCH **1849** The trial of Charles Holbrook took place before Lord Denman at the Somerset Assizes. Holbrook was charged with cutting and stabbing Priscilla Rawlings at Chew Magna on 29 October 1848, with intent to do grievous bodily harm.

Priscilla, a milliner and dressmaker, agreed to go for a Sunday afternoon walk with Holbrook. On their return, Holbrook was keen to see her again and asked her where she would be that evening. Priscilla told him that she would most likely be at church but eventually decided not to go and stayed at home.

Obviously feeling that he had been 'stood up', Holbrook went round to Priscilla's house and asked to speak to her privately. Priscilla's sister urged him to speak out so that everyone could hear him, at which Holbrook pulled out a knife and stabbed Priscilla in the neck. Fortunately, she saw the blow coming and was able to duck, thus avoiding more serious injury. Even so, the knife blow was a violent one and the blade penetrated her neck to a depth of 1.5in. With Charles still threatening to 'be the death of' Priscilla, he was restrained before he could attempt to stab her again.

At his trial, to the consternation of Lord Denman, Holbrook's defence counsel unbelievably described the stabbing as 'a lark'. Neither judge nor jury saw anything remotely 'larkish' about Holbrook's offence and he was found guilty and sentenced to be transported for nine years.

Mr Justice Denman, later Lord Denman. (Author's collection)

1838 The trial of husband and wife William and Rachel Williams, who were jointly charged with the wilful murder of seven-year-old Jemima Davis, was scheduled to take place at the Somerset Assizes.   **31 MARCH**

Jemima was Rachel's illegitimate child by a man named Davis, who had never denied his responsibilities towards his daughter and paid for her to be kept 'at nurse'. When Davis died, the regular payments to Jemima's nurse stopped. Jemima was handed over to her maternal grandmother, Mrs Yeates, who kept her for three months before falling ill. She was then sent to her mother, who had since married William Williams and now lived in Keynsham.

Williams had no idea that his wife had borne an illegitimate baby, so Rachel passed Jemima off as her sister's child. However, William seemed to be the only person who didn't know the circumstances of Jemima's birth and, when one of his work colleagues informed him of her true parentage, it marked the beginning of the little girl's suffering.

From that moment onwards, Jemima was treated with the most unimaginable cruelty and kept without food and water. Concerned neighbours approached Rachel and William and were told that the child was losing weight because she had worms. They assured everyone who complained that Jemima had been seen by a doctor and that she ate voraciously but couldn't gain any weight.

As Jemima grew ever more emaciated, she was forced to beg for food from the neighbours but was beaten whenever her parents caught her doing so. On one occasion, she was punished by being forced to stand barefoot in the snow. She was always bruised and bleeding and cried constantly. Eventually she starved to death. A post-mortem examination showed her to be severely underweight, covered in bruises and missing two toes, probably due to frostbite.

An inquest held by coroner Mr R. Uphill saw a procession of witnesses who testified to trying to help the little girl by giving her food and by remonstrating with her parents about their ill-treatment of the little girl. Yet nobody had reported their concerns to the authorities.

The inquest found a verdict of wilful murder against Rachel and William, who were committed for trial at the Somerset Assizes. However, the Grand Jury, whose job it was to consider the evidence for the prosecution and determine whether or not the trial should proceed, found insufficient evidence; both parents were therefore acquitted and walked from the court free. At the time, Rachel Williams had a new baby by her husband and was pregnant with their second child.

APRIL

Dundry in the 1960s. (Author's collection)

1 APRIL

1831   At the Somerset Assizes, Robert Brewer was charged with maliciously cutting and wounding his wife, Elizabeth, with intent to do her grievous bodily harm. The court heard that forty-two-year-old Brewer was a habitual drunkard, who persistently ill-treated his wife.

On the night of 14 January, Brewer went to bed drunk with a lighted clay pipe in his mouth. Afraid that he would set the bed on fire, Elizabeth took it from him, at which Robert promptly fetched a second pipe. Again, Elizabeth took the pipe, only for Robert to fetch a third, at which Elizabeth's patience snapped. She broke all three pipes and then made a run for the bedroom door to escape her husband's inevitable wrath.

Robert pulled out a clasp knife and tried to cut Elizabeth's throat. As she threw up her arms in self-defence, she knocked the knife upwards and, rather than cutting her throat as intended, the blade went into her lower lip, cutting a 6in-long wound down her chin and throat towards her breastbone.

In his defence, Brewer pleaded both drunkenness and provocation. Found guilty as charged, he was sentenced to death, although there is no record that he was actually executed.

2 APRIL

1897   Two well-known criminals – twenty-year-old Edward Jennings and fourteen-year-old Leah Tregonning (aka Maud Collins) – were arrested at Bristol and charged with highway robbery. On 20 March, photographer Mr Jones was walking on the seafront at Weston-super-Mare when he was approached by a pretty young girl, who asked him to go for a walk with her. Hardly believing his luck, Jones accompanied the woman to the Uphill Road, when they were joined by a young man.

The man accused Jones of being with his wife and punched him in the eye. The couple then demanded money from the photographer, who ran for his life. When they caught up with Jones, the young couple knocked him over, beat him and stole money and other small items from his pockets.

Weston-super-Mare. (Author's collection)

Tried at the Somerset Assizes, both Jennings and Tregonning were found guilty of highway robbery. Mr Justice Day took Leah's youth into account, sentencing her to be kept in a reformatory for five years. Jennings, who had several previous convictions, received six months' imprisonment with hard labour and in addition Day ordered him to be twice flogged, receiving twenty-five lashes with the cat-o'-nine-tails on each occasion.

1882   In the hayloft at Norton Hall in Midsomer Norton was a large cask, which held about forty barrels of grain. The children of the farm occasionally lowered themselves into the cask for amusement. On 3 April, the owner's son, ten-year-old Luie Beauchamp, rushed to his father's dairyman and told him that Frederick Stutley Skye was groaning at the bottom of the cask. **3 APRIL**

Emmanuel Green promptly lowered himself into the cask to rescue Skye, but had barely reached the bottom when he felt himself losing consciousness. Luie ran to another of his father's employees, coachman James Sperring, and as Sperring also went to the cask, Luie went for a doctor.

Sperring managed to hook a chain round what he thought was a leg and Skye was hauled from the cask. Sperring then went back for Green but, feeling ill, climbed out again and found a hatchet, with which he cut a hole in the cask, pulling Green out through the hole.

Seventeen-year-old Skye was dead and, although Green was ill, he recovered after a few days bed rest. The cause of Skye's death was attributed to a build-up of 'carbonic acid gas' in the base of the tank.

1852   Edward Mahoney and William Tudgee were drinking at a public house in Bath when an argument flared up between them. Mahoney pulled out a knife and threatened to run it into someone, then, seconds later, he made good his threat, stabbing Tudgee in the side. **4 APRIL**

Tudgee was taken to hospital, where he died shortly afterwards. However, before his death, he was able to give a deposition, in which he admitted to hitting Mahoney first and making him bleed.

At Mahoney's trial for wilful murder at the Somerset Assizes, judge Mr Baron Platt told the jury that if Mahoney had used the knife for revenge or in anger, his crime would amount to murder. Yet, if he had used the knife in self-defence it would be manslaughter. The jury found Mahoney guilty of manslaughter and he was sentenced to one month's imprisonment.

1827   Throughout Somerset history, there are numerous tales of 'riding the skimmington', an ancient form of punishment meted out to supposed wrongdoers. One such incident is depicted on the wall panels of Montacute House, where a henpecked husband is shown sitting astride a pole and being paraded around the village to the derision of his neighbours. Often, as a prelude to the skimmington, a gang would assemble outside the miscreant's house, banging on household utensils, which they used as makeshift drums. The performance of 'rough music' outside the house was frequently sufficiently shaming to persuade people to move away from the area. **5 APRIL**

On 5 April 1827, the victim of 'rough music' was Thomazine Hawker of Yeovil, who was known as a woman of easy virtue. Thomazine was brave enough to step outside her house to confront the taunting crowd of more than 100 men and women and, as soon as she appeared, a cry went up to play 'the whore's tune'.

Thomazine wisely retreated back indoors, while the band played for two hours outside her cottage, punctuating their music with bouts of stone throwing. Eventually, the local police broke up the gathering and two of the ringleaders, John Mabey and John Collins, were arrested and charged with riotous assembly, assault and ill-treatment towards Thomazine Hawker. Both men were found guilty and sentenced to six months' imprisonment with hard labour.

6 APRIL   **1861**   While collecting water from a pond in a field adjacent to the Carpenter's Arms at Dundry, Hannah Maria Stallard noticed something that looked like a sheep's head floating in the water. She fetched her brother, William, to have a look and he poked the half-submerged object with a stick, eventually manoeuvring it to the side of the pond, from where it could be retrieved. Only then did the Stallards realise that they had discovered the badly decomposed body of a baby girl.

Two surgeons were requested to perform a post-mortem examination on the infant's body, which appeared to have been heavily pecked by the ducks that lived in the pond. John Shorland and Thomas Cowling agreed that the baby was between two and four months old and that she had been an unusually plump baby, suggesting that she had been well cared for prior to her death. The surgeons found wounds to the child's throat from which they deduced that her throat had been cut. They believed that the body had been in the pond for several weeks.

The pond was dragged but nothing of significance was found, although some baby clothes were discovered hidden in the surrounding reeds. Suspicion fell on a Bristol woman, who had visited Dundry some weeks earlier with a baby girl. She had since visited the village without the child, explaining that her baby had died and been buried in Bristol.

At an inquest held at the Carpenter's Arms by coroner Mr Bruges Fry, the jury returned a verdict of 'wilful murder by person or persons unknown'. There is no evidence to suggest that anyone was ever prosecuted for the murder of the unidentified baby.

7 APRIL   **1879**   Twenty-two-year-old labourer James Pattemore had already consumed a large quantity of cider at the Swan Inn, Merriott, when he called for half a pint of gin. When he asked for a second half pint only minutes later, the landlord refused to serve him. Pattemore argued with him and the landlord eventually agreed that he could have the gin, providing he took it home. The gin was poured but Pattemore instantly reneged on the agreement, drinking it in one draught.

Unsurprisingly, Pattemore fell over on leaving the pub but was picked up by his friends and carried home, where he died within hours. At his inquest, the coroner said that he found it disgraceful that 'lads' should be allowed to drink spirits in public houses. His jury returned a verdict that Pattemore's death was caused by drinking a large quantity of spirits.

1875 Four-year-old Ada Jones from Bath had been ill for some time before dying between five and six o'clock in the morning. Ada was the oldest of the three children of Sarah Jones and her husband, although the child's father had left his wife some years earlier. Nevertheless, he regularly sent money for the upkeep of his estranged wife and dependant children, which included two from his previous marriage. **8 APRIL**

Much of this money was spent by Sarah on beer and gin and she also sold clothes and furniture to buy more drink, while her children survived on bread and water or begged in the streets. When Ada died, Sarah threatened ten-year-old Frederick that she would thrash him if he told anybody. However, Frederick disobeyed her and told their landlady, Elizabeth Tooze, who immediately sent for the police.

When PC Stone arrived at the house, he found Ada in a filthy, stinking room. A post-mortem examination noted that the little girl was covered in suppurating bedsores. Most of her right foot had rotted away and she had no skin on her left foot from her toes to her ankle. There was not a trace of food or water in her stomach and bowels.

'I didn't know the child was dying,' was Sarah's only comment when she was arrested for causing Ada's death by neglect, untruthfully assuring Inspector Berry that Ada had been regularly attended by a doctor.

An inquest into Ada's death recorded a verdict of manslaughter against her mother. When Sarah appeared before magistrates, the Mayor of Bath made a point of condemning Elizabeth Tooze, who had never seen any of the children apart from Frederick, but had heard Ada moaning and had complained to Sarah on numerous occasions about the foul smell coming from her room. The mayor also castigated Mr Jones for neglecting his duty as a parent. Only the day before Ada's death, Sarah had written to her husband, 'the children are all well and send their love to you and kisses.'

Sarah was committed to stand trial at the Somerset Assizes on the coroner's warrant but died in Taunton Gaol before the case could come to court.

1924 An inquest was held in Frome on the death of a farmer from Marston Bigot. Twenty-one-year-old Robert Edward Walter from West Forest Farm was found lying dead in a field with terrible gunshot wounds to his head. His own gun lay beside him with both barrels loaded. **9 APRIL**

Superintendent Stewart investigated the mysterious circumstances of the young man's death and explained to the coroner that Walter had been perturbed by damage done to his crops by deer straying from an adjoining wood. He had rigged up a device using an old rifle and a trip wire, intending that any disturbance of the wire by deer would discharge the rifle. Stewart believed that Walter had accidentally activated his own trap, thus shooting himself in the head. The coroner recorded a verdict of accidental death, remarking that Walter was 'evidently a victim of his own ingenuity'.

Cheap Street,
Frome. (Author's
collection)

CHEAP STREET, FROME.

1864   Shepherd Mathew Smith went into a field near Ilchester, where his dog
immediately began digging, as if trying to retrieve something buried in the
ground. When Smith went to investigate, he found that the dog had unearthed
the body of a baby boy.

Smith fetched a policeman, who in turn sent for a doctor. When a post-
mortem examination was carried out on the infant, it was found to be a
full-term baby, who had been buried alive. The baby's windpipe, gullet and
stomach contained earth, which the surgeon Mr Bennett took as proof that
the child had breathed, struggled and swallowed, before dying of suffocation.

Investigations led the police to Mary Thorne, a dairy maid. When asked if
she had been 'with child', Mary stated that she hadn't, adding that she was
willing to be examined by a doctor to prove it. Yet when she was examined
the next day, the doctor confirmed that she had recently been confined. Faced
with this conclusion, Mary admitted that she had given birth, saying that she
didn't know if the child had been born alive or dead.

Charged with the wilful murder of her baby, Mary appeared at the next
Somerset Assizes, where the chief witness was her own mother, who told the
court that Mary had previously given birth to another illegitimate child. Mary
had treated that child kindly but it had lived only a few weeks. Mary's mother
stated that her daughter had told her that she had given birth again, after which
she had fallen asleep. When she awoke, her baby was dead and she had buried
it in the field.

Mr Turner, who acted as counsel for the defence, gave an eloquent speech
insisting that it hadn't been satisfactorily proven that the child had died by his
mother's hands. The jury agreed and Mary Thorne was found not guilty of the
charge of wilful murder but guilty of concealing the birth of her child. She was
sentenced to six months' imprisonment with hard labour.

1879   For many weeks, a rumour spread like wildfire around Somerset
concerning the prophesies of Mother Shipton. The legendary Ursula Shipton
was born in Yorkshire in 1488 and died in 1561. She was believed to be
a great prophetess and many of her predictions were published, mostly
after her death.

It was widely believed that Mother Shipton had predicted that Ham
Hill in South Somerset – then a great stone quarry and now a country
park – would be swallowed up by an earthquake on 11 April 1879. In
spite of assurances by those who had actually read Mother Shipton's
books that no such prophecy was even mentioned, countless
villagers in the area believed that their world was about to end. The
more sceptical among them simply delayed planting their gardens
or moved their family treasures to a safer place, but numerous
families temporarily left the area to avoid the cataclysmic event,
which, of course, never happened.

Mother Shipton.
(Author's collection)

12 APRIL

1908   Soldier Charles Peoples lay in a critical condition in hospital after falling from a train travelling at nearly forty miles an hour. Stationed at Cardiff with the Welsh Regiment, Peoples was returning from a day trip to Plymouth when, as the train neared Weston-super-Mare station, he decided he needed to visit the lavatory. Unfortunately, he mistook the train door for the lavatory door and walked off the train.

He suffered a compound fracture of the jaw and other head injuries in the fall but managed to crawl some distance to a signal box, from where he was taken to Weston-super-Mare Hospital. Fortunately, he survived.

13 APRIL

1878   Market gardener Josh Trask of Merriott came home from work in the evening and called to his mother to bring out a light so that he could stable his horse. Although he shouted three or four times, seventy-seven-year-old Mary Trask didn't hear him and he ended up working in the dark. When he got indoors, he was so exasperated with his mother that he kicked her.

Mary immediately complained of great pain in her stomach. A doctor attended her the following day but she died that evening. Dr Wilson conducted a post-mortem examination and observed heavy bruising on Mary's lower stomach. He determined the cause of her death to be inflammation of the bowels, although could not be certain whether it had resulted from a kick or from natural causes.

Josh Trask was arrested for his mother's manslaughter, although he told the arresting officer, Sergeant Giles, 'On my soul, I never kicked her.' He was tried before Mr Justice Denman at the Somerset Assizes in August, where it emerged that Trask had a previous conviction for failing to contribute to the support of his mother. He was found guilty of her manslaughter and sentenced to be transported for five years.

14 APRIL

1858   At about six o'clock in the morning, a gunshot was heard at Creech St Michael, near Taunton. Soon afterwards, John Baker Bucknall reported to his father that he was unable to gain entrance to his grandparents' inn to keep a prearranged appointment to accompany his grandfather to Bridgwater market.

When Bucknall's father and his employer, Mr Morris, went to investigate, they found all the doors locked. Seeing smoke drifting about inside the property, they broke in. In the cellar lay seventy-two-year-old John Bucknall, a bullet through his head and his coat on fire. His wife was dead in bed upstairs, her throat cut and one of her fingers almost severed. A few rings, a brooch and £40 had been stolen from the cottage.

Suspicion immediately fell on John Baker Bucknall. Bucknall had a previous conviction for housebreaking and was one of the few people who knew that his grandfather had £40 in the house, money that he was planning to use to buy some pigs at the market later that day. There was blood on the boy's clothes and he was known to have recently made a bullet and to have borrowed some gunpowder. The most damning evidence against him was the later discovery of some of the stolen property tied up in his handkerchief, along with a knife and a letter.

John Baker Bucknall approached his trial at the Somerset Assizes before Mr Baron Watson with what was described as 'a jaunty and impudent air'. It took a guilty verdict from the jury and the handing down of the mandatory death sentence by the judge to wipe the smile off his face. Even so, he made no confession of guilt before facing executioner William Calcraft at Taunton Gaol on 24 August 1858.

1864 Soldier Henry Bishop deliberately fired his pistol into the face of his estranged wife, Louisa. After their marriage, Louisa moved from Bath to Henry's posting at Aldershot to be with him. However, after just five days, she returned home alone. On his discharge from the army, Henry joined his wife in Bath but the couple quarrelled on an almost daily basis and Louisa soon left him and moved in with friends. **15 APRIL**

On 15 April, Henry met Louisa in Bath and tried to persuade her to come back to him. When she refused, saying that she had taken a job and, besides, Henry had no home to offer her, he shot her.

Tried at Wells Assizes, it emerged that Henry had attempted suicide on the day after his marriage. Louisa, who lost an eye as a result of the shooting, admitted under cross-examination that she had taken some of his belongings and sold them. Henry was found guilty of shooting with intent to do grievous bodily harm and was sentenced to ten years of penal servitude. On hearing the sentence, he collapsed unconscious in the dock.

1866 Emily Stallard died at Dundry. Her funeral was conducted on the afternoon of 23 April by Revd Boutflower and, as her coffin lay in the grave after the conclusion of the ceremony, some of the mourners believed they saw it moving. **16 APRIL**

By now, Boutflower had left the churchyard. He was hastily summoned back to be assured by several witnesses that there were definite, unmistakable signs of movement from within the coffin. At a loss as to what to do next, Boutflower and the mourners watched the coffin for some time, seeing no further signs of any disturbance. However, the mourners were adamant that they had clearly seen the coffin move and insisted it should be investigated.

Eventually, with the permission of Emily's father, the coffin was lifted from the grave and the lid removed. It was immediately obvious that Miss Stallard had not moved at all – in fact, her body was already beginning to decompose. However, those mourners who believed that they had witnessed the movement could not be easily convinced and Boutflower was forced to send for a mirror, which was held to Miss Stallard's lips. Only when there was no sign of any misting on the surface of the mirror did everyone agree that the deceased was definitely not breathing. The coffin was reburied and Emily Stallard was left to rest in peace.

1883 'I have killed my little boy. He is up at the top of the lane and you will find him in the field with a razor by his side,' said the man who walked into the police station at Wincanton. Albion Wadman then led officers to where his seven-year-old son, James, lay dead, his throat cut with a razor. **17 APRIL**

Wadman was a married man with three sons. His wife had recently been confined to a lunatic asylum, leaving him on his own to raise the children, feed them, clothe them and keep a roof over their heads, while continuing his work as a shoemaker. The two youngest boys had fallen ill and had been admitted to the hospital at Wincanton Workhouse. Yet, even though he now only had James to care for, Wadman struggled, as his own failing eyesight made it almost impossible for him to work.

Charged with the wilful murder of his son, Wadman stood trial at Taunton Assizes. He initially pleaded guilty, but was immediately taken aside by Mr Kitley, the Governor of the County Gaol. After a quiet discussion with Kitley, Wadman tearfully revised his plea to one of not guilty.

Judge Baron Huddleston told the jury that there was no question that Wadman had caused the death of his son and that, in the eyes of the law, this was wilful murder. There was also no doubt that the murder was premeditated. However, the medical witnesses testified that Wadman was suffering from a mental illness that might prevent him from differentiating between right and wrong. If the jury accepted the medical evidence, they should find the defendant not guilty. The jury took only a short time to pronounce Wadman not guilty on the grounds of insanity, leaving the judge to order him to be detained at Her Majesty's pleasure. Wadman was sent to Broadmoor Criminal Lunatic Asylum and is believed to have died there in 1893.

18 APRIL

1938 After falling from scaffolding while working on a school building at Yeovil, John Lucas of Bristol walked a mile to the hospital, escorted by a colleague. On arriving at the Yeovil District Hospital, Lucas collapsed into the arms of the reception staff and later investigations showed that he had broken his neck in three places.

At the time, ninety-nine per cent of broken necks were fatal and a doctor stated that even the slightest movement of the neck was liable to cause death. Staff at the hospital encased Lucas in a full plaster cast and were hopeful that he would survive.

19 APRIL

1875 An inquest was held on the body of a newly-born child, found drowned in a ditch at East Brent. The child's mother was Elizabeth Daunton, who admitted that the baby was born alive and had only kicked a little when she threw it into the ditch. Elizabeth also said that she had expected the child to sink without trace and that no more would have been heard of it.

The jury found a verdict of wilful murder against Elizabeth, an inmate of the Axbridge Workhouse. Tried at the Somerset Assizes, she was found guilty and sentenced to death, although she was later reprieved.

In total, Elizabeth had given birth to four illegitimate children. The first was found dead in bed and the second was removed from her custody after she made repeated threats to kill it. The third child was found dead in a ditch at Lympsham in October 1869. On that occasion, Elizabeth swore that she was sitting at the roadside nursing the infant when it accidentally rolled off her lap into the ditch and drowned. She was found guilty of that baby's manslaughter and sentenced to twelve months' imprisonment.

East Brent.
(Author's collection)

1830 Thomas Vile died at Huish's Almshouses, Taunton, after a fire in his bedroom which reduced his bed and bedclothes to ashes. It was presumed that he had retired for the night without extinguishing his candle, which then set his bed curtains alight. Although the old man's body was dreadfully burned, people sleeping in adjoining rooms had heard no cries for assistance, suggesting that Vile was suffocated by the smoke.

20 APRIL

1880 Zebulun Wood of the Railway Inn, Taunton, appeared before magistrates charged with having unlawfully sold liquor during prohibited hours.

21 APRIL

On 9 April, Sergeant Self happened upon a large bottle containing beer and spirits, concealed under the verandah of the pub. He reported the matter to his superiors and, on the night of 11 April, Self hid on a bridge near the inn and saw Mrs Wood place another bottle in the same place. Soon afterwards, PC Channing approached the pub and took a healthy swig from the bottle and, within a short while, PC Hookway also called for some out-of-hours refreshments.

At the magistrates' court, Mr Cook appeared in defence of Mr Wood, pointing out that he had been the innkeeper for fifteen years without any previous complaints against him. According to both Mr and Mrs Wood, a perfect stranger had visited the pub during licensing hours, ordered and paid for a bottle of beer, asking for it to be left on the verandah for later collection. The customer was definitely not in uniform, insisted Mrs Wood.

The magistrates found that there was insufficient evidence to warrant a conviction and dismissed the case.

1898 Coroner Mr S. Craddock held an inquest at Kingston Seymour on what would have been the sixth birthday of the deceased.

22 APRIL

Three days earlier, Albert Godfrey wandered away from his parents on the farm where his father was employed as a herdsman. Although a search was begun within minutes, it was not to have a happy ending as the little boy was found drowned in a ditch about twenty yards from his home.

His body was pinned down by a grindstone weighing around 2cwt. The grindstone had only temporarily been placed on the side of the ditch an hour or two earlier and the coroner believed that Albert had been playing with it and had fallen into the water, the stone then falling on top of him. The inquest jury returned a verdict of 'accidentally drowned'.

23 APRIL **1937** At the hamlet of Lottisham Green, near Glastonbury, neighbours of William and Lily Rendell were disturbed by screams and groans coming from the couple's cottage. When they went to investigate, they found Lily dead on the kitchen floor, with terrible injuries to her head and throat. A bloodstained hatchet and razor were found nearby.

William and Lily married in 1906 and Rendell served in the army both before and after his marriage, from 1887 to 1899 and again from 1914 to 1919. Although the couple had been married for twenty-one years at the time of Lily's death, they had actually only lived together as man and wife for about twelve months, parting, reuniting and parting again many times during their marriage. (Their first separation came only two weeks after their wedding.) When not living with his wife or in the army, William lived in the workhouse, saying that it was preferable to the dog's life he led at home, where he was subjected to Lily's constant nagging. Nevertheless, only a few weeks before Lily's death, the couple had decided to give their marriage yet another try.

Mr Justice Lawrence. (Author's collection)

Since William had been seen leaving his home shortly before the discovery of his wife's body, he was the prime suspect and was arrested only two hours later. In a statement to police, he alleged that he and Lily had argued about a man she was 'carrying on with' and Lily had told him that, if he didn't like living with her, he could always go back to the workhouse. William lost his temper and hit his wife several times over the head with a small axe. She didn't die immediately, so William 'put her out of her misery' by cutting her throat with a razor.

Tried for wilful murder at the Somerset Assizes in June 1937, Rendell was found guilty. However, the jury recommended mercy on the grounds that William was seventy years old and had been wounded in the head by shrapnel during the First World War. Although sentenced to death by Mr Justice Lawrence, Rendell was later reprieved.

24 APRIL **1830** Twelve-year-old John Lane of Deadman's Post in Buckland St Mary led a miserable life at the hands of his brutal father. Farmer James Lane frequently beat the boy, kicked him and kept him short of food. In spite of this, John was expected to labour alongside his father and, on 23 April, having spent the morning churning butter, he accompanied James to the fields to harvest potatoes.

Later that evening, James Lane called out to neighbour John Ball as he walked past, telling him that there was a dead body in the field. When Ball went to investigate, he found young John lying on the ground beneath a hedge. Ball asked John to get up.

'I can't,' replied the boy.

Ball insisted that James Lane came to tend to his son, at which James shook the boy violently and told him to stand up. When John couldn't, his father punched him hard on the forehead, picked him up and dropped him 6ft into a ditch. Ball rescued him and remonstrated with James, telling him that he would be the death of the child.

'I wish he was dead,' was James's response.

Buckland St Mary.
(Author's collection)

He was persuaded to carry the boy home, where he threw him onto the floor. Eventually, John was put to bed with his two sisters and left unattended until the next morning, when he died at seven o'clock.

Tried at the Somerset Assizes, Lane seemed completely unmoved by the parade of witnesses who catalogued his terrible cruelty. Small, frail and thin to the point of emaciation, John often went to neighbours, begging for scraps of food or for protection from his father. Although James Lane was tried for murder, the jury eventually found him guilty of the lesser offence of manslaughter and he was sentenced to transportation for life.

1881   An inquest was held at Taunton Barracks into the death of forty-seven-year-old Henry Arbery, a quartermaster-sergeant in the 13th Somerset Light Infantry Militia. Having heard that Arbery had complained of severe stomach pains before his death, the jury returned a verdict of 'death by visitation of God'. However, regimental surgeon Dr Hensman was most unhappy that no post-mortem examination had been carried out, and remonstrated with coroner Mr Munckton about this omission.   25 APRIL

After the inquest, Hensman decided to examine the body more closely, finding that Arbery had died from arsenic poisoning. Hensman sent samples of Arbery's stomach contents to county analyst, Dr Alford, who confirmed the presence of a fatal dose of the poison. Yet, since the coroner had already recorded death by natural causes, Arbery's body had already been buried and the coroner had no power to reopen the inquest.

An application was made to Home Secretary, Sir William Harcourt, and, after much legal wrangling, it was decided that the case should be reopened. It was deemed necessary for the new inquest jury to view the body, which was exhumed and found to be very much decomposed.

The inquest jury met for the final time at the Shire Hall in Taunton on 30 September, when they first heard from the sub-actuary of a bank where Arbery had a savings account. James Turle stated that Arbery had approached him, wanting to make a will. Arbery was a widower with three children, who had married his late wife's sister and was concerned that his second wife should be properly provided for after his death. (In fact, Arbery left no will.)

His wife told the inquest that she and her husband had been happily married; a statement confirmed by Henry's two surviving children. (His third child died from natural causes in February 1881.) There was no evidence that Arbery was depressed, or that he had ever contemplated taking his own life, and nor was he known to have any enemies.

The coroner offered to adjourn the inquest again but the police had exhausted every avenue of enquiry. The jury believed that they had heard sufficient evidence to reach a conclusion and returned a verdict that Arbery 'died from inflammation of the stomach, arsenic having been found therein'. But there was no evidence to show how it was procured or administered and furthermore there was no evidence of malice being held towards him by any particular person or persons.

26 APRIL **1853** Six-year-old William Saunders disappeared near Keynsham while walking to school. Since his route took him alongside the river Avon, it was feared that he might have accidentally fallen in.

The river was dragged but no trace of William was found. However, two boys named Evans and Edwin Hucker (or Hacker) watched the dragging operations with great interest. Eventually, after the search had been ongoing for three days, Evans and Hucker mentioned that they had seen William fall into the river at a completely different location.

This revelation aroused some suspicion, as people wondered why the boys had not come forward earlier. It quickly became evident that Evans and Hucker were hiding a very guilty secret. Unable to keep quiet any longer, Evans told his family that he had seen Edwin Hucker deliberately push William into the river. Evans said that he had tried to run for help for William, who was unable to swim and was obviously drowning before his eyes. However, according to Evans, Hucker had held on to his clothing to prevent him leaving and had threatened to push him into the river too if he told anyone what he had just witnessed.

As a consequence of Evans's statement, ten-year-old Edwin Hucker was arrested. By law, children were deemed responsible for their crimes after the age of seven and, in 1748, a ten-year-old had been sentenced to death for murdering another child, although he was later reprieved.

William's body was found several days later, so decomposed that he could only be identified by his boots and schoolbag. An inquest into his death returned a verdict of wilful murder against Edwin Hucker, who was committed for trial at the Somerset Assizes. However, the Grand Jury ignored the bill against him and he was freed without punishment.

27 APRIL **1860** As eleven-year-old Sarah Selwood played with her sisters and a friend near Knowle, a man approached them and asked them for directions, giving Sarah a penny when she pointed out the way. He then asked the children if they would like to see some baby rabbits, singling out Sarah to come with him since she was wearing an apron and would be able to carry the babies back to show her friends. Leading Sarah across a field, the man then gave her a shilling and asked her to lie down. When she refused, he threatened to kill her. The terrified child did as she was told and the man raped her, taking the shilling back and telling her to go home.

The Bristol General Hospital. (Author's collection)

Sarah was so badly injured that she could barely walk and was to spend five weeks in the Bristol General Hospital. Nevertheless, she was able to describe her attacker and, when eighteen-year-old James Thomas was arrested and brought to her hospital bedside, she positively identified him.

Found guilty of rape at the Somerset Assizes in August, Thomas was sentenced to six years' penal servitude. It was intimated in court that this was not his first such offence.

28 APRIL

1824 Joseph Moon and John Beard were executed for highway robbery. On 15 January, Samuel Wyatt from Marksbury had walked the fourteen miles into Shepton Mallet with a sovereign and a £1 note in his pocket. After spending the evening drinking at the George Inn, he set off to walk home.

He could recall very little of subsequent events but vaguely remembered being hit on the head and feeling a hand in the pocket of his breeches. He remembered nothing else until he woke up at the Swan Inn in Shepton Mallet, where he had been carried unconscious. His remaining money had been stolen.

Thomas Lewis, an accomplice of Moon and Beard, turned them in to the police and they were arrested and committed for trial at the Lent Assizes in Somerset. Found guilty, both were hung at Ilchester Gaol.

29 APRIL

1811 Twenty-nine-year-old William Proctor Thomas married Miss Bailey, a beautiful and accomplished woman who was four years his junior. The couple went on to have four children and, at the births of the last three, Mrs Thomas was attended by Dr Robert Tyser.

Although Tyser was married with several children, William Thomas began to suspect that he and Mrs Thomas were having an affair. Thomas eventually banned Tyser from visiting his home but the illicit liaison between Mrs Thomas and her doctor continued, until Thomas felt that he had no choice but to separate from his wife.

As a consequence, Thomas sued Robert Tyser, accusing him of the seduction of his wife, thereby 'depriving him of all the comfort and solace of his life'. The case was tried at the Somerset Assizes in April 1818.

Although there were no witnesses to any immoral acts between Tyser and Mrs Thomas, the testimony of the Thomas' servants left little doubt that the two had conducted a very physical extra-marital affair, mainly when William Thomas was away from home on business. In summarising the case, the judge determined that Thomas was entitled to fair and proper compensation for the 'injury' he had received. The jury agreed and ordered Tyser to pay damages of £2,000.

30 APRIL

1942 Frederick James Austin was executed at Bristol Gaol for the murder of his wife Lilian Dorothy Pax Austin. Twenty-eight-year-old Austin was a soldier from Colchester, who was stationed at Bristol. Rather than be parted from Lilian, Austin arranged a room for her at Redlands.

On 31 January 1942, a single gunshot rang out and Frederick rushed to tell his landlady that he had accidentally shot his wife. Yet, when the scene of the 'accident' was investigated by Professor Webster of the Home Office, Lilian's wound suggested that the rifle had been fired from a normal firing position – in other words, her husband had shouldered the weapon before discharging it. Austin now admitted that, three days earlier, Lilian had found a letter from another woman in his kit bag, which had caused an argument between them. Austin had loaded his rifle in order to frighten her and had then forgotten to unload it again before cleaning it. However, that explanation still did not account for the fact that the rifle had been first shouldered and then fired.

It took the jury more than two hours to decide that they didn't believe Austin's account of his wife's death and to pronounce him guilty, although they recommended mercy on the grounds of provocation by Lilian. Their recommendation was not enough to prevent Austin from hanging.

Bristol Gaol.
(Author's
collection)

MAY

The Square, Crewkerne, 1906. (Author's collection)

1 MAY

1886 The inquest on the death of a baby girl, whose body was found in a pool in the aptly-named Melancholy Lane, was concluded at the George Hotel, Crewkerne.

The child's mother was quickly identified as Jane Nicholls, a servant from Battersea in London. From her yearly wages of £14, Jane supported her elderly mother and father and, finding herself with an illegitimate baby costing 5s a week and no financial assistance from the child's father, she told people in London that she intended to take the baby to her sister in Crewkerne. However, she arrived at her sister's house without a baby and made no mention of having given birth. Even after her sister heard about the discovery of the baby's body, Jane only commented that it must have been left there by a cruel mother.

Jane's written statement was read out at the inquest, in which she claimed to have got stuck in the mud at the edge of the pond and accidentally dropped the baby. When she realised that it was dead, she was too afraid to pick it up in case people thought she had killed it.

The inquest jury returned a verdict of wilful murder against Jane Nicholls. At her trial at the Somerset Assizes in May 1886, she was found guilty of manslaughter and sentenced to twenty years' imprisonment.

2 MAY

1932 Four schoolboys drowned in the river Frome. Tony Horsfield, Charles Sharland, Harold Moore and Stanley Edwards, all from Frome, were playing on the foundations of an old water wheel after school when the masonry gave way, sending the boys plunging into the river.

The river was flooded following recent heavy rains and the boys were rapidly swept away by the current. A passing police officer, PC Edgar Olpin, saw the boys in the water and immediately dived in to try and rescue them. However, they were quickly swept beneath the bridge in the centre of the town and under some houses built over the river. Olpin lost sight of the boys

River Frome at Willow Vale, Frome. (Author's collection)

nd eventually found himself struggling against the current, only reaching he bank with difficulty. He was later awarded the King's Police Medal for his aliant efforts.

The boys died on Harold Moore's ninth birthday.

880 Allegations and accusations continued to fly following revelations by the *Daily Chronicle* concerning the amount of alcohol consumed in the Bristol Workhouse. **3 MAY**

In 1879, almost 8,000 gallons of ale, 119 gallons of wine and 171 gallons of whisky were drunk. This compared to 500 gallons of ale, four gallons of wine and six gallons of whisky consumed during the same period at the neighbouring Barton Regis Workhouse, an establishment of similar size. When the figures were brought to the attention of the Board of Guardians, it was pointed out that alcoholic liquor was only given to inmates when specifically recommended by a doctor. The chairman remarked that several of the workhouse nurses regularly performed their duties while drunk.

On 4 May, the *Bristol Mercury* commented indignantly that if drunkenness was the normal state of the nurses then the guardians must have sadly neglected their duty, adding that it was disgraceful that the workhouse in one of the chief cities of the Empire should be a 'Bacchanalian Temple'.

864 At Hatch Beauchamp, railway labourer Thomas Allen cut his wife's throat and then his own, in the jealous belief that she had been having an affair with one of the couple's three lodgers. However, in spite of the fact that both John and Betsy Allen were 'all over blood' when found, neither of them died. **4 MAY**

Betsy made a good recovery from her injuries but then began to experience breathing difficulties, dying on 17 June. A post-mortem examination revealed that her windpipe, which had been completely severed by her husband's razor, had become so inflamed and thickened that she was unable to get enough air into her lungs or cough up mucus and had therefore suffocated to death.

Thomas Allen was tried at the Somerset Assizes for her wilful murder. There was little doubt that he had cut his wife's throat, since he had made a written confession to a policeman while recovering from his own injuries in Taunton Hospital. However, there was some disagreement between the medical witnesses at the trial as to exactly what had killed Betsy Allen.

That she had died because of breathing difficulties was not in dispute. However, Dr George Cordwent MD stated that he could not be certain whether the inflammation and swelling of her throat was due to her wound or to an illness such as a cold or bronchitis.

The jury believed the other medical witness, surgeon Mr C.E. Mules, who was positive that the injuries to Betsy's throat which were inflicted by her husband of twenty years had caused her death. Thomas Allen was found guilty and sentenced to death, although he was later reprieved.

886 Louisa Padfield gave birth to an illegitimate baby. She kept her son for a few months but found it difficult to work and look after him and so answered **5 MAY**

Mr Justice Day, 1904. (Author's collection)

a newspaper advertisement placed by Louisa Noble of Bath, a 'Christian woman' who was prepared to care for young children.

Louisa Noble agreed to care for Reginald for the sum of 5s a week and the boy went to her in February 1887. However, when Reginald's mother went to visit him, she noticed that he was losing weight and on 1 March 1888, she removed him from Louisa Noble's care and put him with another nurse.

Reginald's new foster mother, Mrs Abbott, called in a doctor who examined the boy and found that he weighed only twelve pounds, exactly half what he should have weighed. He was emaciated and had a burn on his leg and a cut forehead. Reginald survived only a few days with Mary Abbott before dying. The cause of his death was given as chronic diarrhoea, caused by neglect and malnourishment.

Louisa Noble was charged with manslaughter by neglect, appearing before Mr Justice Day at the assizes in Wells. The chief witness against her was her former servant, Alice Davis, who told the court that Reginald was fed only broth and bread given to Louisa Noble to feed her chickens. He was so hungry that he would eat cinders and Alice claimed that Louisa Noble had also beaten him with a cane and held him in a bath of cold water.

The prosecution was not permitted to call witnesses to testify to the condition of four other children looked after by Louisa Noble as this was deemed irrelevant to the case. However, they did call Henry Graham Montague, the Bath 'inspector of nuisances', who told the court that he had seen two apparently starving children at Mrs Noble's in August 1887 and another two who were suffering from diphtheria.

Louisa Noble was not allowed to speak in her own defence but her defence counsel, Mr Bullen, pointed out that Reginald had died from diarrhoea and there was nothing to suggest that his client had been responsible. The jury disagreed and found Louisa Noble guilty. She was sentenced to five years' imprisonment, at which she became hysterical and had to be carried from the dock.

6 MAY   **1868** Shortly before midnight, farmer Benjamin Pollard left the Malt Shovel Inn at Bridgwater in a state of intoxication. He was far from in control of his gig, yet he drove at a furious pace, whipping his horse to gallop faster and faster.

Soon afterwards, a Mr Hurford found Pollard's body lying in a pool of blood on Sandford Hill, Wembdon. Next to him lay a man named Dennis Driscoll, his hand around Pollard's throat. Driscoll's damaged cart stood nearby, while Pollard's gig was later found outside a pub in Cannington, with blood on the front step. Pollard's hat was in the gig and was also bloodstained, as were a cushion and his whip. A post-mortem examination later determined that Pollard had died from a fractured skull.

Horse and gig.
(Author's collection)

At the subsequent inquest, the main witness was Dennis Driscoll, who was cautioned before testifying. Driscoll stated that he had sold a load of mackerel and had spent the evening drinking some of the profits in a public house. He had left at half-past eleven and was driving up Sandford Hill when someone hit him on the head with a stick, rendering him insensible.

When he came to, he found himself lying in the road, his head bleeding heavily and his hat filled with clotted blood. He saw Pollard lying on the opposite side of the road and crawled over to him. He shouted 'Murder!' several times but nobody responded to his cries. The next thing he recalled was being roused by Mr Hurford. If his hand was round Pollard's neck at the time, said Driscoll, he must have been trying to lift the man's head.

Driscoll was medically examined and found to have a lump the size of a duck's egg on his skull, along with a 1 inch-long cut.

The inquest jury ruled that, while in a state of intoxication, Pollard had driven his gig into Driscoll's cart. The collision had thrown both men from their vehicles, causing Pollard to fracture his skull, resulting in his death. They absolved Driscoll of all culpability for the incident.

1868 William Hayward and his wife Ann apparently lived together on the best of terms at their farm at South Petherton. William unfailingly treated his wife with kindness and affection but, during 1868, he became severely depressed and took to wandering around the house sighing heavily and proclaiming, 'Oh, dear, I am fit for nothing at all.' Unable to cope with the running of his eighty-acre farm, William sought help from his wife's brother, George Best, who moved in to live with the Haywards and took over the farm management.

7 MAY

Mr Justice Channell, 1897. (Author's collection)

On 7 May, the three breakfasted together before Best went out to start work, leaving William and Ann in the kitchen. Soon afterwards, William came to the farmhouse door and shouted, 'George, come in, you be wanted.' When Best went back inside, he found his sister dead in a chair by the fire. She had been shot in the back with the farm gun.

Charged with the wilful murder of his wife, William appeared before Mr Justice Channell at the Somerset Assizes looking nervous and vacant. He dozed in the dock, occasionally snoring, as witness after witness testified about his strange behaviour prior to the murder. Hayward was epileptic, suffering from depression, and had attempted suicide several times in the past. In addition, he had a family history of insanity, with a sister in Wells Asylum, a senile grandfather, an epileptic mother and a father who was described as 'paralytic'. Two doctors who visited Hayward in Taunton Gaol, where he had been incarcerated since the murder, both agreed that he was insane.

The jury acquitted Hayward on the grounds of insanity and he was ordered to be detained until Her Majesty's pleasure be known.

8 MAY **1868** Samuel Jacob Reeves, aged fifty-two, was caught in a barn at Trent, near Yeovil, committing an 'unnatural offence' with a farm animal. His workmate Mr Robbins, went to look for him at lunchtime and saw him committing the offence with which he was subsequently charged.

When Reeves appeared at the Somerset Assizes before Mr Justice Channell Robbins was the only witness against him. Once Robbins had testified, the judge asked him if he had recently been discharged from the county police force Robbins admitted that he had and, when pressed by the judge for the reason for his dismissal, Robbins gave it as drunkenness.

'Were you discharged for telling lies?' the judge persisted.

'Not that I am aware of,' replied Robbins.

The judge called Superintendent Bisgood into court. Bisgood informed the court that Robbins had been dismissed for fabricating a story that he had been attacked by two men. When his allegation was investigated, not only was it found to be completely false but Robbins was also found to have been drunk on duty.

With the only witness against him proved a liar, Mr Justice Channell ordered Reeves to be discharged.

9 MAY **1843** Sixty-four-year-old Elizabeth Priest was 'ravished' by the side of a lane about five miles outside Bristol.

She originally came from Devonport in Devon but, when her husband was unable to find work as a blacksmith, the couple travelled north seeking employment. When they reached Upton-upon-Severn, Mr Priest suddenly died. Since then, Elizabeth had been trying to raise the money to go back to Devon by making and selling pincushions and other similar items.

On 9 May, she reached Bristol, where she was given a lift in a cart. When she was dropped off, she continued her journey on foot. Suddenly a man jumped out of the hedge, took her by the shoulders and told her, 'Old woman, I have been waiting for you.'

Some years earlier, Elizabeth had witnessed a murderer hanging at Exeter. According to Elizabeth, her assailant bore such a strong resemblance to the executed man 'Buckingham Joe' that she initially found herself paralysed with fear.

Her attacker threw her to the ground, producing a knife from his pocket and, although Elizabeth struggled, the man threatened to kill her if she resisted. Once he had raped her, she managed to push him into a ditch and ran for her life, leaving all her belongings behind.

Twenty-three-year-old Stephen Berry was eventually arrested and positively identified by Elizabeth as her rapist. Tried at the assizes at Bridgwater, Berry was found guilty and sentenced to be transported for life.

1843 Superintendent William Aberfield was on duty at Bath police station 〔10 MAY〕 when a man came in and asked if there was accommodation for him. When Aberfield said that there wasn't, the man argued that he was sure that room could be found for a murderer.

John Barrow then told the superintendent that he had stabbed his brother William yesterday, after the latter had teased him about a young lady. William had been taken to hospital and John was positive that he had since died.

Luckily for John, William recovered from his seven stab wounds and was the chief prosecution witness when his brother was tried for stabbing with intent at the Somerset Assizes. However, William was a most reluctant witness and told the judge that he had never quarrelled with John either before or since and was quite sure that the incident would not have happened if his brother hadn't been 'in liquor'.

Nevertheless, Mr Justice Coleridge told John Barrow that he was most fortunate not to be facing a charge for murder. The jury found Barrow guilty as charged but was divided, with some jurors for mercy on account of the provocation of William's teasing and the rest disagreeing. After a brief discussion, the jury decided against recommending mercy and, much to William's distress, John Barrow was sentenced to be transported for fifteen years.

1835 Twenty-five-year-old John Plumley was employed as gamekeeper at 〔11 MAY〕 Brockley Hall, a position held by his father, grandfather and great-grandfather before him. By 1834, Plumley had been promoted to head keeper and his future looked set, until another keeper was appointed in the spring of that year.

Initially, Joseph Dunford shared the management of the estate with Plumley but, by the end of the year, Dunford had been promoted over Plumley, who found himself demoted to under-keeper. With the loss of his status came the loss of his right to carry his gun about the estate, a concession only afforded to the head keeper.

Brockley Hall.
(Author's
collection)

Plumley saw his position as head keeper as his birthright and was most unhappy about his demotion, for which he seemed to hold Dunford personally responsible. Plumley's antagonistic attitude led to an uneasy working relationship between the two keepers and, on the evening of 11 May 1835, an argument broke out between them, which ended with Plumley shooting Dunford in the chest.

At Dunford's inquest, the coroner's jury returned a verdict of manslaughter and Plumley was committed to Shepton Mallet Prison to await an appearance at the Somerset Lammas Assizes. Yet when Plumley's trial opened in Bridgwater on 13 August 1835, the charge had been amended by the Grand Jury to one of wilful murder.

Plumley's defence was presented in a written statement. On the evening of the murder, fearing that Dunford was about to attack him, he had raised his gun in self-defence. He could not remember shooting the head gamekeeper and his first memory after raising the gun to his shoulder was of Dunford falling to the ground. Plumley swore that he bore no ill will towards his victim and had not intended to shoot him. Several character witnesses appeared for Plumley, pronouncing him without exception to be a man of good standing and even temperament.

Judge Baron Gurney summed up the case for the jury, advising them that they must decide between verdicts of guilty or not guilty to the charges of both murder and manslaughter. He went on to say that there was no doubt that Plumley had actually killed Dunford, before leaving the jury to deliberate on the two charges. They plumped for guilty of wilful murder.

On 17 August 1835, a very penitent Plumley was taken to the scaffold at Ilchester Gaol where, watched by a crowd of around 500 people, he was sent to his death. His remains were buried within the prison grounds.

1862 As Ann Dunn walked home to Ashton at between eleven o'clock and midnight, John Page suddenly stepped out of the darkness and began to walk with her. When they were only about ten yards from Miss Dunn's home, Page made indecent proposals towards her and, when she told him to go away, he said that he would kill her if she didn't do what he wanted, before proceeding to rape her. During the course of his attack on her, he punched her in the face, making it bleed heavily. When he had finished with Ann, Page picked her up and told her 'Never mind', before following her into her home.

12 MAY

Mrs Perry, who shared Ann's lodgings, took one look at her and asked Page, 'What have you been doing to Ann Dunn?' Page said he didn't know and, putting his arm round Ann's shoulders, he urged her to go to bed with him and make up. 'Go away, you scamp, or I will split your head open with the poker,' Ann responded, at which Page punched her in the face again. Mrs Perry and another lodger, James Coles, leaped to Ann's defence and turned Page out of the house.

When the case came to the Petty Sessions Court at Long Ashton nearly a week later, Ann was still sporting a black eye and appeared to have been 'greatly ill-used'.

The magistrates committed Page for trial at the next assizes, refusing him bail. However, when the case came to court the following August, the Grand Jury ignored the bill and Page was discharged. Although Mrs Perry had heard cries of 'Murder' just prior to Ann's arrival, and she and James Coles were able to corroborate the latter part of Ann's account of the events of 12 May, at the time Ann had only complained to Mrs Perry that Page had struck her and had made no mention of rape. Or perhaps the fact that Ann already had a two-year-old illegitimate child was deemed sufficient reason to give Page the benefit of any doubt.

1839 Edward Cullener took part in a prize fight at Monkton Combe, which went on for 100 rounds. So severely was Cullener beaten that he died within hours of the end of the bout. Henry Coward, Joseph Hicks and Charles Rudge, who had 'aided and abetted' the fight, were jointly charged with Cullener's manslaughter and tried at the Somerset Assizes. All three were found guilty and, calling the fight 'a disgraceful exhibition', Mr Justice Coleridge sentenced them to imprisonment with hard labour. Hicks was sentenced to thirteen months, while Coward and Rudge each received sentences of twelve months.

13 MAY

1913 The bodies of eighteen-year-old baker Ivan Dibsdall and his nineteen-year-old girlfriend Harriet Woolmington were found in the old cricket pavilion at East Coker. Harriet had a single bullet wound in her right temple, while Ivan, who was still clutching a revolver, had a similar injury to his left temple. An inquest on their deaths ruled that Ivan had murdered Harriet before committing suicide.

14 MAY

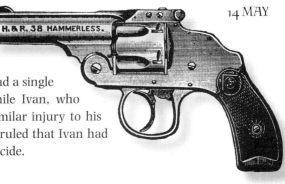

15 MAY

1827   In the parish of Northstoke, Samuel Frankham and George Sealey had a dispute and decided to settle their differences with a boxing match. After several rounds, it was evident that Sealey was coming off worst, so Frankham suggested that they shook hands. However, the spectators were enjoying the spectacle far too much and urged the two men to carry on. Sealey was convinced that he could win and so refused Frankham's offer.

Eventually, Sealey was so badly beaten that he could fight no more. He was taken to the Blaithwaite's Arms public house in Lansdown, where he died two hours later.

Frankham was charged with manslaughter and appeared at the Somerset Assizes on the coroner's warrant. Found guilty, the jury recommended mercy on account of his 'forbearance'.

Lord Chief Justice Best described Frankham as 'the most innocent man who stood on the ground on the day of the fight'. He commended him for fighting like an Englishman and for fairly and generously offering to desist, an offer repeatedly refused by the deceased. Best hoped that Frankham's own feelings would be sufficient punishment for the death he had inflicted and sentenced him to one week's imprisonment.

16 MAY

1885   When postman Albert Bartlett was suspected of stealing letters, the Postmaster-General of Glastonbury prepared a test envelope, containing ninety penny stamps. It was never delivered and, when Bartlett was searched, it was found unopened in his pocket, along with several more undelivered letters.

Bartlett was tried at the Somerset Assizes for stealing letters. However, it was pointed out in court that he had not opened the envelopes and could therefore not be aware of their contents. It was suggested that his offence was more laziness than theft, especially since most of the mail was addressed to people in outlying districts and comprised mainly circulars.

The judge joked that he couldn't imagine anybody being desirous of receiving more circulars. Yet he was not joking when he sentenced Bartlett to six months' hard labour, saying that public officers must understand that their duties were as great as their responsibilities.

17 MAY

1894   Domestic servant Alice Elizabeth Leakey was returning home to Northfield, having been shopping at Timsbury. Suddenly, a man jumped out of the hedge, grabbed her arm and threw her to the ground, where he sexually assaulted her. A member of the Salvation Army, Alice recognised her attacker as fellow Salvationist, George Bull.

Bull stood trial at the Somerset Assizes, charged with criminally assaulting Alice. He assured the court that he knew nothing whatsoever about the offence and called several witnesses to show that he had been at home when the assault was committed. However, the medical evidence proved that Alice had definitely been sexually assaulted and the prosecution called witnesses who testified to having seen Bull in the area at the time.

The jury found him guilty and, sentencing Bull to five years' penal servitude, the judge commented that the fact that Bull belonged to a 'religious association' made his offence all the worse.

1836   Three properties burned to the ground in Templecombe.
One of these was inhabited by Nancy Oliver and her daughter,
both of whom were lucky to escape the blaze alive.

It was immediately obvious that the fires had been started
deliberately and, in due course, three men were arrested and
charged with maliciously setting fire to a dwelling house
with intent to injure Nancy Oliver.

By the time the case came to trial in August 1836, one
of the three accused, Charles Avis, appeared as a witness
for the prosecution. There was deemed insufficient
evidence to proceed with charges against a second,
Samuel Hall, who was therefore acquitted. However,
twenty-one-year-old Daniel Case was found guilty
and sentenced to death. In spite of a recommendation
for mercy by the jury, who considered Avis to have been
equally culpable, Case became the last person in England
ever to be hanged for the crime of arson, meeting his death
at Ilchester on 31 August 1836.

1831   Mr Gugg had been out of work for some time when he found a new job.
On his very first day at work, he was driving his master's horse and cart near
Cheapside in Taunton when the horse took fright and bolted at top speed towards
the High Street. As the runaway horse approached the Market House, one of
Gugg's legs became trapped between a cart wheel and an iron lamp post. His
thigh was so damaged that the splintered bones protruded through the fabric of
his trousers. Gugg was rushed to hospital, where the injured leg was amputated.
However, Gugg survived for only a few hours after the operation. He left a widow
and children.

1881   An inquest was held by coroner Mr R. Biggs at the Old Gaol, Twerton, on
the death of ten-year-old Alfred Hatherell.

An inmate of the Somersetshire Industrial School, Hatherell was severely scalded
on 7 May when he fell into a copper, while trying to get a bucket of hot water
for the weekly wash. Although the scalds were treated by surgeon Mr Lawrence,
Hatherell subsequently developed lockjaw, from which he ultimately died.

The inquest heard that the drains had been 'opened', producing an effluvium
of raw sewage, which had already caused several incidences of blood poisoning
among the inmates, one of which had proved fatal. The inquest jury recorded
a verdict of 'death from lockjaw, caused by accidentally falling into the
copper'.

1881   Harry Quinlan appeared before magistrates at Taunton, charged with
stealing a quantity of bedding and clothing from Daniel Ball of Corfe, near
Taunton.

Quinlan lodged with Ball and his wife, who was described in the contemporary
newspapers as 'a handsome little brunette of about thirty summers'. Ball
obtained employment at Hatch Beauchamp, which necessitated him living

away from home during the week and, when he returned one Saturday, he found his wife of ten years, the lodger and his two youngest children missing, along with several household items.

Ball reported the missing goods to the police, who eventually located Quinlan and Mrs Ball in lodgings at Bedminster, Bristol. Although Mrs Ball stated before the magistrates that it was she who had removed the stolen items from her home, Quinlan was found guilty by the Bench and sentenced to three months' imprisonment with hard labour.

22 MAY   **1861** Mrs Chichester, the landlady of the Wellington Hotel, St Decumans, went into her kitchen just after eleven o'clock at night and found a windowpane broken. As she went to fetch her husband William, she saw a young woman trying to escape from the hotel. Mrs Chichester seized her.

Eighteen-year-old Aminda Webber was arrested and later tried at the Somerset Assizes for burglariously breaking and entering the dwelling house of William Chichester. Found guilty, she was sentenced to nine months' imprisonment with hard labour. Had she escaped, her haul from the burglary would have been one pair of William's cotton drawers.

23 MAY   **1881** A fire broke out at the premises of upholsterer Mr H. White at Yeovil. Fire engines were quickly on the scene and the flames were soon extinguished. However, what nobody realised was that White's young son was in the premises.

Four-year-old Frederick had spent the morning at his father's workshop and had been taken home by one of the workmen at about one o'clock. The boy apparently slipped away almost immediately and returned to the workshop to play with some kittens. He was suffocated in the fire, his body found by a window in an upper room. Tragically, had the firemen known he was there, he could easily have been rescued.

24 MAY   **1848** George Haine of East Coker rushed to tell his neighbours that his wife, Martha, had just died. According to Haine, the couple had been in bed asleep when he was woken by the cries of his baby. Only then did he realise that Martha was dead.

Neighbours noticed that Martha's face was 'as purple as a violet' and that her neck looked grossly swollen. A post-mortem examination revealed that her throat was bruised with what looked like finger marks and Haine was arrested and charged with his wife's wilful murder, appearing before Mr Justice Coleridge at the Somerset Assizes on 4 August 1848.

The medical witnesses determined that Martha had died from 'violence to the vessels of the neck'. However, the two doctors who had performed her post-mortem both agreed that, had Martha been an older woman, they might well have attributed her death to apoplexy. Since Martha's father had only recently died and had 'gone off quick', the jury apparently had some doubts about the cause of her demise.

They asked the judge if they might return a verdict of guilty of the lesser offence of manslaughter rather than wilful murder. Coleridge told them that this was entirely for them to decide, although he personally couldn't see anything about the case to warrant a reduction of the charge. Nevertheless, the jury found Haine guilty of manslaughter and he was sentenced to be transported for life.

1881   Mr C. Young, the medical and vaccination officer of the Polden Hill district, was requested to appear at a meeting of the Bridgwater Guardians, to discuss a charge against him that he had vaccinated an infant no less than twenty-five times.

Young sent a letter excusing himself from the meeting, stating that he was in a weak state of health and much worried in his mind. His written explanation was that, at the time of the incident, he was suffering from poor eyesight due to accidental causes, adding that the child in question was none the worse for being vaccinated in more places than usual.

The complaint was fully investigated by Dr Blaxall, the inspector for the Local Government Board, and it appears that Young's explanation was accepted and no action was taken against him.

1846   Three boys named Baker, Fisher and Doughty were looking for birds' nests at Weston-super-Mare when they stumbled across a decomposing body propped up against a rock. This was a far more exciting find than any bird's nest and the boys examined the body closely, even trying to pull off one of the corpse's boots. However, when the man's leg fell off, the boys decided that it was time to report their find to the police.

The body was so decomposed that the face was unrecognisable. The deceased wore expensive and fashionable clothes, including a coat with silk buttons, a silk waistcoat and dark plaid trousers. Nearby lay a French silk top hat with a mourning band, a small pistol, a meerschaum pipe, a tobacco pouch and a metal vesta case. When the body was examined, it was found to have a small hole at the front of the skull and a larger one at the back, which doctors believed were the entrance and exit wounds made by a bullet from the pistol.

The body had obviously been where it was found for some time and, although there were no reports of any missing men in Weston-super-Mare, a twenty-year-old man had gone missing from Taunton nine months earlier.

An inquest held by coroner Mr Uphill found that 'the deceased committed suicide, but in what state of mind he was in at the time there is no evidence to satisfy the jury'. The deceased was identified by his clothes and pipe as Francis Frederick Warren, who had left Taunton on 27 August the previous year and, in spite of vigorous attempts by his family to locate him, had not been seen alive since. In anticipation of an inheritance that he was due to receive on his twenty-first birthday, Francis had been spending money rather too freely and his relatives had stopped his allowance, causing a 'little altercation', as a result of which Francis left home, never to return.

1857   A club feast was taking place at Bishopswood and police constable Christian Dewey was on duty. When some revellers at the New Inn became a little too exuberant, Dewey went to intervene and was immediately set upon by Walter Wescombe, who shouted, 'Smash the ****** blue coat!' and insisted that he would 'do for' Dewey rather than be taken.

Since there were a lot of people about, Dewey wisely withdrew but, a little later, he met Wescombe again. Wescombe immediately resumed his assault on the policeman, who was unable to affect an arrest. He called for assistance and a man named Vincent came to his aid, but Wescombe's companion, William Willey, knocked Vincent down before joining with Wescombe in a prolonged attack on Dewey, who was severely beaten and kicked.

Charged with assaulting Dewey in the execution of his duty, Wescombe and Willey appeared at the Somerset Assizes. Their defence counsel didn't argue that they had assaulted Dewey but maintained that there had been no intent to murder, do grievous bodily harm or even prevent the lawful apprehension of Wescombe.

They were found guilty of wounding with intent to do grievous bodily harm and each sentenced to five years' penal servitude.

28 MAY   **1894**   Four-year-old Ernest Kingston and his five-year-old brother, Walter, walked home from school in the afternoon. The two little boys – the sons of the landlord of the Compass Inn, North Petherton – were probably tired and their older sister doubtless thought she was helping them when she perched them on the back of a passing timber wagon.

The driver, who had on previous occasions forbidden the boys to ride on the wagon, knew nothing of their presence until he heard a child cry out. When he looked behind him, he saw both boys lying on the road. Although the driver immediately pulled up his horses, he was unable to stop quickly enough to prevent the rear wheels of the heavy carriage passing over Ernest.

Doctors Hawkins and Sincock were summoned and found that, although Ernest had been crushed and badly mangled, he was still alive. Walter was dead, his neck broken. Sadly, Ernest later died from his injuries.

29 MAY   **1880**   George Salmon attended his regular rifle target practice at the Frome Selwood Rifle Corps. Fourteen ball cartridges were issued to him and Salmon fired them all. Then, instead of handing back his rifle at the armoury as he should have done, Salmon stole six cartridges from the drill inspector's magazine and took them home with him.

Later that day, George went to visit Mr Newport, along with his brother John and a friend, Arthur Hancock. George was still carrying his rifle and the men were keen to fire it, so Newport fetched them a piece of board, which they propped in a tree. The men then walked 100 yards and aimed at their makeshift target.

In a garden nearby, ten-year-old William Wells had climbed an apple tree to water a rose. His sister heard the first shot, which passed through the apple tree, causing a few leaves to fall. She shouted to ask William if he was all right and he replied that he was. Moments later, the second shot was fired and William fell from the tree dead. He was shot through the head from a distance of 393 yards.

There was no way of knowing which of the three men had fired the fatal shot, hence when they appeared at the Somerset Assizes at Wells on the coroner's warrant, charged with wilful murder, nobody seemed entirely sure how the trial should proceed. The presiding judge, Lord Coleridge, consulted with Mr Justice

Grove, who was sitting in the other court and advised the jury to find all three prisoners guilty of manslaughter. He then released all three on bail while an appeal was made.

Eventually it was ruled that the conviction against all three men was justified on the grounds that they had acted with 'wicked and culpable negligence'. They were recalled to the assizes in February of the following year, where each was sentenced to spend one month in prison, without hard labour. The defendants were treated so leniently because they were all of good character and the court accepted that they had no previous intent to 'do mischief'.

1878 Suffering from crippling rheumatism, twenty-year-old Sarah Leighton from Windsor came to the Bath Mineral Water Hospital. Her condition much improved, she was discharged from the hospital and announced her intention of spending a few days relaxing in Bath before returning home.

30 MAY

On the night of 30 May, she was heard shouting for help and was found in the river Avon, struggling desperately to get out. A policeman held out a pole to her but she was unable to grasp it, so he stripped off his uniform and dived in. However, it was a very dark night and the river was swollen and fast flowing, and he was unable to reach her.

At an inquest held at Twerton by coroner Mr Biggs, nobody could confirm or deny a rumour that the woman had recently been caught stealing. The jury returned a verdict of 'found drowned', adding that they could not determine how or why she came to be in the water.

Bath Mineral Water Hospital. (Author's collection)

31 MAY   **1878** Eighty-year-old housekeeper Elizabeth Hardwick from Cheddar was found head down in a well in her garden by a neighbour, the soles of her feet just protruding above ground. At an inquest held by Mr Craddock at the Cheddar Valley Inn, it was surmised that Elizabeth, who was partially paralysed, had knelt at the side of the unguarded well and had overbalanced while bending forwards to draw water. The inquest jury returned a verdict of 'accidentally drowned'.

JUNE

High Street, Porlock, 1960s. (Author's collection)

1 JUNE

1853 Poet and theologian Sir Charles Abraham Elton died in Bath. One of his most memorable works was *The Brothers: A Monody*, written in 1820 after the deaths of Abraham and Charles, the eldest of his thirteen children.

In 1819, the two boys, aged fourteen and thirteen, decided to explore Birnbeck, a small island off Weston-super-Mare, to which it was possible to walk along a causeway at low tide. As they examined the rock pools, a young woman realised that they were in danger of being trapped by the incoming tide and shouted a warning, but the boys didn't hear her. By the time they realised their predicament, the causeway was already underwater.

Although the young woman raised the alarm, the water was still too shallow for a rescue boat to be launched. The two teenagers made a desperate attempt to reach the shore but the youngest was swept away by the incoming tide and carried out of his depth. His brother stripped off his jacket and plunged into the water to try and rescue him but to no avail.

By the time a boat could safely be launched, the boys had completely vanished and, when the case was reported in *The Times* over a week later, their bodies had still not been found, although Abraham's jacket had been recovered. The boys were described as 'handsome and accomplished youths, with rare talents and amiable dispositions'.

2 JUNE

1846 James Smith arrived home to Radstock after an absence of nearly forty years, claiming to have made a fortune of £50,000 in America and the Indies. He was warmly welcomed by his brother and sister and their families, to whom he promised untold riches.

After James had enjoyed their hospitality for almost a week, one of his nephews, Joseph Carter, became a little suspicious about the truth of his uncle's claims and, after intense questioning, James Smith was proved to be an impostor who was not related to the Smith or Carter families in any way. Documents sewn into the waistband of his trousers identified him as John Giles, a native of Cornwall. Giles was forced to apologise to the families he had duped and was 'given a good dressing of soot and grease' before being run from the town.

Carlingford Terrace, Radstock. (Author's collection)

Carlingford Terraces, Radstock.

1914 Henry Quartly of Porlock shot his neighbour Henry Pugsley in the back then walked across the street to his own home, where he turned his shotgun on himself. He survived to stand trial for Pugsley's wilful murder. 3 JUNE

There had been a six-month feud between Quartly and the Pugsleys arising from a summons on Quartly (initiated by Mrs Pugsley) for using indecent language within the hearing of the highway. At the Somerset Assizes, Quartly stated that he only wished he had shot her too. Against the advice of the judge, Quartly insisted on pleading guilty, leaving Mr Justice Atkin with no alternative but to sentence him to death. He was hanged at Shepton Mallet on 10 November 1914.

1899 The body of a new-born baby girl was found floating in a Fry's chocolate box in the river Tone at Taunton. A post-mortem examination failed to establish whether or not she had been born alive and, in spite of exhaustive enquiries by the police, her identity was never discovered. At an inquest on the baby's death, the jury returned a verdict of 'found in the river', adding that that there was no evidence to show how it came to be there. 4 JUNE

1880 Fitter Thomas Nunn was bolting together two curved pieces of iron at the foundry in Frome owned by E. Cockey & Sons. Each piece weighed more than five tons and, as Nunn worked, he accidentally kicked one of the three supports holding the iron in place. One of the pieces toppled and Nunn's head was crushed, killing him instantly. The inquest jury recorded a verdict of 'accidental death' on Nunn, who, fifteen years earlier, had been convicted of manslaughter after striking a man named Thomas Wallace with a shovel. At the time, the courts considered that there were extenuating circumstances and, since Nunn was of previous good character, he served only one month in prison. Now, Wallace's relatives insisted that justice had finally been meted out by a higher authority than the courts of law. 5 JUNE

1896 At Weston-super-Mare Hospital, coroner Mr Craddock held an inquest on the death of Eugene Augustine O'Sullivan. 6 JUNE

O'Sullivan was a blind organ grinder, a great favourite in the town. On 5 June, he arrived at one of his regular spots in Station Road and began playing his barrel organ for loose change from passers-by. Unfortunately, cabman Reuben Carter accidentally crashed into O'Sullivan, crushing him between the wheel of his vehicle and a tree. Although O'Sullivan was rushed to hospital, he died from his injuries within hours. The inquest jury recorded a verdict of 'accidental death'.

1877 People attending the Bath and West Agricultural Show crossed the Widcombe Suspension Bridge, a wooden toll bridge, which was a much-used shortcut from the station to the showground. Soon after the arrival of the 10.30 a.m. train, a crowd surged onto the bridge. 7 JUNE

The toll house was nearest to the showground, which led to large queues of people waiting on the bridge while halfpennies were collected at the far end. Suddenly, the middle of the bridge gave way, plunging between 100 and 200

The fall of Widcombe Bridge at Bath – after the accident. (Author's collection)

people some 30ft into the river below. Some landed on the stone pavement or the quay wall, which ran alongside the river, while others clung desperately to the collapsing woodwork.

Those who had not been involved in the disaster immediately sprang into action. Some dived into the water to rescue people, while others dragged survivors onto pleasure boats, which were quickly launched from nearby boathouses. Three railway workers dangled ropes over the broken bridge and pulled several people to safety.

An inquest was opened on 8 June by coroner Mr A.H. English, at which time eight bodies had been recovered. Dozens more people lay injured in the Royal United Hospital at Bath, many of whom were not expected to survive. There were more fatalities over the next few days and it was feared that bodies may have been washed further down the river, which was drained at the site of the tragedy in order to search for more victims. Several more people were reported missing, including two gentlemen from London.

The privately-owned bridge, which had a 90ft span, was opened in 1863 and had undergone extensive repairs in 1876. It later emerged that there had been an argument over payment between the toll keeper, Mr Tanner, and a person crossing the bridge, and that several people had expressed anxiety at the time that the bridge would collapse under the weight of foot traffic. 'I intend to have my money,' argued Tanner when people voiced their concerns. It was alleged that one man was so worried that he pulled a handful of sovereigns from his pocket and offered to pay for everyone to cross.

The inquest eventually returned a verdict of manslaughter against the bridge owners and the toll keeper. However, the Grand Jury at the next Somerset Assizes determined that there were no charges to answer.

8 JUNE 1842   A fire broke out at one o'clock in the morning at the New Inn, Ilchester. Such was the ferocity of the blaze that several neighbouring properties caught fire and it was only the quick actions of the residents, who borrowed ladders from Ilchester Gaol and doused the roofs of the surrounding houses with

buckets of water, that prevented the destruction of much of the town. The flames spread so quickly that, having first been alerted to the fire by a lodger, landlord James West and his wife were forced to flee the pub in a state of near nudity. It was believed that the fire was the work of an arsonist, since windows had been maliciously broken at the pub on three previous occasions.

1890   The arrival of Fossett's Circus in Taunton caused great excitement and a large crowd gathered on Station Road to watch the parade of performers and animals, which included a caged leopard. Unfortunately, some spectators decided to poke the leopard with sticks through the bars of its cage. The animal became enraged and managed to push aside a cage bar and escape.

9 JUNE

In the ensuing panic, people flung themselves into the river Tone to try and get away. Others climbed onto the roofs of the circus wagons or up trees, or just concealed themselves in the long grass of an adjoining field. Initially, the leopard seemed somewhat bemused by its new-found freedom and stayed close to its cage. It then ambled across the field, jumped a ditch and hid in a bean patch in a nearby garden. Two circus employees went after it armed with stakes – one was bitten but not seriously injured, while the other was seized by the shoulder and badly mauled.

Having evaded capture, the leopard jumped a wall into Camel Road, eventually ending up in the garden of a house. By now, several people had armed themselves with guns and one took a pot shot at the leopard with a revolver. The animal was hit but, rather than disabling it, the shot simply maddened the animal even further and it leaped through a closed glass window into the front parlour of the house. Now confined, the leopard presented an easier target, and a man managed to poke his rifle through the broken window and fire two shots, one of which killed the animal. It was reported that much of the furniture in the room was damaged and the carpet was stained with blood. The circus had purchased the valuable leopard only a week earlier.

1846   Workmen were building a new church at Widcombe, Bath. One man climbed a ladder, balancing a large stone on each shoulder while another, James Hillier, stood at the foot of the ladder to steady it. Unfortunately, one of the stones slipped as the workman climbed and it hit the crown of Hillier's head, fracturing his skull. He died within minutes.

10 JUNE

1923   William Joseph Button and Bertram Berryman were friends who worked as shot firers at Wells Colliery, positioning and detonating explosives underground to dislodge coal. The two men were working the night shift together when Berryman apparently made a fatal error, firing a shot that accidentally killed his workmate.

11 JUNE

Berryman was so overcome with grief that he committed suicide, placing a detonator in his mouth and firing it. The two men's mutilated bodies were later found by their colleagues. A note in Berryman's handwriting, found close to his body, related the details of the accident, ending: 'Not to cause any trouble, I take my own life as I truthfully say that it was an accident. All my belongings are to go to my wife and children. God bless them all and forgive me.'

12 JUNE   **1843**   The town of Street held a party and, during the afternoon, a fight broke out among a number of drink-fuelled revellers. When it ended, one of the combatants, Thomas Warman, offered to fight anyone who was prepared to accept his challenge. John Tinney immediately stepped forward, saying that although he had just recovered from an attack of the 'ague', he thought he could beat Warman. With William Bath, Robert Godfrey, Thomas Ganfield and Robert Reed acting as seconds, the battle commenced. It was a short but fair fight until Tinney decided he would fight no more. Bath picked up Tinney, who was sprawled on the ground, and put him on the footpath out of harm's way before leaving. However, Tinney was seriously injured. Spectators carried him to the stable of a nearby inn, where he died two hours later.

All five men appeared at the Somerset Assizes, charged with Tinney's manslaughter. The jury acquitted all except Bath, who had been seen to kick Tinney as he lay on the ground. The single kick cost William Bath nine months in prison.

13 JUNE   **1836**   There had long been a rivalry between the youths from East and West Coker, which periodically erupted in fights between the two warring factions. John Withey of East Coker had beaten the best fighter from West Coker, and since then the West Coker youths had taken every opportunity to goad him. However, Withey had been bound over to keep the peace and managed to avoid any further fighting, even when directly challenged by a West Coker youth named John Apsey.

When the time period for which he was bound expired, Withey sent Apsey a note saying that he was ready to meet him, and a crowd of men assembled in a field at West Coker for a boxing match that lasted for eighty rounds. It ended when Withey hit Apsey in the throat and knocked him down. When he fell, Apsey banged his head hard on the ground. He was carried home in a chair and a doctor was called but he died without regaining consciousness. Withey was also badly injured and, for a while, it was thought that his injuries would prove fatal.

He recovered to be tried at the Somerset Assizes for Apsey's manslaughter, where it was stressed that Apsey had been the instigator of the fatal encounter between the two men, having bet Withey 10s that he wouldn't fight. Accordingly, when Withey was found guilty, he was given a nominal sentence of four months' imprisonment.

14 JUNE   **1880**   In Widcombe, Bath, Harriet Plucknett was found dying in her rented rooms in the home of assistant parish overseer Mr H. Catley.

Miss Plucknett, who was about seventy years old, had occupied two garrets of the house for the past twenty years. She was somewhat eccentric and suffered from delusions, in spite of which she supported herself by working as a needlewoman.

Not having seen his lodger for a couple of days, Catley went to check on her and found her door locked from the inside. Unable to gain admittance to her apartment, he called the police and PC Newton broke down the door. Newton and Catley were immediately assailed by a foul stench and, when they entered the apartment, they found Miss Plucknett lying on the floor almost naked. She was emaciated and her breasts and face were heavily bruised. One eye was swollen shut and her left shoulder appeared to have been struck.

Surgeon Mr Hanham was summoned and declared her condition to be hopeless. The cause of Miss Plucknett's death was recorded as 'apoplexy' but, given that she was found in a room locked from the inside, nobody could offer any explanation for her apparent injuries, other than suggesting that they were self-inflicted during a hallucination or the result of struggling during a fit.

1945 Mexican soldier Aniceto Martinez was hanged at Shepton Mallet for the rape of Agnes Cope, a seventy-five-year-old woman from Rugeley, Staffordshire. He became the last American serviceman to be hanged at Shepton Mallet Prison and the last man to be hanged in the United Kingdom for the crime of rape. (*see* entry for 12 MARCH.)

15 JUNE

1899 Twenty-five-year-old Edwin Hayward was employed in the construction of the new granary at Avonmouth. An experienced carpenter and joiner, he was working on the roof of the building when he suddenly fell over, slid around 22ft down the roof and disappeared off the edge. He landed headfirst on another roof, some 47ft below. His fellow workers found him still alive and rushed him to the Bristol Infirmary, where he died before he could be admitted for treatment. A post-mortem examination found that he had a large wound on his forehead, heavy bruising to his chest, and had fractured both arms and his right thigh. Doctors attributed his death to shock.

16 JUNE

Hayward was a steady, sober man who had seemed in perfect health before the accident and was used to working at heights. Colleagues who had been near to him when he fell stated that he had made no sound and that he had been working safely. Doctors theorised that Hayward had probably fainted due to sunstroke. It was an extremely hot, sunny day and the roof on which he was working was made from galvanised iron. At the subsequent inquest, coroner Mr Maitland supported this theory and the jury returned a verdict of 'accidental death'.

1898 Bargeman Mr Gay watched in astonishment as an elderly cripple seated herself carefully on the banks of the river Avon at Bath, threw away her crutch, removed her bonnet and shawl and slipped into the water. Unbeknown to sixty-five-year-old Jane Cox, the river was only a couple of feet deep at the spot where she had chosen to commit suicide and Gay was able to fish her out and hand her to PC Gibson, who took her to hospital. She was distraught, telling Gibson, 'I would rather die than go back to the Union.'

17 JUNE

Jane appeared before magistrates at Bath, charged with throwing herself into the river Avon with intent to kill herself. Recently released from the workhouse, by the time she was brought to the police court, she had obviously realised that she could face a prison sentence for her attempted suicide. She promised the magistrates that she would never do such a thing again if she could go back to the workhouse, and was bound over to keep the peace for six months and sent back.

18 JUNE   **1864** Sarah Susan Coles married John Tooling (or Toole) at Bath. Unfortunately, Sarah was still married to her first husband.

Having left John Coles because he abused her, Sarah was told that he had died and assumed that she was free to marry again. However, Coles was still very much alive and Sarah was charged with bigamy and sent to prison to await her trial at the next Somerset Assizes. There, Mr Baron Bramwell called Tooling to the witness stand and established that he had given Sarah no money or gifts and that the only real harm done was that Tooling had been 'scandalised' for marrying a woman who wasn't legally entitled to wed.

Sarah was most apologetic and, when the jury found her guilty of bigamy, Bramwell dealt with her leniently. Telling her that she had not really harmed anyone – although she had disgraced herself – he admonished her, 'Don't do it again.' Taking into consideration the three months she had already spent in gaol, he sentenced her to one month's hard labour.

19 JUNE   **1878** Labourer Isaac Smith was brought before magistrates at Taunton, charged with permitting his house to become so overcrowded as to be dangerous or injurious to the health of the inmates. Magistrates heard that the two-roomed house slept ten men and women and that, rather than each person having the statutory 300 cubic feet of air, the accommodation in Smith's home allowed only seventy cubic feet per person. It was the first case of its kind to come before magistrates in Somerset and Smith was ordered to 'abate the evil' immediately. Although he wasn't fined, he was ordered to pay 7s 6d court costs.

20 JUNE   **1898** At just seventeen months old, Richard Spurrell of Avon Street, Bath was already very good at walking. Even his mother didn't fully appreciate just how proficient he was and, when she put him down so that she could do some housework, she had no idea that he would wander out of the house and continue walking for some distance along the road outside.

Unfortunately, the toddler was so small that carter Mr Welch didn't notice as Richard walked into the side of the water wagon he was driving and was knocked over. There was a second horse tethered to the rear of the wagon and, as it passed, it stepped on the child's head, crushing it completely. Richard was rushed to hospital but was dead on arrival. An inquest on his death determined that it had been accidental and that Mr Welch was in no way to blame.

21 JUNE   **1894** Elizabeth Ann Plummer gave birth to a baby at Coleford. Elizabeth was the servant of Thomas William and Agnes Tottle and there was little doubt that her employer was the child's father.

Agnes Tottle attended Elizabeth in labour but was called away on an errand at the last minute, hence Elizabeth gave birth alone. When Agnes arrived back in her room minutes later, she informed Elizabeth that her baby had been stillborn.

Dr James Howard Kenrick had examined Elizabeth at eleven o'clock that morning and passed an opinion that she would not give birth for some time yet. He was sent for again at four o'clock but was out and didn't arrive until after ten o'clock at night, by which time Thomas had buried the baby in his garden. Kenrick demanded to inspect the infant and found that it been buried face downwards in quicklime and had a large piece of paper in its mouth. Kenrick performed a post-mortem and, based on the fact that the baby's lungs floated in water, decided that the child had been born alive.

Thomas and Agnes Tottle were charged with wilful murder and appeared before Mr Justice Grantham at the Somerset Assizes. It emerged that, in January 1894, Thomas William Tottle had approached Kenrick and offered him a stack of hay to 'get rid of the trouble he was in'. It was alleged that Kenrick had told the Tottles more than once that the child would be born dead and that he had not mentioned the offer of hay at the inquest or the magisterial hearings. Called to give evidence, Kenrick now stated that it was possible that the child had suffocated during birth, adding that the test he had used to establish that the child was born alive was not completely reliable.

With no way of establishing conclusively whether the baby had ever lived a separate existence from its mother, there could be no trial for murder and the defendants were both acquitted. The judge censured Kenrick for his performance on the witness stand, adding that if he had attended Elizabeth when he was sent for, he would have seen the baby for himself.

1880 The *Bristol Mercury* reported that a house in Coker Hill, Yeovil, was haunted. At certain times of the day, the female occupant witnessed strange manifestations, by which she was rendered 'powerless'. One of the main phenomena was the sound of someone scrubbing, which frequently occurred at around midnight. **22 JUNE**

In an effort to banish the ghost, the Lord's Prayer was written out backwards and concealed under the woman's bed. A man called in for assistance claimed to have seen strange apparitions throughout the house, although the newspaper reported that the frequency of the incidents seemed to be decreasing.

1840 Edward Garrett of Norton St Philip, known as a kind and affectionate father to his three children, attempted to murder them all by giving them laudanum. Neighbour Elizabeth Smith sent for surgeon Thomas Hill, who administered emetics. Only the youngest child, Edwin, succumbed to the poison and Garrett was charged with his wilful murder. **23 JUNE**

Garrett and his wife lived in abject poverty and, just four days before Edwin's death, Edward had been certified as 'of unsound mind' by Hill. At the time, Garrett told Hill that he and his family had been on the brink of starvation for some time and Hill felt that Garrett was severely depressed and at risk of committing suicide.

At his trial, a letter he had written to his sister while in custody was read to the court:

You know I made an application to you for a few pounds, but in vain; if
my own flesh and blood would not help me, where am I to go for aid? ... My
children have gone to bed crying for food, my creditors were pressing me
and I had nothing to give them. All these things were pressing on me and
drove me to distraction. I attempted my own life and that of my children –
the younger is dead, poor little soul.

The jury found Garrett guilty but recommended mercy on account of his
distressed state of mind at the time of the murder. Although Mr Justice
Coleridge awarded the mandatory death sentence, there is no evidence
that Edward Garrett was executed and it seems likely that he was deemed insane.

24 JUNE   **1864**   Fifteen-year-old James House was receiving *2s 6d* parish relief every
week until the Board of Guardians decided to stop the payments. Furious,
House went to assistant overseer Thomas Hucker Baruxtaple to complain and
Baruxtaple promised to investigate.

Baruxtaple kept his promise and sought out House on 24 June to tell him
that his money had been stopped by the relieving officer, Mr Stagg. House didn't
believe him and followed Baruxtaple to his home, shouting abuse at him. His
parting shot was to tell Baruxtaple, 'It wasn't Stagg, it was thee and I'll make
thee rue for it.' Thus, when Baruxtaple's barn was found to be on fire later that
day, the police had an obvious suspect and House was taken into custody. His
mother saw him being arrested and asked, 'Did anyone see thee do it?' When
House replied no, she advised him, 'Thee stick to that.'

At House's trial for arson at the Somerset Assizes, Mrs House denied saying
any such thing. She insisted that what she had actually said was, 'If you did it,
speak the truth and nothing but the truth and God will protect you.'

The evidence against House was entirely circumstantial but the jury found
him guilty, although they recommended mercy on account of his age. He was
sentenced to six months' imprisonment.

25 JUNE   **1944**   *Old Faithful*, a United States Flying Fortress plane, crashed on Bayford Hill
near Wincanton, claiming the lives of all nine of its crew. Lt Peter Mikonis, Lt
Frank E. Pepper Jr, Lt Will H. Stevens, Lt Joseph E. Sullivan, S/Sgt R.C. Anderson,
S/Sgt Douglas K. Deurmyer, Sgt Dean A. McDowell, Sgt Richard A. Mehlberg and
Sgt Ralph Stein from the 401st Bombardment Group, based at Bassingbourn in
Cambridgeshire, were returning from a sortie over Toulouse in France. The crew
were making for RAF Zeals in Wiltshire but, with their disabled plane in flames,
deliberately turned into Bayford Hill to avoid crashing in the town of Wincanton.

26 JUNE   **1859**   At half-past three in the afternoon, a ferocious hail storm struck Bath and
the surrounding areas. Hailstones averaging 1.5in in diameter fell for several
minutes, causing particular devastation to windowpanes. Two nurserymen, Mr
Drummond and Mr Griffin, each had more than 5,000 panes broken in their
glasshouses, while Mr Turgett lost a further 300 panes from his greenhouse.
The combined cost of the damage incurred by these three men alone was said to
be in excess of £900.

1934   Eighteen-year-old Edward Douglas Macey had worked for Benjamin and Therese Golledge at their farm in Broadway for four years. His time at the farm was insufferable as, according to Macey, Mr Golledge sexually abused him. In 1934, Edward fell ill and, nursed by Mrs Golledge, the two began an illicit affair, which left Edward a nervous wreck. Still subject to Benjamin's sexual demands, Edward was terrified that his affair with Therese would be discovered. The boy finally cracked on 26 June, when he told both Mr and Mrs Golledge about his associations.

Mr Golledge forgave him but insisted that Edward would have to leave the farm, the only home he had known for the past four years. Brooding in his room overnight, Edward decided to commit suicide and the following morning, he threw himself into the farm pond. Benjamin Golledge pulled him out, only for Edward to confess that he had just shot Therese. When the police were called, Edward greeted them with the words, 'Good morning, Sergeant. I am your culprit.' He later made a statement saying that he had picked up the farm gun, with the intention of shooting himself. Hearing Therese moving about upstairs, he went to beg her forgiveness for telling her husband about their affair. When she refused, he shot her.

In the immediate aftermath of the murder, Edward was so depressed that he simply didn't care whether he was hanged or not. However, by the time his case came to trial, he had changed his story and now said that the gun had gone off accidentally.

His defence counsel was able to prove that the gun had an exceptionally light pull and that there was a protruding piece of wood on the banisters at the farm, which could have caught the trigger, causing the gun to fire.

When the jury retired, Macey's defence counsel, J.D. Casswell, found himself in an awkward position. The jury sent a question to the judge, asking if it was possible to find Macey guilty of manslaughter, when it was noticed that there was a policeman with them in the jury room. This was sufficient grounds for the judge to declare a mistrial and Casswell was approached and asked if he wanted to exercise this option. In the belief that the jury would convict Macey of the lesser offence of manslaughter, Casswell declined, a fortunate decision, since the jury eventually acquitted the young farm labourer.

[It should be noted that Benjamin Golledge vehemently denied Macey's allegations against him, none of which were ever substantiated.]

1847   A number of men were drinking in The George public house, in Bathampton, when a quarrel broke out between two of them. Solomon Dayton and John Potter agreed to adjourn to a nearby field and settle their differences with a fight.

The fight attracted seventy to eighty spectators and had been underway for some time when PC Thomas Smith arrived and tried to break it up. He was immediately knocked over. PC John Bailey was next to try and intervene, and he too was knocked over by a man named Maurice Perry. At some stage in the melee, Bailey was kicked while lying on the ground, rupturing a large vein located just beneath his collarbone. Blood flooded the inside of his chest, preventing him from breathing and he died within minutes. He also had a head injury, which caused an effusion of blood at the base of his brain and which doctors believed to have been the result of a fall. Since Perry had been seen to knock PC Bailey over, he was arrested and charged with the constable's murder. Another two men, Samuel and Henry Crawley, were charged with aiding and abetting him, while Dayton and Potter were charged with causing a disturbance.

Perry was tried for wilful murder before Chief Justice Wild at the Somerset Assizes, his crime all the more serious as his victim was a police officer killed while executing his duty. After debating the case for half an hour, the jury announced that, while they believed that Perry was involved, they could not be sure that he had dealt the fatal blow. The judge insisted that, if the jury believed that Perry were in any way 'concerned' in the murder, they should find him guilty and, after further deliberation, the jury reluctantly complied and he was sentenced to death. However, the jury were far from happy and several members signed petitions for a reprieve. Perry's sentence was ultimately commuted to one of transportation for life.

There was insufficient evidence to proceed with the charges against the Crawleys, and Dayton and Potter were released after the trial – the time they had already served in custody deemed to be sufficient punishment for their offence.

29 JUNE   **1951**   An explosion at the Royal Ordnance Factory at Puriton, near Bridgwater, claimed the lives of six men involved in the production of an explosive known as RDX. The cause of the explosion remained a mystery, even after a full investigation by the Chief Inspector of Explosives, who could find no evidence of electrical discharge, lightning or sabotage. It was eventually concluded that the breakdown of a stirring machine may have contributed to the disaster.

30 JUNE   **1876**   Twenty-nine-year-old Emma Jarvis was found drowned in the river Froom, her baby Walter clutched in her arms. At an inquest held by coroner Dr Wybrants, the jury learned that Emma had a long history of depression and mental weakness. Her husband Francis was addicted to drink, spending his pay as soon as he received it, with no concern for the financial support of his wife and child. So unhappy was her marriage that Emma had threatened to drown herself and her baby several times.

The jury determined that Emma destroyed herself and her child while in an unsound state of mind and asked the coroner to reprimand her husband for his brutal treatment of her. Francis Jarvis, who sobbed bitterly throughout the proceedings, promised that he would never touch another drop of intoxicating liquor as long as he lived.

JULY

Cheddar. (Author's collection)

1 JULY **1854** Elizabeth James of St Decumans lost eight sovereigns and, since there was no sign of any break in, she immediately suspected her servants of having robbed her. A search revealed the missing money concealed in the belongings of thirteen-year-old Elizabeth Jones. Elizabeth was arrested and stood trial at the Somerset Assizes, where the jury found her guilty, tempering their verdict with a recommendation for mercy on account of her age. The judge sentenced her to six months' imprisonment, the first and last three days to be in solitary confinement.

2 JULY **1859** It was a scorching hot day and Frank Wall from Cheddar was helping with the haymaking. He was sent to purchase a gallon of cider but didn't return for nearly three hours, by which time he had drunk almost six pints of the cider. Frank spent the rest of the afternoon cavorting round the hay field 'like one deranged'. Several times he jumped into the nearby river and had to be hauled out.

Eventually, at ten o'clock at night, one of the labourers bothered to take him home, where he was put to bed by his mother. Unable to rouse him the following morning, she sent for surgeon Mr Lawrence, but sadly Frank died within hours. Mr Lawrence was of the opinion that the cause of his death was apoplexy arising from immersion in cold water while intoxicated, coupled with overheating.

At the subsequent inquest, the coroner's jury returned a verdict according to the medical evidence. The coroner had been unable to substantiate the rumours that whisky had been added to the cider for 'brutal sport' and that Frank had been deliberately thrown into the river. He was just nine years old when he died.

3 JULY **1897** As Mary Holbrook picked flowers outside her house, watched by her father, James, and sister, Dorothea, they noticed a cyclist approaching. There was a hill outside the Holbrooks' home and, as the man reached the top, he took his feet off the pedals and freewheeled down. There were no brakes on the bicycle and it was obvious that the rider was travelling far too fast. The cycle ploughed into Mary at speed, the front wheel passing over her and the back wheel dragging her along the road. Cyclist Samuel Voke of Bedminster, Bristol, ended up in a hedge. Fortunately, nineteen-year-old Mary survived the accident, although nearly two weeks later, when Voke appeared before magistrates at Axbridge charged with 'furiously riding a bicycle', she was still confined to bed and in severe pain. Voke was fined 20s and ordered to pay 21s 6d costs.

4 JULY **1881** Ann Wright, also known as Ann Workman, was brought before the Bench at Bath charged with having been drunk and disorderly in Cheap Street on 2 July. When magistrates sentenced her to one month's imprisonment with hard labour, she immediately expressed her thanks and further demonstrated her gratitude by dancing in the dock until she was forcibly removed. Since her husband had several convictions for violent assault on her, it was not difficult to understand why she was so pleased at her sentence.

1945 Two pilots stationed at Yeovilton were killed in a plane crash at Charlton   5 JULY
Horethorne. Petty Officer Pilot Kenneth J. Hutley and Temporary Acting Sub-
Lieutenant Ronald J. Thaxter (both aged twenty) of 759 Squadron Fleet Air Arm
were circling their aircraft over the village when the wing tips of the two planes
touched briefly. One plane immediately crashed to the ground and burst into
flames, the second crashing into a corn field soon afterwards. Both men died
instantly.

1864 Elizabeth Harris of Long Ashton went to work, leaving her six-year-   6 JULY
old daughter, Sarah, at home. When Elizabeth returned, there was no sign of
Sarah and, when the child came back that evening, she complained of being
'sore'. Elizabeth examined her and found evidence that she had been sexually
assaulted and, when questioned, Sarah told her mother that Joseph Mitchell
had taken her to look for mushrooms and had hurt her.

When Elizabeth confronted Mitchell the next morning, he admitted to
taking Sarah mushrooming but insisted that he hadn't harmed her in any
way. He then asked Elizabeth to forgive him, offering to forget the rent for the
potato patch she leased from him if she would let the matter drop.

Although Mitchell was originally charged with assault with intent, the
Grand Jury found insufficient evidence to proceed with the case, thus his trial
at the Somerset Assizes was for the lesser offence of indecent assault. The
chief witness for the prosecution was young Sarah, who was so small that
she had to stand on a chair in the witness box. Sarah assured the judge that,
although she couldn't yet read, she knew her catechism and realised that it
was wicked to tell lies. She then proceeded to give a very clear and detailed
account of the events of 6 July.

Mr T.W. Saunders, acting in Mitchell's defence, told the court that Mitchell's
wife had been bedridden for almost a year and was therefore incapable of a
normal marital relationship. Besides, Saunders complained to the court, the
only real witness was a six-year-old girl – surely it wasn't safe to convict a man
on the testimony of such a young child? Unfortunately for Mitchell, the jury
disagreed and found Mitchell – a father and grandfather – guilty as charged.
He was sentenced to imprisonment with hard labour for twelve months.

1898 Annie Holmes and her husband Thomas spent the evening drinking   7 JULY
before returning to their home in Avon Street, Bath at about nine o'clock.
When they arrived, Thomas, who worked as a rag and bone man, demanded
that Annie take off her dress, so that he could tear it up.

Annie refused. Only the previous evening, Thomas had torn up all the
clothes she possessed and the dress she was wearing was the only one she had
left. At her refusal, Thomas flew into a rage. Grabbing a shovel, he hit his wife
four or five times over the head until the shovel broke, at which Thomas began
kicking her in the ribs.

Fortunately, neighbours intervened before Annie was too seriously injured
and Thomas was arrested and charged with wounding. When Thomas
appeared at the police court in Bath, he pleaded guilty to assaulting his wife
and was sentenced to one month's imprisonment.

8 JULY

1878 After spending the day together haymaking, William Allen and his father, James, returned to their home near Wells and began quarrelling. In the course of the argument, William struck James, who fled from the house in fear for his life. William followed his father and caught him in the road outside their house, where he began biting him. By the time William's brother intervened, William had bitten several large chunks of flesh from his father's face and arms, leaving wounds of between 2 and 3in long. He also bit his brother's thumb before being subdued.

Brought before magistrates on charges of assault and doing actual bodily harm, William sheepishly pleaded guilty, saying, 'It was the drink that done it.' Charitably, his father and brother decided not to press charges and William was bound over to keep the peace for a period of six months and ordered to pay 7s 6d court costs.

9 JULY

1828 A storm of great ferocity hit Bath at eight o'clock in the evening, continuing unabated for four hours. A large volume of water poured down Widcombe Hill at such a rate that houses at the bottom were quickly flooded to a depth of 12ft or more. Although there was catastrophic damage to property, most of the residents escaped unscathed but, when the water finally receded, seventy-year-old James Moody and his wife were found dead in their bedroom in Sussex Place. Such was the fury and speed of the flood that they had drowned in their bed.

10 JULY

1862 George Morris, aged twenty, was a footman in the service of Colonel Jones at Kelston Park, Kelston. With the colonel away, Morris and butler John Loveless spent the morning shooting rabbits. When they returned, Loveless asked Morris to post some letters. Meanwhile, Loveless went into the garden to pick fruit with some of his fellow servants, including Ellen Roan and gardener John Croom. Croom locked the garden door after him and, within minutes, Morris was rattling the door, asking to come in. Croom told him to go and post the letters as he had been asked but Morris continued to demand entrance to the garden. When Croom didn't open the door, Morris fired his shotgun, blasting a hole through the door. Ellen's leg was peppered with shot and she fell unconscious into the arms of the coachman. Surgeons were later to find twenty-two pellets in her legs, all but one of which were too deeply embedded to be extracted.

Morris was charged with maliciously shooting with intent to do grievous bodily harm to Roan, Croom and Loveless and further charged with having injured the person of Ellen Roan. At his trial at the Somerset Assizes, the court heard that he had been devastated by the consequences of his actions, having only meant to fire at the door and frighten his colleagues. The judge accepted that he had not intended to do bodily harm and sentenced him to three months' imprisonment.

11 JULY

1881 Fifteen-year-old Edward Brain and his friend, Gorton Cross, were enjoying riding the swing-boats at the funfair on Weston-super-Mare pier. However, as they stood face-to-face in the swing, Edward slipped and fell out, knocking himself unconscious. He soon recovered and the boys walked to the end of the pier and caught a cab to Heal's Coffee House, where they had arranged to meet Edward's brother, Shadrach. No sooner had the boys arrived at the restaurant than Edward began to feel ill and, although Shadrach immediately summoned a doctor, the boy died before medical help arrived. A post-mortem examination found that he had died from compression of the brain resulting from a fractured skull.

1899 Domestic servant Kate Palmer cleaned the upstairs windows of her employer's home at Weston-super-Mare by sitting on the windowsill. Unfortunately, she lost her balance and fell backwards, plummeting nearly 30ft onto a stone-paved yard at the back of the house. Although a surgeon was immediately sent for and arrived within minutes, there was nothing he could do for Kate, who died without regaining consciousness from a fractured skull. **12 JULY**

1854 William Henry Brooks and John Kerridge both worked for Mr Bevan at Wells, Brooks as an apprentice and Kerridge as a journeyman cabinet maker. On 13 July, the two men argued and Kerridge ordered fifteen-year-old Brooks to get out of his sight. When Brooks refused, Kerridge seized him by the throat, dragged him out of the workshop and threw him on the floor. Brooks immediately returned to the workshop and, in a fit of temper, threw a lump of mahogany at Kerridge, hitting him on the temple and drawing blood. Kerridge bandaged his head and continued working for an hour or so when, feeling unwell, he went to the doctor. He died within a couple of days and Brooks appeared at Somerset Assizes charged with his manslaughter. Found guilty, he was sentenced to two weeks' imprisonment with hard labour, the last three days to be served in solitary confinement. **13 JULY**

1828 An inquest was held at the Rising Sun public house in Taunton on the death of carter William Dymond at the Taunton and Somerset Hospital on 12 July. **14 JULY**

Dymond was driving his cart loaded with coal towards Wellington when his horses were frightened by a dancing bear. Dymond jumped off the cart to try and calm them but was crushed between a cart wheel and a metal post and fell to the ground, the cart then running over his leg. He was taken to hospital but died the next morning, when a post-mortem examination revealed that he had ruptured a large blood vein in his liver and died from internal bleeding.

The inquest jury returned a verdict of 'accidental death' but added a rider to say that they felt the blame for Dymond's death lay with the town beadle, James Wood, whose duty it was to prevent such itinerant exhibitions on the streets. Meanwhile, the bear was captured and locked up. Its owners were informed that they would not be permitted to leave town until the conclusion of the inquest, but in the early hours of the morning after the accident they liberated the bear from captivity and absconded.

15 JULY

1920 Sanger's Circus had come to Taunton and there was an afternoon performance before an audience of almost 1,500 people. At 3.40 p.m., the clowns were performing their act when someone cried 'Fire!' There were only two exits from the big top and the crowd flocked towards them. An Indian doctor, visiting the circus with his son while on holiday in the West Country, was later to say that, although people were obviously in a hurry to get out of the blazing tent, there was no panic and no stampede for the exits. Nevertheless, a fourteen-year-old schoolgirl, Mildred Drew, was caught up in the crush and trampled. Unable to move, she burned to death.

There were four more deaths from the fire. Mark Henry Maltravers (six), Arthur Gray (twelve) and Jane Vickery (thirty-nine) perished in the flames, while Edward Crabb (seventy-nine) later died from his burns in hospital. At an inquest held by the coroner for West Somerset, Mr Foster Barham, Mark's mother stated that she had led her son out of the tent. However, when she reached the exit, she was knocked over by the crowd and lost her grip on the boy's hand.

The presence of a strong breeze, which blew the flames into rather than away from the tent, ensured that the big top was entirely consumed by flames within four and a half minutes, and it took only a matter of seconds for the fire to spread from the ground to the roof.

Circus manager Edward Sanger stated that the tent was made from strong, waterproofed canvas and that smoking was permitted inside it. The risk of fire was thought to be so small that the circus held no insurance against it. The coroner stated that he believed the fire was started by a carelessly discarded lighted match and returned a verdict of 'death from shock and burning arising from misadventure' on the victims.

16 JULY

1858 Pregnant Susan Rendle slipped quietly from her home in the parish of West Coker, carrying her two-year-old son, Robert. When she reached the mill pond at Hewhill, she took off her bonnet and shoes, leaving them on a wall, before wading into the pond with Robert in her arms. Their bodies were discovered later that morning.

Susan had apparently contemplated suicide for some time. On the previous morning, she had given a brooch to her mother and some other items to her sister. At an inquest into the deaths, conducted by coroner Mr D.H. Ashford, the jury returned an open verdict of 'found drowned'.

17 JULY

1839 In Worle, a young servant, Eliza Pain, was sent by her master, Josiah Reeves, to purchase a few items from a shop. Soon afterwards, Samuel Norman, the relieving officer for Worle, came across a man clambering out of a ditch in Snatch Lane, who told him, 'I must die.' Further down the lane, Norman spotted a young girl staggering about in obvious distress.

The man, Charles Wakeley, who was also employed by Josiah Reeves as a servant, asked Norman to check on the girl's condition. Norman rode back down the lane; there he found Eliza Pain slumped on the ground, blood gushing from wounds in her throat. Norman called for assistance and his shouts were answered by nearby residents Sarah Bowden and Sydney Tripp.

While Sarah stayed with the dying girl, Sydney ran to fetch Josiah Reeves and Norman took Wakeley to the nearest police constable. Although Wakeley went quietly, as soon as Norman tried to hand him over to the policeman he began to fight ferociously, pulling Norman from his horse. Eventually the policeman was forced to knock him down with his staff before he could handcuff him.

A post-mortem examination showed that Eliza had several superficial wounds on the left-hand side of her neck, as well as severe bruising on her left temple and five stab wounds over her left eye. The injury that had actually killed her was a 3in cut on the right-hand side of her throat, which severed her jugular vein.

Tried before Mr Justice Coleridge at the Somerset Assizes, Wakeley insisted on pleading 'Guilty' to the murder of Eliza Pain. In spite of entreaties from the judge and the governor of Ilchester Gaol, Wakeley refused to change his plea and was consequently sentenced to death. He was hanged at Ilchester Gaol on 4 September 1839, the last ever public execution to be held here.

1936 Three people were found dead in a house in Frome. Post-mortem examinations revealed that Albert John Williams, a steward at the United Services Club, had died in his bed from asphyxiation, while his wife, Alice, and six-year-old son, David, hung from coat pegs behind the door of another bedroom. **18 JULY**

Police and doctors were mystified by the three deaths. There were no signs that any struggle had taken place in the house and a teapot containing tea in the kitchen waited for boiling water to be added. The only remotely strange thing was the presence of a newspaper on a table in the living room, in which there were two references to hanging.

At an inquest held before coroner Mr C.L. Rutter, the jury determined that Alice Williams had hanged her son and then herself while of unsound mind. However, they were unable to determine either how or why Albert Williams had died.

A previously healthy man, he had seen his doctor in February 1936 with an attack of quinsy, and again on 15 July, when he complained of pain in his shoulder. Dr Beddard had prescribed medicine for the pain and told the inquest that, had Williams drunk the whole bottle at once, it would have proved fatal. However, analysis of the dead man's stomach contents showed no trace whatsoever of any poisonous substances or drugs. There were no marks of violence on Williams's body and, according to county pathologist Dr Godfrey Carter, it would be impossible for an otherwise healthy man to asphyxiate simply by rolling face down onto a pillow. Death from asphyxia could occur after an epileptic fit but Williams had no history of epilepsy, nor did his body show any signs that he had suffered from a seizure.

The Williams family were known to be devoted to each other and Alice had often been heard to say that she didn't know what she would do if anything happened to her husband and son. Thus coroner Mr Rutter could only speculate that either Alice Williams had killed her husband while her mind was unsound or she had simply woken up and found him dead in bed, deciding to end her life and that of her son rather than go on living without him.

19 JULY   **1862**   Samuel Thomas called at the New Inn in Worle to pay for some bacon. Once there, he decided to stay for a while and was soon drinking with a group of young men, generously treating them to beer and tobacco. When the landlord called time, the youths followed Thomas out of the pub and jumped him. They rubbed dirt into his mouth and nose, turned out his pockets, stole his money and threw him into a pond before running off. (One at least had the conscience to return minutes later and pull him out before he drowned.)

Thomas was able to describe his assailants to the police, who quickly arrested William Lancaster, Albert and Frederick Knowles, Benjamin Day and Edward Hewlett, all of whom were also known to the pub landlord. The youths, who were aged between seventeen and twenty, stood trial at the Somerset Assizes charged with robbing and assaulting Samuel Thomas with intent to kill and murder him.

Only Lancaster, Day and Hewlett were defended, their counsel Mr Prideaux describing the attack as 'a drunken frolic'. The court heard that Day had taken little part in the assault but had acted as a lookout and he was therefore acquitted, while Lancaster, Hewlett and the Knowles brothers were found guilty. Hewlett was sentenced to two years' imprisonment with hard labour, while the others, who all had previous convictions, each received three years.

20 JULY   **1898**   Deputy coroner Mr Wallace held an inquest on the death of twenty-three-year-old Albert Grist. Grist worked as a signalman on the construction of the new road between Hewish and Worle, his job being to precede the steam roller, signalling with flags if it should stop or go.

During their meal break, Grist and his workmates each consumed a quart of cider at the Full Quart Inn. Having resumed work, Grist signalled the roller to stop as a horse and trap approached, then, before it had come to a halt, he stepped out into the road in front of it. As he did, his left foot was caught by the roller and his entire lower body from the stomach down was crushed to a pulp. Amazingly, he was still fully conscious, telling his workmates that he didn't think he was too badly hurt. Grist, who was newly married, died from his injuries within the hour. The inquest jury returned a verdict of 'accidental death'.

21 JULY   **1871**   Rounding a slight bend shortly after leaving Highbridge station for Wells, the engine driver saw three men on a trolley on the line just in front of him. He put the train into reverse but was unable to reduce its speed and it ploughed into the trolley. One of the three men managed to jump clear, but the other two – Mr Norris and Mr Edwards – were killed instantly. The inquest jury returned verdicts of 'accidental death' on both men.

1929   Late at night, Revd Richard Trafford heard footsteps in the grounds of the Downside School near Bath, where he was headmaster. He shone a torch outside and recognised two of his pupils, Peter Awdry and Philip Neilson, who appeared to be running away. Revd Trafford called to the boys, who didn't respond, and although the school grounds were searched, the boys had vanished. Peter's body was discovered in Weston-super-Mare around thirty-six hours later.

The two boys were described as normal and happy, but both apparently enjoyed adventure and had been in trouble at school for previous escapades. Now it seemed as though they had gone to Weston-super-Mare and stolen a canoe, which they then took to sea. The canoe's owner, Mr Robert Chance, told the inquest on Peter's death that his white canvas canoe seated four people but was not safe for use in rough seas.

The inquest jury returned a verdict of 'found drowned' on Peter and the coroner added that he held out very little hope for Philip's safety, since the two boys were usually inseparable. Philip's body was found floating at Burnham-on-Sea a week later.

1811   *The Times* printed the sorry saga of Phenis Adams, a private in the 1st Somerset Militia.

Adams applied for surgical aid for an ulcerated wound on his arm. On examination by doctors, it was thought that the wound was self-inflicted. Knowing that he faced dismissal for his deception, Adams deserted and, once recaptured, was placed in Wilton Gaol. By then he had a second wound, this time on his leg, which was also thought to have been self-inflicted.

On 24 April, Adams contrived to fall downstairs and, when he was picked up, he had blood oozing from both ears. He was put to bed and, after a couple of days rest, it was determined that he had no apparent injuries as a result of his fall. Adams disagreed, saying that he believed that he was going deaf.

'Are you very deaf?' asked the doctor in hushed tones.

'Yes, very,' confirmed Adams, falling into the trap set by the doctor.

Realising that he had been rumbled, Adams immediately fell into a state of insensibility. From April through to the date of the article, he remained almost in a coma, drinking only an occasional sip of tea or broth and eating just a little bread and butter. His respiration remained easy and constant and the pupils of his eyes were very slightly dilated. Doctors tried every means they could think of to rouse him but to no avail. Snuff and strong salts were placed up his nose, which had no effect apart from making his eyes water. Strong electrical shocks were administered and blistering chemicals were applied to his head and back, yet he still barely moved a muscle.

On 14 July, it was decided to administer 'nitrous oxyd gas' [*sic*], which was known to 'excite an extraordinary degree of mental and bodily excitement'. However, Adams's teeth were so tightly clenched that it was impossible to get him to inhale the gas, even when his nostrils and lips were pinched shut. Adams flatly refused to breathe and, when it became evident that his pulse was slowing, the doctors were forced to stop the experiment for fear of suffocating him.

At the time of the article, Adams remained completely insensible.

24 JULY

1899 The funeral of John Murphy took place in Bristol. Unfortunately, Murphy had died at one o'clock in the morning on 14 July and, as his wife was unable to afford the cost of his burial, his body had remained at his home for nearly eleven days during an almost unprecedented heatwave.

The house in Hotwells was occupied by Mr and Mrs Peacock and their five children, who let their upstairs rooms to Mr and Mrs Murphy, who had three children of their own. As Murphy lay decomposing, the Bristol Sanitary Officer made regular visits but, in the face of Mrs Murphy's inability to pay for a funeral, was able to do nothing more than spray the house with disinfectant to mask the horrible stench. To the relief of the entire neighbourhood, a decision was finally made by the authorities to bury the corpse regardless of the cost.

25 JULY

1871 Seventy-one-year-old Rebecca Payne was killed instantly at Frome by the coal train from Radstock. At about ten o'clock in the morning, Miss Payne was crossing the Great Western Railway line, having chosen not to use one of the three level crossings in the immediate vicinity. She was known to be somewhat deaf and it was supposed that she didn't hear the train approaching. The jury at her inquest returned a verdict of 'accidental death', adding that they believed the engine driver to be blameless.

26 JULY

1858 An inquest was held at Hinton Blewett by Mr Bruges Fry on the death of Edward Simmons.

Simmons was a notorious character, described as 'the terror of the neighbourhood' and 'a great bully'. At a beer-house skittle alley, Simmons began to pick on a man named John Wookey. Having struck Wookey in the face, Simmons continually pestered him to fight, according to witnesses, asking him more than twenty times.

Wookey refused again and again but when Simmons punched him a second time, he lost patience and proceeded to give Simmons a good thrashing. Simmons fell over several times during the fight before finally giving up and sloping off home, where he died some days later. A post-mortem examination conducted by surgeons Mr Hunt and Mr Perry showed that he had a perforated intestine, probably caused by falling onto a hard surface while fighting.

The jury took into account the extreme provocation, deciding that Wookey had acted in self-defence and returning a verdict of 'justifiable homicide'.

27 JULY

1858 Elizabeth Card, the wife of a Nailsea collier, cut the throat of her four-year-old son, James, before attempting suicide.

Mrs Card had six children and was heavily pregnant with her seventh. On 27 July, she sent the three oldest to their grandmother's house, taking the three youngest children upstairs with her. She cut James's throat with a razor almost beheading him, and then turned her attention to six-year-old Melinda, who fortunately managed to escape her mother's clutches. Mary, aged one year and eight months, was unharmed. Neighbours heard the children screaming but, by the time they arrived, Elizabeth had cut her own throat. Although her wound was serious, it was not life threatening.

An inquest into James Card's death returned a verdict of wilful murder against his mother and she was committed for trial at the next assizes. There the court was told that Elizabeth was badly treated by her husband, George, who was described as a 'drunken, worthless fellow'. Elizabeth was terrified of his violence and had recently left him, only returning on the day of the murder. Elizabeth seemed only sorry that she hadn't succeeded in killing herself, saying that she had sent her child out of a wicked and miserable world. She claimed that her head was 'bad' at the time and that she didn't know what she was doing. She sobbed bitterly throughout her trial, which ended with the jury acquitting her on the grounds of insanity and the judge ordering her to be detained during Her Majesty's pleasure.

1928   A butcher's boy called at the home of the Banks family in Alcombe. He was on the verge of leaving when he heard someone tapping on a window to attract his attention. Eventually, a man opened the window, saying, 'Get the police at once. I am in trouble.' When PC Dredge arrived at the house minutes later, the man told him, 'For God's sake, constable, come in. A terrible thing has happened. I have shot my wife and daughter.'   **28 JULY**

Inside the house, Dredge found two women lying dead in separate bedrooms. He sent for a doctor and arrested their killer, fifty-one-year-old Albert Spencer Banks, the newly appointed manager of the labour exchange at Minehead.

Banks professed to remember little about the murders, although, when asked about the death of his fifty-three-year-old wife, Edith, he admitted to Inspector Fry, 'I believe I did kill her but I cannot remember properly.' Having established that Banks could remember very little about the murder of his wife, Fry then questioned him about his daughter's killing. 'It is just the same as the other,' replied Banks tearfully.

Banks was committed for trial at the Autumn Assizes in Wells and appeared before Mr Justice Shearman. Although initially charged with two murders, his trial dealt only with the murder of his wife and it quickly became apparent that his counsels were relying on an insanity defence. Banks was universally known as a man of the highest character, described on his discharge from the army as 'a steady, sober, honest, intelligent, reliable, hard-working man'. However, in previous years, he had experienced at least two periods of mental illness. In 1926, he was hospitalised for thirty days and, in 1913, he spent nineteen days undergoing treatment for what was described as 'delusional insanity'. On that occasion, he had become convinced that his wife and daughter had been killed by native Indians and had spent two or three days absent from his army post while he scoured the nearby jungle looking for the culprits.

It seemed perfectly obvious to everyone in court that Albert Banks had not been in his right mind when he shot his beloved wife and daughter. Thus it came as no surprise when the jury found Banks guilty, adding that he was insane at the time of murdering his wife. Mr Justice Shearman ordered Banks to be

Above & below: Two views of Alcombe, Minehead. (Author's collection)

etained during His Majesty's pleasure, ruling that the murder of his daughter, Marian Banks, was to remain on file.

1883 In the early hours of the morning, John Dunsford, the manager of the *Bridgwater Mercury* offices, was woken by the smell of burning. Realising that the premises were on fire, he tried to go downstairs, but was driven back by the intense heat and flames. He went to the bedrooms of his children and woke them but, as he led them to the relative safety of an upper floor, he tripped several times and lost his grip on them. Beatrice Ellen (four), Florence Ethel (six) and Rosina Maud (twelve) were overcome by smoke and perished in the flames. Eventually, Dunsford made his way to the very top of the house with his wife, one daughter and the family servant. He shouted for help from a window, asking the crowd assembled below to fetch the fire escape. Unfortunately, this had been locked away and the custodian of the key couldn't be found. In desperation, Dunsford threw a mattress out of the window and urged his wife to jump. She did but missed the mattress completely, landing on the pavement, breaking her right arm, leg and several ribs and injuring her head. Rushed to Bridgwater Hospital, she later died from her injuries.

Beatrice's twin sister was tossed out of the window and caught by a member of the crowd. Meanwhile, John Dunsford hung onto the window sill for several minutes, the heat scorching his hands, until a ladder was brought to rescue him. The family servant managed to get to the roof, from where she too was rescued.

It was thought that the fire had originated in the shop below the Dunsfords' living quarters and that the conflagration had been worsened by the actions of a policeman who, with the best of intentions, broke down the outside door to try and get to the survivors. Verdicts of 'accidental death' were recorded on the deceased.

29 JULY

1873 Fourteen-month-old Harriet Tovey of Bedminster, Bristol, was suffering from measles and had a nasty cough. Her mother, Sarah, gave her a few drops of balsam of aniseed but, within minutes, Harriet was unconscious. Only then did her mother realise that she had accidentally given her daughter a mixture of opium and vinegar instead of cough mixture. Harriet was rushed to Dr Thomas S. Floyd 'in a state of profound slumber'. For more than ninety minutes, the doctor tried every method he could think of to rouse the baby, including attaching her to a 'galvanic battery', but his efforts were in vain and Harriet died from an overdose of opium.

At Harriet's inquest, Sarah Tovey said that she kept opium in the house to relieve her grown-up son's cough. She could not explain how the opium and vinegar mixture came to be in the cough medicine bottle. The jury returned a verdict of 'death by misadventure'.

30 JULY

1885 A fast passenger train on the Somerset & Dorset Railway collided with a stationery goods train at Binegar station. It was later shown that signalman William Applebee had accidentally moved the wrong lever, diverting the speeding train from the up line onto the down line.

31 JULY

One female passenger was killed instantly. Twenty-four-year-old Annie Charles, who was travelling to join her husband, Joseph, a coastguard in Cork, Ireland, died from a fractured skull, with additional fractures to one arm and leg. Four other people were seriously injured, including guard Thomas Beakes, who had served with the railway for thirty years. Beakes had both legs amputated after the crash but died soon afterwards.

It emerged at the later inquest into the disaster that the line had only that morning been passed safe by Government Inspector Colonel Rich. Rich had recommended some minor alterations to the signal locking, although he was quite happy for the line to be opened while these were carried out. The inquest jury concluded that Applebee was guilty of culpable negligence; he was charged with manslaughter and sent for trial at the next Somerset Assizes. However, the Grand Jury ignored the bill and Applebee was not penalised for his part in the disaster.

AUGUST

The Town Bridge, Bridgwater, 1959. (Author's collection)

1 AUGUST

1808 A cart horse took fright in the village of Banwell and bolted. As it galloped past James Chipper, its flapping harness caught around his waist and he was dragged for nearly half a mile at great speed, literally being dashed to pieces. When the horse was finally halted, so little remained of Mr Chipper that he was scarcely recognisable as a human being and could only be identified by the remnants of his clothes.

2 AUGUST

1846 Mr Fowles visited the privy at his lodgings in Wellington Place, Bath and found a new-born baby boy. Fowles extracted the infant, who was still alive, and sent for a doctor. The baby died shortly afterwards and surgeon Mr Harris determined that he had suffered a head injury, with a resultant accumulation of blood on the brain.

When the occupants of the house were questioned, suspicion fell on Ann Coles, the niece of the owners, who worked as a servant during the day and slept at Wellington Place. At first she denied having given birth but later admitted that she believed her baby was stillborn and that it was dead when she threw it down the privy. Amazingly, in order to dispose of her baby, Ann would have had to pass through an apartment rented by Mr and Mrs Francis. Somehow, she had managed to walk through their room without disturbing their sleep, unlocking then relocking their door on her way. Having just given birth, she had accomplished this feat without leaving as much as a spot of blood in her wake.

At Ann's trial for wilful murder at the Somerset Assizes, surgeon Mr Harris was unable to state with any certainty whether the baby's injuries were wilfully inflicted, produced by a fall or accidentally inflicted during childbirth. He further stated that the bleeding on the baby's brain could have given the appearance that the baby was dead, after which it might have experienced a temporary revival.

Since Ann's son was found alive, she could not legally be charged with concealment of the birth, which only applied to dead babies. Hence Mr Baron Rolfe instructed the jury that they must either find Ann guilty of wilful murder or acquit her altogether. The jury immediately returned a verdict of not guilty.

3 AUGUST

1894 Fourteen-year-old Frederick Lyons was at work at Blagdon Waterworks, helping to fill a trench with puddle clay to make it watertight. The clay was lifted in a skip by a large crane and deposited in a wagon. As one wagon was being loaded, its brakes failed. The driver shouted a warning to the men working nearby but the front of the wagon caught the skip, which rebounded into Frederick, knocking him over, fracturing his spine and left leg and injuring his chest. He later died from his injuries at the Bristol Royal Infirmary.

It was shown that the wagon brake – a leather belt on a drum – had become wet after a rainstorm, causing it to slip. At the subsequent inquest conducted by deputy coroner Mr A.E. Barker, the jury returned a verdict of 'accidental death', adding a rider that in future the wagon brakes should be inspected before use to make sure that they were in working order.

Bristol Royal
Infirmary. (Author's
collection)

1862 'The Female Blondin' – a tightrope walker – gave a performance at   4 AUGUST
Bridgwater, walking across a rope suspended 30ft from the ground. Heavy
weights were attached to the rope to steady it, secured by guy ropes stretching
to the ground and, as people flocked for a better view, someone stumbled into
one of the support ropes. A twenty-eight pound weight fell, crashing onto the
head of twenty-four-year-old ship's carpenter George Wilkins.

Wilkins fell to the ground unconscious, blood streaming from his head. He
was taken to Bridgwater Infirmary, where he was initially expected to make
a full recovery but sadly he died two days later from an effusion of blood to
the brain. At the subsequent inquest held by Mr J.E. Poole, the jury recorded
a verdict of 'accidental death'. They pointed out that when Mr Blondin
performed, his rope and its supports were safely fenced and suggested that this
practice could be adopted by his female counterpart.

1927 Five-year-old Olive Irene Watts of Twerton-on-Avon went to Keynsham   5 AUGUST
with her parents and, as a treat, was given a halfpenny ice cream cornet. By
the following day, she was complaining of stomach ache, and within twenty-
four hours, she was suffering from convulsions and her temperature had risen
to 105°. Although she was rushed to hospital, she died on 7 August.

By then, more than 200 people in the Keynsham area were unwell. All
were suffering symptoms similar to those of gastroenteritis and nine were
sufficiently poorly to be admitted to hospital. A further fifty cases of suspected
poisoning had been recorded twenty-four hours later and all but one victim
had eaten ice cream made by one particular vendor.

Alfred Miller stated that he had been producing and selling ice cream for
twenty years without a single complaint. He used only the freshest, natural
ingredients – new milk, new-laid eggs, sugar, cornflour and vanilla. All of his
utensils were scrubbed with boiling water and soda before every use and his
premises regularly passed inspections by the sanitary inspector.

Laboratory analysis of samples of a subsequent batch of ice cream isolated
a bacillus from the salmonella group. Recording a verdict of 'death by

misadventure' on Olive Watts, the coroner stated that he was satisfied that Miller was in no way to blame.

6 AUGUST   **1844**   George Gulliford of Ilchester was a notorious criminal who, although only twenty years old, had a string of convictions behind him. Having served a term in gaol, he was released from prison and enjoyed only five days of freedom, during which he committed three counts of burglary and one of sacrilege.

On 6 August 1844, Gulliford appeared at the Somerset Assizes in Wells, where, having been found guilty, the judge told him that, were it not for a recent change in the law, he would have been sentenced to death. In view of his persistent offending, the judge decided that he should be transported for life and thus George became the seventh member of the Gulliford family to be transported.

7 AUGUST   **1863**   The prolonged torture of Sarah Webber, an elderly woman described as being 'weak of intellect', came to an end when her employer, Thomas Cook, was sentenced to six months' imprisonment with hard labour.

Sarah had worked for the Cooks at Langford Budville for nine months and was supposed to earn £3 a year. Yet, throughout her entire employment, she had been paid only 3s. Sarah was treated with extreme brutality by her employers. On one occasion, when she was ill in bed, Cook forced excrement into her nose and mouth and she frequently had buckets of cold water poured over her. She was kicked and beaten and had her hands tied to a beam in the cheese-making room at the farm, where she was left for hours until the Cooks' daughter took pity on her and released her. One of the worst atrocities was allegedly perpetrated by Mrs Cook, who forced a piece of honeycomb containing bees into her mouth and laughed as Sarah was stung.

At Wellington Police Court, both Thomas Cook and his wife were charged with a series of aggravated assaults. The Bench ignored the charges against Mrs Cook, as there was no corroborating evidence and they believed that she had acted under the influence of her husband. The decision to incarcerate Thomas Cook was greeted with loud applause and people were so incensed by what the magistrates described as his 'barbarous conduct' that he needed police protection to enter and leave the court.

8 AUGUST   **1835**   Thirteen-year-old William Hodges was tried at the Somerset Assizes in Bridgwater for 'killing and slaying Sarah Davis at Wells on 23 July by riding over her with a horse.'

William's boss had asked him to take the horse to its field, specifically warning him to go quietly. However, he chose to ride at a full gallop, kicking the horse on in an effort to make it go even faster. Sarah Davis was walking at the side of the road when William's horse barrelled into her, knocking her over. William didn't even stop to see if she was all right and, when he was later told that Sarah had died from her injuries, his only comment was, 'I don't care a damn.'

Found guilty, William was sentenced to twelve months' imprisonment with hard labour.

1879 John Albert Walter of the 3rd Battalion Somerset Volunteers had spent a long period on guard duty but insisted that he wasn't at all tired. To demonstrate his vim and vigour, he turned a somersault over a pile of blankets. Unfortunately, as he was tumbling, his bayonet fell out of its sheath and Walter landed on the point, which penetrated his spine and led to peritonitis, from which he later died. At an inquest held by the deputy coroner Mr R. Biggs, at the hospital in Weston-super-Mare, the jury recorded a verdict of 'accidental death'.

9 AUGUST

1825 Hannah Taunton was tried at the Somerset Assizes in Bridgwater, charged with the manslaughter of her husband, Henry.

10 AUGUST

Ninety-five-year-old Henry and fifty-seven-year-old Hannah married in April 1825 but Hannah quickly realised that she had made a dreadful mistake. On 13 May, Henry tried to cut his throat but was thwarted by a policeman. Brought before magistrates in Bath the next morning on a charge of attempting to commit suicide, Henry pleaded for his wife to come back to him but Hannah was resolute and, on 15 May, she took drastic steps to end her marriage by pushing her husband down a flight of steps in Walcot Parade, Bath. Henry died on 18 May from the injuries he received.

At her trial, Hannah insisted that her husband's fall had been accidental. However, Elizabeth Smith testified that she was within two yards of the incident and had seen Hannah give Henry a hefty push between his shoulder blades, which sent him toppling down the steps to land on his head at the bottom. Another witness, Mr Hawkins, tended Henry as he lay injured and testified that Henry had accused Hannah of throwing him down the steps, and both Smith and Hawkins stated that Hannah had made no move to assist her husband after his fall.

The jury found Hannah Taunton guilty and, in view of her age, Mr Justice Littledale sentenced her to only six months' imprisonment.

1896 Frederick William Hann bought a toy pistol through a newspaper advert, which he fired at apples in the orchard across the road from his home. On 18 July, Frederick accidentally shot his thirteen-year-old brother, Charles. Frederick immediately fetched a doctor to attend to his brother and initially the wound didn't seem too serious. However, infection set in and Charles died in Yeovil General Hospital on 11 August. At an inquest held at the White Lion Hotel by coroner Mr E.Q. Louch, the jury returned a verdict of 'death from misadventure', adding a rider that representations should be made to the Home Office to ban sales of these pistols to children.

11 AUGUST

Yeovil General Hospital. (Author's collection)

12 AUGUST   **1836**   John Gill was found guilty of maliciously wounding his wife, Sarah, with intent to disfigure her. At his trial before Mr Baron Alderson at the Somerset Assizes in Wells, the court heard that he had deliberately bitten off most of her nose after an argument. Thirty-year-old Gill was sentenced to two years' imprisonment.

13 AUGUST   **1881**   On the road near Vobster, carter Albert Thomas Lambert indecently assaulted ten-year-old Mary Elizabeth Day.

At the police court in Frome later that week, magistrates found insufficient evidence to support the charge against Lambert, although they were in no doubt that Lambert had indecently exposed himself to the little girl and had otherwise insulted her. Lambert's employer, Major Paget and Paget's bailiff, Samuel Kingston, both provided excellent character references and the magistrates agreed that the act had been committed on a sudden impulse due to temptation from the Devil rather than with malice aforethought. Nevertheless, the magistrates insisted that little girls on the highway must be protected and fined Lambert £2 plus costs.

14 AUGUST   **1828**   Sarah Mitchell was tried before Mr Justice Park at the Somerset Assizes in Wells, for the wilful murder of her son.

Sarah was taken to Shepton Mallet Prison after being convicted of stealing some plates and, since she was still breastfeeding her seven-month-old son, the child went too. Sarah was suffering from 'milk fever' at the time – something that we today would probably call post-natal depression – and her condition was aggravated by having drunk some beer and having been 'much jolted' in the vehicle conveying her to prison. Confined to a dark cell on arrival, she seized her infant son by the heels and repeatedly dashed his head against a bed post.

Sarah was acquitted on the grounds of insanity and Mr Justice Park observed that solitary confinement frequently seemed to cause madness, adding that such a punishment should only be resorted to with the greatest caution.

Some contemporary newspapers reported that this was the second infant that Sarah had killed in similar fashion.

15 AUGUST   **1913**   The coroner returned a verdict of accidental death on Henry Frederick Millar, aged twenty-four, who died from injuries received in a motorcycle accident near Kingsweston. Charles Stack was driving his horse and cart, when he saw Mr Millar approaching from behind. Knowing that his horse was nervous, Stack raised his hand to signal Millar to slow down. However, Millar either did not see or ignored the signal and tried to pass the cart, at which the horse shied and knocked him from his motorcycle. The cause of his death was attributed to bleeding from lacerations to his internal organs.

16 AUGUST   **1861**   At Wiveliscombe, Robert Sully committed the latest in a long series of sexual offences against children, this time choosing ten-year-old Mary Jane Stook as his victim.

Seventy-one-year-old Sully had been detained in Wiveliscombe Union as a pauper lunatic from 1853 until 1856 and, according to medical witnesses at his subsequent trial at the Somerset Assizes, continued to be weak-minded. Yet he was still sufficiently sane to understand that what he was doing was wrong.

Court House, Wiveliscombe. (Author's collection)

The jury found Sully guilty as charged, at which Mr Justice Williams revealed that Sully had a previous conviction in 1857 and, at the time of the trial, there were indictments against him for a further two similar offences of the same revolting nature. He sentenced Sully to be kept in penal servitude for four years.

1832 The trial of Maria Spurlock took place at Wells before Mr Justice Taunton. Maria pleaded not guilty to the wilful murder of her husband, George, on 10 August 1832.

17 AUGUST

The fatal argument between the couple started over a pair of George's breeches, which Maria was supposed to have mended but hadn't. When George remonstrated with her and called her 'damned lazy', Maria went to the kitchen and picked up a butcher's knife. Elizabeth, one of the couple's seven children, asked her where she was going with it, at which Maria lashed out, cutting her daughter's forehead. Her father rushed to her assistance and Maria plunged the knife into his chest.

The children's screams attracted the attention of neighbour, Frederick Roe, who found that the fight had now spilled out into the Spurlocks' garden. Maria still held the knife in her hand and George was tightly gripping her wrist, trying to prevent her from using it against him. Roe managed to disarm Maria then escorted George indoors and sat him in a chair, where he died minutes later.

It emerged in court that Maria had given birth to twins four years earlier, after which she had suffered from what would now be recognised as post-natal depression. She made several attempts to commit suicide, including trying to cut off her own head, as a consequence of which her family became accustomed to hiding the house knives. Maria had then tried to drown herself and was certified insane by a surgeon in 1830. Doctors who had examined her since the murder agreed that she was nervous, agitated and 'in a violent, distracted state'.

In the face of such evidence, Mr Justice Taunton instructed the jury to acquit Maria Spurlock on the grounds of insanity and ordered her to be detained until His Majesty's pleasure was known.

18 AUGUST   **1881**   An inquest was held by coroner Dr Wybrants at East Coker on the death of fifteen-year-old farmer's son Alexander William Marsh.

Alexander and his brother had been amusing themselves by jumping over a barrier that they had made by balancing a stick on two poles. Instead of clearing the barrier, Alexander landed astride the stick, which splintered and penetrated his groin. In spite of treatment by Dr Colmer of Yeovil, Alexander died from his injuries.

19 AUGUST   **1789**   John Walford was executed near Nether Stowey for the murder of his wife.

Walford was a charcoal maker, spending six days every week living and working alone in the woods. Although he was betrothed to Ann Rice, he was seduced by Jane Shorney, who deliberately set out to trap him into marriage. Jane gave birth to John's baby and, when he impregnated her again, he had no choice but to marry her.

Castle of Comfort Inn, Doddington. (Author's collection)

The wedding took place on 18 June 1789 but, having got her man, Jane made his life a misery by constantly criticising him and taunting him about his lost love, Ann. Only three weeks after her marriage, Jane persuaded John to accompany her to buy cider from the Castle of Comfort Inn at Doddington. Only John returned, having beaten Jane senseless with a fence post on the way home, before cutting her throat with his pocket knife.

After a three-hour trial at Bridgwater, John was found guilty of wilful murder and sentenced to hang near to where his wife's body was found. The place of his death has since become known as Walford's Gibbet.

Memorial to Jane Walford at Doddington. (© N. Sly)

1891 Seven-year-old Lily Maud Burgess was kidnapped in Bristol by Emily Pople, who was later charged with taking Lily by force, with the intent to deprive Emma Pearson of the said child. **20 AUGUST**

Emma Pearson was Lily's mother and a respectable married woman. However, she had given birth to Lily in December 1883 while unmarried and her husband was not the child's biological father.

Emma's mother lived in Burlington Street, Weston-super-Mare and, when Lily was eight or nine months old, she was boarded with her grandmother's next-door neighbour, Emily Pople. Both Lily's mother and biological father contributed financially to her upkeep until 1888, when Emma decided that she wanted Lily to live with her and her new husband.

Emma asked her mother to collect Lily but Emily Pople refused to give the child up. Mr Pople was a beach entertainer and the couple had taught Lily a number of acrobatic tricks. At Emily Pople's court hearing, it was alleged by prosecution counsel Mr H.R. Wansbrough that the little girl earned the Poples far too much money for them to willingly hand her back to her mother. Emma and her mother made repeated attempts to get Lily back but without success. Then, in August 1891, Emma Pearson went to Weston-super-Mare and, happening to see Lily on the streets, snatched her and took her to Bristol. Emma left Lily in the care of her aunt, Mrs Elizabeth Westbury, while she made arrangements to return to her new home in Fulham. However, in the meantime, Emily Pople travelled to Bristol and snatched Lily back.

Emma went straight to Weston-super-Mare, where she confronted Emily Pople and demanded her child. Emily refused to relinquish Lily, telling Emma, 'I'll tear your liver out if you dare to touch the child again.'

Summonsed to appear at Bristol Police Court on a charge of kidnapping, Emily Pople was persuaded to hand over the child to her natural mother and all charges against her were dropped. During the court hearing, Lily clung to Emily Pople sobbing hysterically and had to be prised away to be handed over to Emma Pearson. Emily Pople immediately fainted and was assisted out of court, almost insensible with grief.

21 AUGUST
1873 Thomas and Annie Penelope Crocker were inexplicably taken ill at their home in Alfred Street, Burnham-on-Sea. The two children, aged five and four, died the next day and it was suggested that they might have taken insect-destroying powder, which had been accidentally left outside their bedroom.

An inquest was opened by coroner Dr Chaddock and adjourned to allow the police to communicate with Reade Brothers in Wolverhampton, the manufacturers of the powder. Unbelievably, the company refused to tell Superintendent Gillbanks the active ingredient, saying only that it was one of the poisons allowed under the 1868 Pharmacy Act. Thus samples of the powder and the contents of the children's stomachs were sent to Bristol analyst Mr Stoddart. Stoddart confirmed that the common denominator was arsenic and, at the resumed inquest, the jury returned an open verdict that 'the deceased children died from the effects of arsenic'.

Burnham Esplanade and Sands. (Author's collection)

Burnham, Esplanade and Sands.

22 AUGUST
1826 James Gibson was tried at the Somerset Assizes, charged with stealing an iron chest and other items from the home of a merchant.

The merchant was awakened on the night of the offence by an enormous explosion outside his house. He quickly realised that he had been burgled and that the thief had stolen the chest, along with two canisters. What the thief did not know when he struck a light outside the property to examine his haul was that the canisters contained gunpowder.

The arrest of the culprit was a fairly easy exercise for the police. James Gibson was found dreadfully scorched, his hair and beard burned away and his eyelids completely destroyed. He also had a wound on one of his legs and a button missing from his charred jacket, which was identical to one found in the debris of the explosion. Found guilty, Gibson was sentenced to be transported for seven years.

1939   Two people were killed in Cheddar Gorge when more than half a ton of rocks fell 400ft from a cliff face. Five-year-old Arthur John White from Combe Down, Bath died instantly, while Mrs Kate Scott of Corsham, who was visiting the Gorge on a day trip, died in hospital a couple of days later.

Cheddar Gorge. (Author's collection)

23 AUGUST

Dr F. Wallis, the Deputy Director of Bristol Museum, stated at the inquest that, although the fall was exacerbated by excessive rain widening the joints between the rocks, in his opinion, the immediate cause was the sheer weight of ivy and other vegetation. Mr T.G. Gill, the agent for Lord Weymouth, who owned the cliff, told the inquest that as much vegetation as was practical had been cut from the rocks and almost 300 tons of loose stones had been removed from the cliff earlier that year. A barrier had also been erected around the cliff.

The coroner recorded verdicts of 'death by misadventure' on both victims.

1787   *The Times* reported the executions of three 'malefactors' at Gallows Field, Ilchester. John Cary, aged twenty-three, was sentenced to death for highway robbery. He eventually admitted to committing a string of robberies around the Bath and Bristol area, including eleven in the nine-week period prior to his arrest. He was accompanied on the gallows by Edmund Connell, who was executed for burglary, and Grace Bootle, aged forty-five, who was convicted of receiving stolen property.

24 AUGUST

1869   Williton farmer Mr Pile employed William Crocombe to dip his flock of sheep. Two days later, seventy of the sheep were found dead in their field and, within a week, 200 had died. When Pile tried to claim compensation, Crocombe denied any liability, suggesting that Pile had tampered with the sheep dip and added extra chemicals without his knowledge. Eventually, Pile sued Crocombe and, when the case was brought up at Williton Police Court, the presiding magistrates found Crocombe liable for the full amount of Pile's loss and awarded damages of £50 plus costs. They hoped that the case would serve as a caution

25 AUGUST

against the careless use of chemicals, particularly sheep dip, of which the principal ingredient was arsenic.

26 AUGUST **1872** William Lace, aged forty-three, was executed by William Calcraft at Taunton Gaol for the murder of his wife at Blagdon on 23 April.

William and Eliza had four children and were apparently very happily married. However, on the day before Eliza's death they had a minor quarrel when William arrived home from work earlier than expected and found that his supper wasn't ready.

On the day of her murder, William accused his wife of 'being out in the hundred acres with a hundred fellows a month ago'. When Eliza said that she didn't understand what he meant, William flew at her in a rage. Eliza escaped to a neighbour's cottage but William pursued her and ordered her home, promising not to beat her. However, as soon as they reached their garden, he knocked her down, kicking her head as she lay on the ground with a baby in her arms. The couple's twelve-year-old daughter grabbed the baby and ran for help. Eliza managed to get up and returned to her neighbour's house but now the door was locked against her. Another family also locked their door then watched from their cottage as William dragged his wife back home, where he kicked her to death. When his daughter came back with another neighbour, William was throwing pails of water over Eliza in an attempt to revive her. Told that Eliza was dead, he insisted that she was only 'dead drunk'.

When Lace appeared at the Somerset Assizes in Wells before Mr Justice Mellor, the principal witness against him was his daughter. Known as a sober, even-tempered man of exemplary character, he was found guilty as charged and stated that he was ready to die for what he had done. At the trial, Mr Justice Mellor criticised the conduct of several of the Laces' neighbours, who had not intervened to save Eliza's life.

27 AUGUST **1829** At Twerton, a boy named Joseph Skrine was throwing sticks at a walnut tree, in the hope of dislodging the nuts, when the tree's owner spotted him and shouted at him to stop. Joseph immediately took to his heels, with the owner of the tree close behind him, threatening to thrash him if he caught him. Eventually, Joseph ducked into a privy to try and hide. When his pursuer opened the door, Joseph gave three deep sighs and died from fright.

28 AUGUST **1884** Members of the Salvation Army were the cause of a riot in Frome. A few days earlier, two Salvationists appeared before magistrates, charged with obstructing the town's main thoroughfare by preaching. There had been a long-standing conflict between the police and the Salvationists and, while the police had no objection to the Army marching, they would not permit them to stop and obstruct the streets. The Army promised that they would abide by this agreement but it was a promise that was broken again and again. Eventually, the police lost all patience and Captains Smith and Cozens were arrested. Each man was fined 6d by the magistrates but each stated that he did not have enough money to pay the fine, leaving the magistrates no alternative but to send them to Shepton Mallet Prison for seven days.

Market Place, Frome. (Author's collection)

When the two men were released, the Salvation Army made martyrs of them, throwing a banquet in their honour and parading them through Frome, dressed in convicts' uniforms and accompanied by brass bands. They eventually halted outside the police station, where they booed and hissed and the band played 'We Shall Conquer'. Unfortunately, their actions drew large, hostile crowds and, as the band struck up, the Army was attacked from all sides. Their banners were seized and ripped to pieces and the bandsmen's instruments were flattened.

At the height of the pitched battle that ensued, the Salvationists sent a desperate plea for help to the police station. However, with only one constable on the premises, the duty sergeant thought better of sending him out alone to face two angry mobs.

When the Army were finally able to escape to the safety of their barracks, the crowd gave three cheers, followed by a rousing chorus of 'Rule Britannia'. The contemporary newspapers fervently hoped that the events of 28 August did not herald a return of the rioting and 'rowdyism' which had disgraced the borough during the previous winter.

1936 Six-year-old Samuel Windsor James Burrows from North Petherton **29 AUGUST** was accidentally shot dead by another child. The owner of the shotgun, Richard James Baker, had last used it two days earlier, leaving it in a place that was readily accessible to children. He also neglected to unload it, leaving it containing a live cartridge. When the gun was picked up and accidentally fired by a child, the shot hit Samuel, who was standing more than 40ft away at the time.

In recording a verdict of 'accidental death', the foreman of the inquest jury suggested that Baker should be severely censured for his carelessness.

1847 An inquest was held on the deaths of three children at Norton St **30 AUGUST** Philip two days earlier. Their mother, Mrs Doggett, went to work early in the morning and, unable to find anyone to look after the children in her absence, she left them alone at home, locking them in for safety. Later that day, neighbours noticed smoke issuing from the cottage. They broke down the door and discovered a fire, which was quickly extinguished. Tragically, the three children, all aged under seven, had already been suffocated by the smoke.

31 AUGUST   **1896** Albert Dyer was renovating a property known as The Green in Somerton. As he lifted the floorboards in a recessed cupboard in the attic to lay some gas pipe, Dyer found a small cloth-wrapped bundle. Curiosity compelled him to open the bundle, which contained the skeletonised body of a baby. Dyer went straight to the new owner of the house to report his gruesome find, and Mr E.W. Valentine summoned a doctor and the police. When Dr Wade and Sergeant Comer examined the attic, they were horrified to find a further three bundles lying beneath the floorboards, each containing more skeletonised remains.

The four bodies were taken to the local police station, where they underwent a thorough examination by Dr Wade. He found it impossible to glean much information from the collection of tiny bones, although he was to state at a later inquest that he believed that two of the bodies were those of prematurely born infants, while the other two were full-term babies. He was unable to determine whether any of the infants had been born alive, nor was he able to state with any certainty how long the bodies had been concealed in the attic, saying that it could have been any period of time between five and twenty years, possibly even longer. One of the bodies was wrapped in a child's napkin, which was bound with tape. A second was wrapped in a piece of bed curtain and a third in an apron and a towel. A search of the house and garden revealed no further clues.

The previous owner of the house, Thomas Welsh, had recently died, aged eighty. An eccentric bachelor, he had shared his home with housekeeper Eliza Edwards (aka Eliza Martin) for the last thirty years of his life. On his death, he left Eliza a cottage and an income of £100 a year and, although Eliza was still alive at the time of the discovery, she was suffering from dementia and was unable to contribute anything to the police investigations.

The coroner's jury eventually recorded an open verdict on the deaths of the four unidentified babies and the mystery remains unsolved.

Somerton. (Author's collection)

SEPTEMBER

High Street, Weston-super-Mare. (Author's collection)

1 SEPTEMBER   **1924**   An inquest held at Knapp, near North Curry, returned a verdict of 'wilful murder' against George Henry Derham, who shot his seventy-year-old mother dead in the kitchen of their farmhouse.

Mary Derham's seventeen-year-old granddaughter, Elizabeth, told the inquest that she was brushing her hair when she heard a shot fired in the next room and saw Mrs Derham fall. As she ran from the house to seek help, she saw her Uncle George standing with a shotgun in his hands and heard two further shots. Having apparently shot his mother, George then turned the gun on himself. Gravely injured, he was rushed to Taunton Hospital, where he died from his injuries soon after the inquest.

2 SEPTEMBER   **1891**   Thirty-five-year-old Henry 'Harry' Dainton was released from prison after serving a one-month sentence for assaulting his wife, Hannah, who had been granted a separation order in his absence. It was the latest in a long line of assaults on his wife by Dainton, who violently objected to Hannah's drinking, which he thought excessive. Just six days after his release, Dainton found Hannah in a public house, drinking with a group of friends. An argument broke out between them and Hannah was later seen with a bloody nose.

At ten o'clock on the evening of 8 September, a couple were seen fighting by the river Avon at Bath. The woman was shouting 'Murder!' and onlookers saw both of the combatants topple off the bank into the river. Soon afterwards, Harry returned to his home in Avon Street dripping wet and told his fourteen-year-old son that he had jumped into the river intending to drown himself.

Hannah's body was later recovered from a shallow part of the river. There were marks of a struggle on the bank nearby, as well as signs that someone had fallen into the river and then climbed out again. Footprints in the area exactly matched those of Harry Dainton's boots.

Charged with wilful murder, Harry Dainton was tried at the assizes in Wells before Mr Justice Cave. Found guilty, he was sentenced to death, although the jury recommended mercy on the grounds of Hannah's provocative conduct. There is no evidence to suggest that Harry Dainton was executed, indicating that the jury's recommendation was heeded.

3 SEPTEMBER   **1753**   Susannah Bonford was burned at the stake at Cure Green, near Wells, for the wilful murder of her husband by poison. Wearing a black dress, with a black hood over her head, she was dragged to the place of execution on a sledge. Before 'a prodigious concourse of spectators', she was permitted to spend half an hour in prayer with a clergyman before being seated on a stool with a rope around her neck and strangled. She was then surrounded by faggots, under which was placed a barrel of pitch. Two iron plates were put around her body and nailed to the stake, so that she would remain upright, then the fire was lit. The flames burned for about an hour, almost totally consuming the body. When they died down, what little remained of Susannah was placed in a box, which was later buried.

4 SEPTEMBER   **1844**   Joel Fisher was hanged at Taunton Gaol for the murder of his wife, Mary, at Weston-super-Mare on 5 June.

The couple argued constantly. Mary had an explosive temper and frequently went out of her way to antagonise her husband. More than once, she left Joel then later persuaded him to take her back, promising to control her temper. However, her promises were never kept.

The couple ran the Devonshire Inn in Weston-super-Mare and, on 4 June 1874, a long-term lodger left, claiming that he could no longer tolerate Mary's rudeness towards him. The Fishers argued and, refusing to sleep with Joel, Mary eventually retired to bed with their servant and Joel's two young sons from his first marriage. At five o'clock the next morning, Joel burst through the bedroom door wielding an iron bar, with which he smashed Mary's skull. Realising that he had not killed her, he then fetched a carving knife and cut her throat, before sending one of the pub's lodgers to fetch the police.

At his subsequent trial before Mr Justice Pattison at the Somerset Assizes, his defence counsel admitted that his client had killed Mary but tried to persuade the jury to consider a verdict of manslaughter, on the grounds that Mary had provoked Joel. Doubts were also raised about Fisher's sanity but the jury found him guilty of wilful murder and he was sentenced to death. He told the judge that he would rather hang than live with such a wicked woman.

1851 Sarah Ann Roberts had lived in Wrington with her two children since being abandoned by her husband, who, having run away to America, later died there, leaving her a widow. Sarah supported herself and her family by working from home as a shoe and boot binder.

She was distantly related by marriage to eighteen-year-old Charlotte Birch from neighbouring Churchill, who was in service as a housemaid at Weston-super-Mare. However, in 1851, the family she worked for discovered that Charlotte was pregnant and she was instantly dismissed from her job. When Charlotte told Sarah Roberts about her predicament, Sarah confided that she too was pregnant. Anxious to avoid the shame and scandal of producing illegitimate babies, Sarah suggested to Charlotte that they should each take a dose of her homemade concoction. 'If it does you no good, it will do you no harm,' Mrs Roberts convinced Charlotte.

On 5 September, both women took a large swig of the mixture and, within a short time, both were seized by agonising stomach pains. Charlotte returned to her family home and, although both women summoned a doctor, in spite of the attentions of surgeons Mr Chadwick and Mr Coates, both died.

Sarah, who died on 6 September, admitted to the doctors on her deathbed that she had personally collected the weeds and herbs from which she had made the potion that she believed would induce an abortion. Indeed, when her house was searched after her death, no less than four quart bottles of the mixture were found. Charlotte, who had taken a slightly smaller dose, died at home on the morning of 7 September.

At the inquest into the deaths of the two women, the coroner fervently hoped that 'this fatal calamity' would act as a deterrent for other women intending to adopt any such dangerous practices.

6 SEPTEMBER **1878** After a night spent drinking with his friends in numerous public houses, twenty-seven-year-old Edward Adams was bet 6*d* that he would not jump off the Newton Bridge in Bath. Although several members of the public urged him not to do so, Adams jumped into the river Avon and drowned. An inquest on his death returned a verdict of 'death whilst in a state of intemperance'.

The Avon from Newton Bridge, Bath. (Author's collection)

7 SEPTEMBER **1892** Eighteen-year-old Martha Elizabeth Alford left Bishopston in Bristol, where she was employed as a domestic servant, intending to walk to her parents' home at Norton Malreward. She was seen by two women at Whitchurch, Keynsham on 9 September, when she appeared very ill. She told the women that she had spent the previous night in Bristol with her boyfriend Harry, who was a soldier. Harry had given her a glass of beer, which 'nearly drove her mad'. Martha arrived home later that evening, complaining of feeling ill, and died the next morning. A post-mortem examination revealed the apparent presence of an irritant poison in her stomach.

An inquest was opened at the Black Lion, Whitchurch by coroner Mr Craddock and adjourned so that Martha's remains could be examined by county analyst Mr J.W. Gatehouse. Gatehouse was unable to extract any known poison from her organs but testified that her stomach contained a quantity of black liquid, rich in fungus spores, which bore some of the characteristics of extract of ergot, an agent often used to induce abortion. In addition, there appeared to have been 'manipulative interference' with her womb. The coroner suggested that Martha had been pregnant and that either she or someone else had tried to bring about a miscarriage.

In spite of exhaustive enquiries, the police were unable to identify 'Harry' or any other boyfriends Martha might have had. The cause of her death seemed to be the ingestion of a poisonous fungus, although there was no evidence to suggest how or by whom this had been administered. Thus, on the advice of the coroner, the inquest jury returned an open verdict.

1929 Seventeen-year-old Gwendoline 'Molly' Phillips left Rock's Farm at Exford where she was employed, telling the housekeeper that she was going to visit her aunt. Molly never arrived at her aunt's house in Cutcombe, nor did she return to the farm. In spite of intensive searches of the surrounding moorland on foot and on horseback, Molly had apparently disappeared into thin air.

In March 1931, a human skeleton was found in a shallow bog on Codsend Moor by farm workers burning gorse. The body was identified as that of Molly Phillips by her mother, Mrs Ford, who recognised the remnants of her blue dress. Establishing a cause of death proved more difficult. Dr Godfrey Carter, a pathologist at Taunton Hospital, examined the remains and found no obvious signs of injury or broken bones. The bog in which Molly was found was shallow enough for her to have extricated herself without difficulty and Carter theorised that Molly had caught her foot on a stone at the edge of the bog and tripped, probably dying from shock and exposure. Carter also felt that Molly might have been fleeing in fright from someone or something.

An inquest returned a verdict of 'death by misadventure', although the police continued to search the moor and investigate the mystery. They found strands of hair, a brooch, a button, some pieces of women's underclothes and a pair of spectacles – all of which Molly's mother identified as belonging to her daughter. A man also came forward to say that he had witnessed a struggle between a man and woman at Dunkery Beacon on the day of Molly's disappearance. Along with many local people, the police came to believe that Molly had been murdered.

It was widely reported in the contemporary newspapers that both the police and Molly's mother applied to Attorney General Mr Lovat Fraser for the inquest to be reopened. In a statement made to the House of Commons in mid-May 1931, Fraser confirmed that he had received such an application. Yet, rather than coming from Mrs Ford or the police, the request had been sent by a newspaper reporter. When the Attorney General contacted Mrs Ford

Dunkery Beacon.
(Author's collection)

directly, she claimed to have been hounded by the press and stated that she had no wish for the case to be reopened.

9 SEPTEMBER   1896   A funeral carriage bearing the coffin of a child headed from Saltford to Arno's Vale Cemetery in Bristol. As it reached Keynsham, the horses were startled by a steam roller and bolted. The coachman and undertaker, who were riding on the outside of the coach, fell off, while the child's father jumped from inside the coach, cutting his hand badly. As the runaway coach neared the Lamb & Lark public house, saddler Mr W. Phelps managed to grab the reins and bring the coach to a stop. As it slowed, the child's mother leaped to safety but stumbled on landing, a wheel passing over one of her legs. A doctor was summoned and, after treatment, everyone was well enough to proceed with the funeral. It was apparently the second time that week that Mr Phelps had stopped a runaway horse.

10 SEPTEMBER   1878   An inquest was held in Frome by coroner Dr Wybrants on the death of two-year-old Albion Francis Lapham. The child's mother told the court that Albion was standing by the back door of his home when Carey Millard went to a nearby well to draw up some water. Having pulled up one bucketful, Carey walked off with it, leaving the cover of the well open. By the time he returned for a second bucketful less than thirty seconds later, Albion had toddled over and fallen 44ft into the 8ft-deep water in the well. Although a young man named John Bennett immediately volunteered to be lowered into the well, by the time he reached the child, Albion had drowned.

11 SEPTEMBER   1926   Police broke into a cottage in The Mount, Frome, after concerned neighbours approached them to say that they had been unable to rouse either the owner, Mrs Ellen Thorne, or her two lodgers. On entering the cottage, Inspector Parfitt found fifty-six-year-old widow, Mrs Thorne, and one lodger, seventy-two-year-old widower Isaac Bray, lying dead on the kitchen floor. Mrs Thorne had a single fatal wound on the back of her head, while Bray's head had apparently been struck twice with a bloodstained hatchet that was found in the kitchen sink. When the police went upstairs, they discovered the body of the second lodger, William Hoddinott, on the floor of a bedroom, his throat cut and a bloody razor nearby.

Hoddinott, an unemployed coachman, had lodged with Mrs Thorne for about a year. During the First World War he served at Salonika, where he was believed to have contracted malaria. Since losing his job early in 1926, he had been living on his savings and, according to his brother, Walter, was depressed because he was almost completely out of money. Mrs Thorne had mentioned to neighbours in the past that Hoddinott's behaviour could be a little 'odd' at times – on one occasion, he insisted that people were trying to kill him by poisoning his food. Yet, Mrs Thorne didn't appear to be afraid of him and apparently had no concerns for her own safety.

The jury returned two verdicts of wilful murder against William Hoddinott, who then feloniously took his own life.

1855   News of the victory at Sebastopol during the Crimean War reached Weston-super-Mare, causing great jubilation. Fireworks were let off and pistols and cannons were fired on the streets in celebration. Twelve-year-old Charles Henry Poole was warned to stay away from the cannons, in spite of which he walked in front of one as it was being fired and was struck on the head by the wadding. The blow was sufficient to render him unconscious but he recovered within a few minutes and was well enough to walk home. However, later that evening, he fell into a coma and died.

At the subsequent inquest, coroner Mr Bruges Fry was appalled to find that a post-mortem examination had already been carried out without his orders, stating that this would probably compromise any charge of manslaughter against the firer of the cannon. Nevertheless, the jury were satisfied with the medical evidence that Charles had died from concussion of the brain and recorded a verdict of 'accidental death'.

1886   The Braysdown coal pit near Radtsock employed 150 miners. On Monday 12 and Tuesday 13 September 1886, a boiler fire was lit to test a new engine that had recently been installed in the pit for the purpose of drawing loaded trucks to the surface. What was reported was 'a quantity of carbon oxide gas' [*sic*], built up underground, causing the deaths of four miners – Job Riddle, Elijah Harding, James Moore and Ernest Emery.

The men were working the night shift and had been sent to stop up a passage. When they did not return, bailiff George Webber was sent to find them. Webber found all four men lying dead, their tools by their sides and their candles still alight. All but twenty-year-old Emery wore peaceful expressions, as though they had just fallen asleep.

1861   When seventeen-year-old farm labourer Robert Clode was caught in the act of committing an 'unnatural offence' with a mare at West Hatch, the police were immediately called and Clode was handed over to the local constable. Once in custody, Clode tried to cut his throat and had to be physically restrained to prevent him from succeeding.

At Clode's trial at the Somerset Assizes, on a charge of attempting to commit a detestable offence, Mr Justice Williams expressed his regret that so many people in court were forced to listen to the particulars of such a revolting crime. After debating the evidence, the jury announced that they found Clode guilty of actually committing the offence. However, Williams told them that the defendant had only been charged with attempting to commit, therefore could not be guilty of the more serious charge. He was found guilty of 'attempting' the offence and sentenced to twelve months' imprisonment.

1868   Fourteen-year-old Elizabeth Newport was the domestic servant of Mr Thomas Smith – the National Schoolmaster from Castle Cary – and lived at the schoolhouse with Smith and his wife, their four children and their lodger. At about two o'clock in the morning, Elizabeth was asleep when her bedroom door opened and Mr Smith came in, carrying a candle. Elizabeth asked him if it was

time to get up, but Smith didn't reply. She thought he looked a bit strange, so she got out of bed and started dressing. Smith told her to get back into bed again, saying that he was going to get in with her. Frightened, Elizabeth began to cry, at which Smith put his arms round her and kissed her several times. Frozen with fear, Elizabeth finally managed to tell Smith that she was going home. Smith immediately left the room, although he returned a couple of minutes later, dressed only in his nightshirt, and tried to get into bed with her again. Only when Elizabeth threatened to scream did he leave her room.

After Elizabeth complained to her mother, Smith was charged with having unlawfully assaulted Elizabeth by kissing her against her will. He appeared at Wincanton Police Court, protesting his innocence, but Elizabeth was a convincing witness and the Bench found him guilty as charged. He was fined 50s.

16 SEPTEMBER **1886** An inquest was held at the Butcher's Arms, Dundry, by deputy coroner Dr Francis Wickstead, on the sudden death three days earlier of nineteen-year-old farm labourer Thomas Clarke.

The inquest heard that Clarke had tethered a horse to a gate in the village and that the animal had become restless, pulling the gate off its hinges and dragging it into the lane. This angered Clarke, who went to release it, jerking the horse's head and causing the animal to prance excitedly and rear up. As it did so, Clarke suddenly collapsed across the gate. Assuming that he had suffered a fit, several people rushed to help him. His collar was loosened and he was given a little brandy, in spite of which he remained insensible, foaming at the mouth, his face purple. Only then did people realise that his shirt front was soaked with blood. Clarke died minutes later, before a doctor could reach him. A post-mortem examination revealed a single stab wound just below his left nipple, which had penetrated his heart. Two penknives were found in his breast pocket and, although the blades of both were folded closed, one was stained with blood.

The inquest concluded that Clarke had opened one of his knives, intending to cut the rope tethering the horse to the gate. As the horse panicked, it had jerked its head and caught Clarke's hand, driving the knife into his chest. Being somewhat angry at the time, it was likely that Clarke didn't immediately realise that he had been stabbed and thus had sufficient time to close his knife and replace it in his coat pocket before collapsing.

The inquest jury recorded a verdict of 'accidental death'.

1850   Eighty-four-year-old Hugh Haymans was buried at Kewstoke near Weston-super-Mare. At his own request, Mr Haymans was buried wearing his first wife's wedding gown, described in the contemporary newspapers as an 'old-fashioned light chintz printed cotton'. He also asked for his late wife's apron to be placed in his coffin.   17 SEPTEMBER

1820   In common with many other local newspapers countrywide, the *Bristol Mercury* carried an advertisement for Boerhaave's Red Pill No. 2, a drug that purported to be able to cure what was euphemistically referred to as 'a certain complaint'. The advert stated: 18 SEPTEMBER

> It is a melancholy fact that thousands fall victim to this horrid disease, owing to the unskilfulness of illiterate men, who, by improper treatment of this direful calamity, not unfrequently cause those foul Ulcerations and Blotches, which so often appear on the Head, Face and Body with Dimness in the Sight, Noise in the Ears, Deafness, Strictures, obstinate Gleets, Nodes on the Shin-Bones, ulcerated Sore Throat, Diseased Nose, Nocturnal Pains in the Head and Limbs (frequently mistaken for other disorders) till at length a general debility and decay of the constitution ensues, and a melancholy death puts a period to suffering mortality. [*sic*]

By following the directions included, a patient could speedily cure himself of venereal disease for the cost of 4s 6d a box. 'This remedy acts with equal mildness, certainty and expedition, requires no hindrance of business and is taken without exposure,' continued the advertisement, adding, 'Its amazing sale for the last fifty years, though seldom advertised, is the proof of its surprising efficacy.' As a postscript, the advertisement also proclaimed the usefulness of Red Pill No. 2 in chronic rheumatism, glandular obstructions and scurfy eruptions, adding, 'in short it has succeeded when salivation and other means have failed'.

19 SEPTEMBER 1878 Frederick Salway of Fivehead appeared at the Petty Sessions in Ilminster charged with brutally ill-treating his nine-year-old son. Described as 'a terror to the neighbourhood', Salway had several previous convictions for violence, including an assault on a policeman, for which he was fined £5 and an assault on a labourer, during which he bit off one of the man's fingers. Now he had beaten his son black and blue with a belt, as well as punching him in the face, giving him two black eyes. Salway was fined £2 plus costs for what the magistrates referred to as 'a most brutal case'.

Ilminster. (Author's collection)

20 SEPTEMBER 1825 Farmer Robert Cording, from Huish Champflower, was happily married until his wife became associated with a bizarre religious sect whose teachings completely turned her mind. Twenty-nine-year-old Ann Cording became so deranged that it was necessary to commit her to an asylum. However, after less than two weeks she escaped, fleeing to her mother's home in Batheaston. On 20 September, Robert went to visit her there to try and persuade her to return to the asylum for treatment, but Ann became upset and rushed out of the house, throwing herself into a nearby fish pond. Robert dived in to rescue her but was unsuccessful and both he and Ann drowned. At an inquest on their deaths, the jury's verdict was 'That the wife drowned herself when in a state of mental derangement and that the husband accidentally drowned in his endeavours to rescue her'.

1855 An inquest was held at Bath by coroner Mr A.H. English on the body of Mr Tristram Whitter, aged eighty-one.

Whitter had been ill for some time and his doctor, Mr George Leighton Wood, prescribed a mixture of syrup of poppies, camphor and solution of acetate of morphine. The prescription was taken to druggist Mr Steele of Milsom Street, who passed it to his apprentice, Robert Gane.

Milsom Street, Bath.
(Author's collection)

On the morning of 7 September, after taking his first dose, Whitter was comatose. Wood was unable to rouse him and, finding this highly unusual, contacted Mr Steele to check the contents of the medicine. Robert Gane was out at the time and Steele assured the doctor that the medicine had been prepared according to the prescription. It was only when Gane returned and Steele questioned him that it was discovered that Gane had mistakenly used pure morphine instead of acetate of morphine. In spite of desperate efforts by several surgeons, Whitter died from an overdose of morphine and the inquest jury returned a verdict of manslaughter against Robert Gane, even though Whitter's brother appealed for the boy to be treated as leniently as possible.

Gane was tried at the Somerset Assizes, where the question for the jury was whether or not his fatal error constituted criminal negligence. The jury decided that it did not and Gane was acquitted.

1887 As maid Ann Chapman was walking downstairs at the home of her employer, Miss Stevens in Frome, she stepped on the front of her long dress and fell. Ann was carrying a tray of glass and china at the time and landed face first among the broken shards, cutting her face and neck badly. One piece of glass pierced her jugular vein and Ann lost a great deal of blood before reaching the Cottage Hospital. Surgeons struggled to stop the bleeding and, for a while, it was thought that she might die from her injuries. Fortunately, she survived.

23 SEPTEMBER 1862   Mary Ann Saville (alias Day) told neighbours at Stogumber that the Devil had visited her that morning and tempted her to poison her infant son. As the baby seemed in its normal rude health, her 'wild speaking' was ignored. Later that day, John Lewis, Mary Ann's landlord, arrived home and, soon afterwards, he heard a baby cry in apparent distress. Lewis sent his daughter to the room that Mary Ann shared with her common-law husband, Henry, and three-month-old son, where the girl found her sitting on the bed rocking the baby. Just seconds later, Mary Ann followed her landlord's daughter downstairs and appeared to be in such a state of distraction that John Lewis sent for the police. When the constable arrived, he and Lewis went up to Mary Ann's room, finding that she had cut her son's throat with a sword.

Mary Ann appeared at the Somerset Assizes, charged with wilful murder. The court heard that she was suffering from a 'suppression of milk', which had so turned her mind that she was not responsible for her actions. The judge ordered her to be detained for as long as Her Majesty might see fit.

Stogumber.
(Author's collection)

24 SEPTEMBER 1851   John and Leah Watts set out from West Woodlands to sell their produce at Frome market, leaving their fourteen-year-old daughter behind. When they got home that afternoon, it was to find Sarah lying raped, beaten and strangled in the dairy.

A detective was appointed by the Home Office to investigate the brutal murder and, on searching the Watts' home, he found a silk handkerchief on the kitchen table and a bloody handprint on the dairy door. A watch, clothes and some bread, butter and cheese had been stolen from the house. Suspicion immediately fell on three local men, Robert Hurd, William Sparrow and William Maggs, who had been seen near the Watts' home on the afternoon of the murder. Later, all three men had changed their clothes and several people identified the handkerchief as belonging to Sparrow, although he denied ownership.

A few days later, Sparrow spoke to a woman at North Bradley Fair about the murder, apparently revealing details of the crime that only Sarah's killer would know. At about the same time, Maggs told someone that he was afraid that Sparrow was intending to 'split' on his partners in crime, thereby earning a pardon and claiming the £50 reward. Maggs was most indignant about this, saying that it had been Sparrow who had actually killed Sarah after she recognised him. Sparrow was then found with a watch in his possession, which was thought to be the one stolen from the Watts' house. Sparrow insisted that he had bought it from Hurd, in Maggs's presence. All three men were arrested, when it was noted that Sparrow's hand bore a bite mark dating to around the time of Sarah's murder.

At the trial of the three suspects, it emerged that the watch that had prompted their arrests was not the one stolen from the Watts family. This fact alone seemed to cause the collapse of the prosecution's case against the three defendants, who were all acquitted. The murder of Sarah Watts remains unsolved, although at the assizes in 1852, Sparrow was sentenced to be transported for twenty-five years, having been found guilty of burglary.

25 SEPTEMBER 1830 Thomas Searle, a forty-nine-year-old father of seven, was seriously affected by the sermon preached at his local church – so much so that he felt that every word of it was directed at him personally. He came to believe that he had committed a sin against the Holy Ghost and that he could never be forgiven, either in this world or the next. This drove him to such a state of despondency that his family feared for his safety.

On 25 September, Searle woke his twelve-year-old daughter and asked her if she wanted to go to heaven. When the child said yes, Searle kissed her affectionately then cut her throat. Her younger sister tried to seize the knife from her father, cutting her hand in the attempt. Fortunately, both children survived.

Tried at the assizes in Taunton before Mr Justice Park, Searle was horrified by his actions. He was normally a man of excellent character, known as a kind, loving father and the child he had attempted to kill was a particular favourite. (Called into court to give evidence, she took one look at her father standing in the dock, burst into tears and fainted.) The jury acquitted Searle on the grounds of insanity and he was ordered to be detained until His Majesty's pleasure was known.

26 SEPTEMBER 1881 At the Axbridge Petty Sessions, three farmers were charged with cruelty to animals. William Knowles was fined £1 plus costs for beating his horse at Banwell, Henry Beacham was fined 10s plus costs for beating a cow at Congresbury and Thomas Nipper was fined 10s plus costs for ill treating a mare by working her in an unfit state.

On the same day, John Maidment was charged at Wells with beating his twelve-year-old son, Arthur. Maidment's wife had recently left him and her two sons, and Maidment admitted to leaving the boys alone from early morning until late at night, while he was at work as a farm labourer. Eventually, Arthur went to his mother's house and complained that his father had hit him.

On examining the boy, Mrs Maidment found that he was covered with bruise
and had obviously been severely beaten. Maidment admitted to thrashing the
boy with a stick as a punishment for playing truant from school. He was ordered
to pay the court costs but given no other penalty, having agreed to employ a
woman to watch the children while he was at work.

27 SEPTEMBER 1856   The town of Watchet was rocked by a huge explosion at the premises
of Messrs Wansborough & Co.

Finding that the existing boiler was not powerful enough to operate their
heavy machinery, the owners of the paper mill had recently installed another.
They economised by using a second-hand boiler and several of the mill
workers had expressed an opinion that it would not be strong enough. They
were unfortunately proved right when the boiler exploded.

Weighing four tons, the boiler was blown 80ft into the air by the force
of the explosion, narrowly missing a nearby cottage where several children
were asleep in bed. Nearly thirty men were working at the mill at the time,
two of whom were erecting a new roof directly over the boiler. Luckily, they
had descended from the roof only seconds before the explosion. One man was
blown almost twenty yards but, by a miracle, he sustained no more serious
injury than a few bruises. None of the workforce was seriously injured and the
greatest damage of all was financial, as the cost of damage to the buildings
and machinery from the fire that resulted from the explosion was estimated
at £1,000.

28 SEPTEMBER 1837   Almost 300ft above the river Avon at Clifton is a cave known as 'Giant's
Hole' and, in 1837, the attraction was visited by an elderly gentleman
accompanied by a much younger lady. Attendants at the cave noticed that the
man appeared to be 'in a great state of excitement' and that he was muttering
to himself. When it was suggested that perhaps he might be ill, and should
therefore defer his trip into the enclosed cave and remain in the fresh air, the
woman thanked the attendants for their concern but reassured them that her
husband was 'prone to fits of absence'.

The subsequent events were widely reported over the following few days by
newspapers the length and breadth of the country. As the couple leaned over
the balustrade at the cave's outer entrance admiring the view, the man was
seen to be using violent gestures towards his wife, who sank to the floor in a
state of terror, clinging desperately to the iron railings. Watched by horrified
onlookers at the bottom of the cliff, the man grabbed his screaming wife by
the waist and threw her over the balustrade, to land on the ground below 'a
disfigured mass'. Bystanders ran to her aid and heard her say, 'My God, I am
innocent,' before dying.

The man had watched as his wife almost floated through the air towards the
ground. However, her piercing screams had attracted the attention of the cave
attendants, who rushed to apprehend him. They were on the point of seizing
him when, 'with a spring and a demonical laugh', he hurled himself over
the balustrade. Newspapers called it 'just Providence' that he hit a pointed

pinnacle of rock where, 'impaled and writhing', he hung for nearly a minute before falling to the very bottom of the cliff, landing about ten yards from the mangled body of his wife.

It was reported that the couple had arrived in the area from London only the night before the tragedy and were staying at the nearby Gloucester Hotel. However, when reporters from the *Bristol Mercury* made enquiries, they were unable to verify the identities of the dead couple, nor were there any missing guests. It took a couple of days of probing by reporters from the local paper to reveal that the entire story was a complete fabrication and that no murder had ever been committed.

882 Twenty-five-year-old Samuel Silas Phippen farmed sixty acres near Frome. His sister, Ada, served as his housekeeper and a second sister, Lucy, was staying at the farm as a guest.

Previously a teetotaller, Samuel had recently taken to drinking. On 23 May, he suffered a violent bout of *delirium tremens*, which lasted for four days and necessitated treatment from a doctor. He suffered a second attack at the beginning of September, although he recovered without medical assistance. Nevertheless, he continued to drink heavily and, on 28 September, he spent much of the night drinking and playing cards with friends. The following morning saw him visiting the local pub and drinking three pints of beer. He ate lunch with his two sisters, then slumped over the table and fell asleep. Ada went out, while Lucy busied herself about the house. Shortly afterwards, she heard a loud bang and, when she looked out of an upstairs window, she saw her brother crouched by a wall in the farmyard.

The bang was also heard by fourteen-year-old labourer George Greenland, who rushed to investigate. As he entered the feed store from where the noise had originated, he saw his workmate Christopher Hill lying dead on the floor. Running to fetch help, he bumped into Phippen and told him that Hill was dead. 'I know. I've been and shot he and now I'm going to shoot you,' Phippen replied.

Fortunately, the shot had hit Greenland in the arm and he was able to escape. In the lane outside the farm, he met Henry Gunstone, who raised the alarm. Meanwhile, Phippen had taken another pot shot through a hedge and killed a second man, carter Charles Sheppard. He then walked to the New Inn at Southwick and calmly ordered a pint of beer and a cigar. Landlord Mr Lusty had heard about the murders and sent for the police. When PC George King arrived, Phippen surrendered his gun, although he denied shooting anybody, saying, 'That's got to be proved – nobody saw me do it.'

Phippen was tried at the Somerset Assizes, charged with two counts of wilful murder and with shooting at George Greenland with intent to murder him. His defence counsel, Mr Collins KC, was able to demonstrate a history of familial insanity and also called several medical witnesses, who unanimously believed that Phippen was insane at the time of the murders. The jury found him not guilty on the grounds of insanity and he was sentenced to be detained during Her Majesty's pleasure.

30 SEPTEMBER 1863   At the inquest on the death of a baby found in a toilet at Leigh Court near Bristol, the jury found a verdict of wilful murder against servant Emma White, who was committed for trial at the next Somerset Assizes.

Emma was employed by Sir William Miles Bart MP and, for some time, her fellow servants had suspected that she was pregnant. Emma vehemently denied that she was with child but, in the early hours of the morning of 28 September she finally went to Cook Agnes Brown and admitted that she had given birth. Agnes asked where the child was and Emma led her to the toilet. Having removed the baby from the water closet and established that it was dead, Agnes placed it on the toilet seat and locked the door. Surgeon Mr William White Day was summoned and confirmed that Emma had recently given birth. He believed that the baby was born alive and had died from extreme pressure on its throat.

At the assizes in December, the Grand Jury ignored the bill against Emma White and she was therefore acquitted.

OCTOBER

High Street, Yeovil. (Author's collection)

1 OCTOBER **1864** The annual drill of the North Somerset Yeomanry Cavalry terminate at Wells, having been a chapter of accidents almost from start to finish.

A trooper accidentally ran his sword into the thigh of another troope Captain Helbert was thrown from his horse and seriously injured, Colonel Si William Miles was knocked off his mount, and Captain Haviland's horse fe on him at Farrington Gurney.

The week ended with a fatality. Corporal James Blinman from Hallatrov was riding a high-spirited young horse, which bolted. Lewis Cole spurred ou his own horse in pursuit but was unable to overtake Blinman, whom he foun lying insensible in the road about a quarter of a mile away. Blinman had fracture at the base of his skull, along with extensive wounds to his face. H was taken to his home, where he remained alive, although insensible, unt the following afternoon.

2 OCTOBER **1869** After a trip to Yeovil market, butcher John Williams went to the Marke Inn. During the course of the afternoon, Williams commented that he ha a million nuts, at which another drinker, John Slade, began to tease him fo exaggerating, saying that he had no idea how many a million actually wa: Cross words were exchanged between the two men, which culminated in Slad punching Williams on the cheek, knocking him briefly unconscious. When h came round, witnesses noticed that he seemed to be having difficulty raisin his head.

Williams eventually left the pub but early the following morning he wa found cold and stiff in the outside toilet, having obviously been dead fo some time. Surgeon Mr Tomkins found that he had bruising and swellin to his left cheekbone, along with a 1.5in-long skull fracture on the right hand side of his head. Slade was arrested and charged with manslaughte However, at his trial, Slade's defence counsel maintained that Williams ha suffered a fit of apoplexy while sitting on the toilet and had fallen forwar cracking his skull.

The medical witnesses were unable to determine whether the fracture ha occurred as the result of a blow or a fall and they additionally testified tha Williams's skull was much thinner than a normal skull. The jury found Slad guilty of manslaughter but recommended mercy. He was sentenced to thre months' imprisonment with hard labour.

3 OCTOBER **1886** Baptist minister William Ernest Glenville married Elizabeth at th Church of St Andrew in Montpelier, Bristol. At the time, Glenville was servin at Ashton Bampton in Oxfordshire, but the couple soon moved to a nev parish in Wells. It quickly became evident to Elizabeth that marriage wa not all what she had expected it to be. William treated her with indifferenc and, within two weeks of the wedding, had struck her. On another occasior he threw a pint bottle at her, which shattered on her knee, leaving he lame for several days. Due to William's excessive sexual demands, Elizabet often left their marital bed at night and went to sleep with the servants to ge some peace.

While working in Oxfordshire, Glenville became friendly with a family named Wade, who had three nubile daughters. Glenville made a point of sitting the girls on his knee and caressing them and, when his wife protested, he told her that it was only done in friendship and was part of his ministerial duties. Besides, as a man, he should be able to do as he pleased without her interference.

Elizabeth soon tired of her husband's antics and began divorce proceedings on the grounds of his cruelty and adultery. Glenville vehemently denied all the allegations against him but unfortunately his case was somewhat weakened by the fact that he had contracted 'a certain disease'. Hence, when the petition was heard before Mr Justice Jeune in March 1891, it was not contested and Elizabeth was granted her *decree nisi* for the dissolution of her disastrous marriage.

1863   Elizabeth Fox, a servant at The Rectory at Rimpton, announced her intentions of going to visit her parents in Dorset. The trip home was a ruse, since twenty-year-old Elizabeth was pregnant and unmarried. Instead she went to herbalists Robert Slade Colmer and his wife, Jane, who practised their trade at Yeovil.   **4 OCTOBER**

On 4 October, Elizabeth suddenly died. The Colmers' son was a qualified doctor and, called to attend Elizabeth shortly before her death, Dr Colmer found her in bed, complaining of stomach pains. She appeared to be bleeding internally, so he gave her brandy and ergot of rye and pressed on her lower abdomen, which caused blood to gush from her vagina. Elizabeth died in spite of his efforts.

Dr Colmer notified the police of the sudden death and a post-mortem examination was carried out. It was found that Elizabeth had been around six months pregnant but had lost the baby, and that death had resulted from a tear in her womb, made by instruments of some kind. It was impossible for the injury to have been spontaneous, or for Elizabeth to have caused it herself.

At the subsequent inquest, Robert Colmer explained that Elizabeth had miscarried, expelling a foetus the size of a pigeon's egg. Following his training as a herbalist, Colmer had burned the foetus and afterbirth, in the belief that doing so would prevent Elizabeth from suffering pain or infection. The coroner stated that the law expected every medical man to be competent at handling any cases he undertook, be that man a qualified surgeon or a quack. If the jury believed that Elizabeth had gone to the Colmers for the sole purpose of procuring an abortion and Robert had carried out this procedure, he was guilty of wilful murder. If, on the other hand, the jury found that Elizabeth had taken something of her own accord to induce an abortion and had then died as a result of Robert's gross ignorance, then the proper verdict would be manslaughter.

The inquest found a verdict of manslaughter against Robert Colmer, who was later tried at the Somerset Assizes. However, once the prosecution had presented their evidence, the judge intervened, saying that he could see nothing to connect the accused with the ruptured womb that ultimately killed Elizabeth Fox. The only offence that he could see was concealment of the birth, resulting from the fact that Colmer had burned the miscarried child. The jury immediately acquitted Colmer and he walked from the dock a free man. He was not so fortunate in 1880, when he was sentenced to death for committing a similar offence, although his sentence was later commuted to one of life imprisonment.

5 OCTOBER   1855   Twenty-nine-year-old Mary Jennings from Wiveliscombe had three illegitimate children, a situation she felt stood in the way of her finding a husband. So she decided to reduce her burden by pushing her oldest child into a cesspit.

She began screaming for her neighbours on the evening of 5 October and, when they ran to see what the matter was, she pointed to the cesspit and told them that her son Robbie was in there. The neighbours peered in but saw no sign of the child, who was completely covered by raw sewage. Eventually, he was dragged from the depths of the pit, fortunately still alive.

Tried at the Somerset Assizes for attempted murder, Mary Jennings stood in the dock nursing a young baby, apparently unconcerned by the proceedings. The prosecution claimed that the cesspit was normally covered by a large stone that would have been far too heavy for the child to lift without assistance. In the days immediately before the incident, Mary had spoken to several neighbours, telling them that Robbie was preventing her from marrying and that she hoped she would one day find him dead – she also mentioned that she had recently been troubled by dreams in which Robbie drowned in the cesspit. However, the key point for the jury was that she had made no effort whatsoever to rescue her son from the pit, claiming to have been too afraid to do so. Instead, she had simply shouted for her neighbours and stood idly by while they pulled the child out.

Mary still seemed unconcerned as the judge sentenced her to be transported for the rest of her natural life. However, young Robbie, who had been brought to court to speak to the judge, burst into noisy sobs and seemed inconsolable at his mother's fate.

6 OCTOBER   1896   In the early hours of the morning, Mr Cunningham of Combe Down, Bath, was awakened by his wife, who told him that their two sons were calling 'Da-da'. Cunningham lit a candle and went to see what the boys wanted. As soon as he opened his bedroom door, he noticed that it was extremely hot and he immediately deduced that the house was on fire. Although there was no smoke or flames, he alerted his wife and then ran to the boys' bedroom, taking them downstairs. As he passed the open door, he saw that the living room was blazing.

Cunningham left his sons in the front garden and ran back to his wife, who handed him their baby. He took the baby to his sons and was about to go back for his daughter when he spotted her in the garden. By then, Mrs Cunningham was standing at their bedroom window. 'Why don't you come down?' asked her husband.

'I can't. Shall I jump?' Mrs Cunningham replied.

'If you can't come, jump,' said Mr Cunningham, which she did.

Although the family had now escaped, as had the Crisp family, who occupied the adjoining house which was also on fire, nobody had rescued the Cunninghams' two servants, Eliza Gerrish and Emily Jordan. They were seen at various upstairs windows and were encouraged to jump, but although ladders were put up to the upper floor, rescuers were unable to locate them and both servants perished in the flames. Mrs Cunningham also died soon after the fire from injuries received when she jumped from the window.

At a subsequent inquest, held at the Guild Hall in Bath by coroner Mr B.H. Watts, it was determined that the source of the fire in the Crisps' house was shared joists. The fire had originated in the Cunninghams' home but it was impossible to determine how it had started. The jury returned verdicts of 'accidental death' on all three victims.

1896 A man who gave his name as John Tuckey, and purported to be an engine fitter from County Cork in Ireland, was found acting very strangely on Wells Hill, Radstock. John Hillier, who first observed Tuckey, reported his behaviour to the police and he was taken into custody. Dr Worger later examined him and pronounced him insane. Tuckey was brought before magistrates at the police court in Kilmersdon and charged with being a wandering lunatic and with attempting to commit suicide. Magistrates ordered his removal to Wells Asylum.

7 OCTOBER

1878 An inquest was held at the Guild Hall in Bath on the suspicious death on 6 October of Mary Ann Mills of Corn Street.

On the day before her death, a Saturday, Mary Ann worked at the Crystal Palace Inn, where she was said to be in her normal state of health. However, on Saturday night and Sunday morning, she complained to two of her daughters that their father had 'ill-used' her, showing them a bruise on her forehead.

Dr Willes of the Royal United Hospital in Bath was called to see Mary Ann on the Sunday afternoon and found her unconscious. Her husband, John Mills, explained that she had fallen over and banged her head. Mary Ann died that evening and Dr Willes refused to issue a death certificate without conducting a post-mortem examination, when he found that Mary Ann had died from compression of the brain caused by bleeding. Unfortunately, the injury to Mary Ann's brain could have been caused by both a blow from a fist and a fall onto a hard surface. Mary Ann's complaints to her daughters were considered hearsay and were not admissible as evidence at the inquest. In spite of the fact that Thomas Viner, another resident in her lodgings, testified to having heard Mary Ann being abused by her husband during the night before her death, the inquest jury inexplicably returned a verdict of 'death by natural causes'.

8 OCTOBER

1881 Eleven-year-old Jemmy Davis of Banwell was described in the contemporary newspapers as 'more than half an idiot'. Nevertheless, he was entrusted to drive a sow from Banwell to Barton, a distance of about two miles. Since the sow knew its own way home it was assumed that Jemmy would simply be able to follow it – unfortunately nobody had given any thought to

9 OCTOBER

how the child would find his way home again without the pig to guide him. When Jemmy didn't arrive home as expected, searchers scoured the area. He was eventually found the following evening by a farmer, roughly five miles away at Cheddar. 'Wearied, forlorn and faint from hunger and fatigue,' he had taken shelter in a haystack. The farmer notified the police and Jemmy was taken home.

10 OCTOBER **1857** Thomas Miller was a herdsman at Warleigh House, near Bath, living with his parents in one of the estate cottages. Known for being a little strange at times, on the night of 9 October, Thomas suddenly became very ill, complaining of terrible pains in his head. His mother sat up with him all night as he raved about seeing angels and being attacked by Indians. Although he was too ill to go to work in the morning, by the afternoon Thomas seemed much better and his mother left him reading his Bible while she went to run an errand.

Andrew Border also worked at Warleigh House as a groom and under-coachman, as did his wife Sarah, a maid, and, on the afternoon of 10 October, the Borders called at the Millers' home to ask how Thomas was. As they waited at the door, Thomas suddenly rushed out of the cottage brandishing a large knife. Before the Borders could react, he stabbed Sarah in the heart and she fell to the ground, fracturing her skull. Thomas then turned the knife on Andrew, stabbing him in the belly. Andrew managed to escape but died later that evening from loss of blood.

Miller ran away but, soon afterwards, faint groans were heard coming from some bushes. Miller had cut his own throat and plunged the knife into his belly. He was carried home and put to bed. Although Miller's wounds were serious, he survived to stand trial at the Somerset Assizes for the wilful murder of Andrew and Sarah Border. Nobody was able to conceive any motive for the murders, although there were several theories. One was that Miller and Sarah were former sweethearts but Sarah had preferred Andrew, and another was that Sarah had teased Miller about his likeness to the perpetrator of a recently reported murder. However, by all accounts, Miller and his victims were friendly towards each other.

After hearing medical evidence and learning that Miller had a family history of insanity, the jury acquitted him, finding him insane at the time of the murders.

11 OCTOBER **1890** Neighbours of James Andrews from Bruton heard the sounds of a fight coming from Andrews's house, where his brother, Richard, was visiting. When Richard was found dead in the street shortly afterwards, sixty-two-year-old James was charged with 'feloniously killing and slaying' him.

James gave several conflicting accounts of the argument with his brother, who was supposedly very drunk at the time. He first denied having hit Richard, then said that he had a 'middling tussle' with him, in order to get him to leave his house. Finally, he admitted to hitting Richard with a stick, but insisted that he had only hit him twice on his knee.

The medical evidence showed that Richard had a number of bruises and grazes, along with a contused wound at the back of his head. In addition,

BRUTON, RIVER BRUE & BRIDGE.

Bruton. (Author's collection)

both of his lungs were weak and he had unmistakable signs of heart disease. The cause of his death was given as heart failure accelerated by violence and, in the doctor's opinion, the wound at the back of his head was the result of a fall. The jury found James guilty as charged but recommended mercy. He was sentenced to six months' imprisonment with hard labour.

1858 Mary Govier, the landlady of The Wheatsheaf at Taunton, had five children, all of whom were suffering from 'the itch'. On the advice of a friend, she contacted James Sweetland, a thatcher who was also a 'quack' doctor. Sweetland visited Mrs Govier and it was agreed that he would cure her entire family for 17s 6d. He gave Mrs Govier four pots of ointment, advising her to use one of them first as it was strongest. He then suggested that she and her husband should also use the ointment to prevent them from becoming infected. Mrs Govier was especially careful to ask whether it was safe to use on her youngest child, thirteen-month-old Emma, and Sweetland assured her that it was, saying that he had even cured infants at the breast with it. Mrs Govier rubbed some of the ointment onto her own hand and noticed that her skin immediately reddened. Again, Sweetland reassured her, saying that it would soon go back to its normal colour.

Mrs Govier's older children became restless and uneasy after she applied the ointment but Emma vomited a couple of times during the night and died the following morning. Surgeon Mr Foye examined her and found what looked like burns on her stomach, arms, legs and back. The Goviers' older children had similar, although less severe, symptoms and Mary's husband John's arm was blistered. Foye had the ointment analysed and found it to be a mixture of nitric acid, mercury and lard, which was approximately seven times stronger than it should have been. Foye therefore had no hesitation in stating that Emma's death resulted from application of the ointment.

Sweetland was charged with Emma's manslaughter and appeared at the Somerset Assizes. His defence counsel insisted that Emma's death was not due to any negligence or lack of skill on his client's part but maintained that, in her anxiety for her child, Mary Govier had applied far more of the ointment than she had been told to do. The jury had already heard that Emma was a delicate, rather sickly child and, after some deliberation, acquitted Sweetland.

13 OCTOBER   **1892**   The Society for the Prevention of Cruelty to Children initiated the prosecution at the Bristol Police Court of Sarah Witchell and her husband for the ill-treatment of Sarah's thirteen-year-old sister, Mabel Snook.

Mabel moved in with her sister in Old King Street, Bristol to act as a nursemaid to Sarah's children and, in the six months that she lived there, she was regularly beaten with a poker, a flat iron and brushes. Permanently covered with cuts and bruises, she was threatened with death if she ever revealed how she got them and was instructed to tell anyone who asked that she had fallen down. Mabel was usually kept locked indoors and, although a few people noticed that she was poorly dressed, dirty, crawling with vermin and battered, she made no complaint to anybody, even her own mother.

Mr Witchell denied ever having beaten Mabel, although he admitted to magistrates that he 'might have spoken a word out of place to her'. Sarah Witchell admitted that she had beaten her sister on occasions, but told the magistrates that she had only done so as chastisement because Mabel hadn't looked after the children properly.

The magistrates discharged Mr Witchell, having found little evidence against him, although they censured him for standing by and watching Mabel being beaten, calling his conduct disgraceful. Sarah Witchell was sent to gaol with hard labour for one month.

14 OCTOBER   **1862**   Caroline Nicholls lived at Batheaston and, although she was married, she did not live with her husband. In 1862, she unexpectedly found herself pregnant by another man. She discussed her embarrassing situation with a friend, Sarah Caseley, asking her what she could do. Sarah told her that she would find her some lodgings until the child was born and would then take the baby and raise it.

The two women met just outside Bath on the night of 14 October. As they walked along, Caroline was suddenly gripped by agonising labour pains and asked Sarah if they might go to her house. Sarah said that they couldn't but reassured her that the lodgings she had found were not far away. However, Caroline's baby couldn't wait and literally fell onto the gravel path. Sarah immediately bent down, shouting to Caroline, 'Now, run!' As Caroline took to her heels, Sarah scooped up the baby and tossed it over some nearby railings, where it hit a tree and fell to the ground. Yet, unbeknown to the two women, their actions had been watched by a Mrs White, who chased after them and managed to catch Sarah.

Sarah was marched back to the railings, with Mrs White hanging on to her to prevent her escaping. Once there, Mrs White asked another female passer-by to climb over the railings and retrieve the baby, which was fortunately still alive. The police were summoned and Sarah Caseley was arrested. Caroline Nicholls was also apprehended and both women were charged with attempting to murder a newly-born child.

They appeared at the Somerset Assizes in Taunton before Mr Justice Byles. In his summary of the case for the jury, Byles told them that their verdict hinged on whether or not there was satisfactory evidence that the prisoners had intended to murder the child, and in Caroline's favour was the fact that a bundle of baby clothes was found on the path where she gave birth. It was obvious that Caroline at least intended to clothe the baby when it was born and the jury acquitted both defendants. They were then both immediately tried for unlawfully abandoning an infant and endangering its life. Caroline Nicholls was again acquitted but Sarah Caseley was found guilty as charged and sentenced to twelve months' imprisonment with hard labour.

1808 At Downside in Backwell, six-year-old Sophia Weaver went to pick blackberries in the fields near her home. When she didn't return, a search was initiated and a dog belonging to Sophia's father led the searchers to a deep pit, made by the extraction of lead ore. The searchers noted that the grass around the pit had recently been trampled, but it was ten o'clock in the evening by then and very dark. The search was resumed at first light and two men were lowered into the pit on ropes. They found Sophia standing at the pit bottom, totally unharmed except for a few bramble scratches. The child had spent fourteen hours almost 100ft underground, and the fact that she was uninjured was even more remarkable since, in the course of their descent, her rescuers had dislodged several large boulders from the walls, which had crashed to the pit bottom close to where the little girl stood.

15 OCTOBER

1899 The Bristol Police Court dealt with three cases of assaults on police officers, which occurred on Saturday 14 October. George Thomas was sent to gaol for fourteen days for a drunken assault on PCs Bird, Wall and Davis.

In another drink-fuelled incident, James Leslie assaulted PCs Zelly, Adams and Harvey. The main complaint against him was that he had bitten PC Harvey's thumb and refused to release it until a passer-by managed to put him in a chokehold. Leslie, who was additionally charged with being drunk and disorderly, was sent to prison for twenty-eight days.

Albert Price was also being drunk and disorderly. In assaulting PCs Smith and Piper, he allegedly 'acted like a madman', for which he was fined 40s or one month in prison with hard labour.

Magistrate Mr Hosegood afterwards commended the few members of the public who had assisted the police, commenting that, in all of the cases, the

16 OCTOBER

majority of witnesses had taken the side of the offenders and made every effort to help them avoid arrest.

17 OCTOBER   **1898**   Thirty-eight-year-old Annie Fisher died in the Royal United Hospital in Bath from blood poisoning, arising from an ulcerated leg. Although she had been ill for about five weeks, she had received no medical attention until two hours before her death, when her sister-in-law, Mrs Mitchell, called at her house and insisted that she was sent to hospital.

Dr Dodson, who admitted her, believed that Annie's death was due to neglect and that, had she been treated earlier, she would have recovered. Asked why he had let his wife get into such a state, Alfred Fisher replied, 'She's a woman and can look after herself.' Thus, at the inquest on her death, held by Mr B.A. Dyer, the jury's verdict was one of manslaughter against Alfred.

Fisher appeared at the next Somerset Assizes, charged on the coroner's warrant. The prosecution stated that he had caused Annie's death by his 'gross and wicked neglect'. However, it was shown that Annie herself had refused to allow a doctor to be called. The Fishers had three sons and Annie was regularly visited by friends, neighbours and relations, any one of whom could have summoned medical help.

Mr Justice Kennedy stated that Alfred Fisher was a drunkard who did little or no work, preferring to live on the earnings of his wife and children. Yet, although there might have been a fault in his behaviour, the jury must be satisfied that there was a criminal fault. The jury were not and Fisher was acquitted.

The Royal United Hospital in Bath. (Author's collection)

1848 Disillusioned with the conduct of his wife, a man took her to Shepton
Mallet market with the intention of selling her to the highest bidder. The woman
had apparently enjoyed several extra-marital affairs and, although her husband
had always forgiven her in the past, they had mutually decided to separate.
Having discussed the best way to go about this, both husband and wife agreed
that a sale was the only legal means. The bidding started at half a crown and
eventually rose to 5s. The successful buyer was the wife's brother but instead of
paying his money, he attacked the husband. He was soon joined by his 'purchase'
and one of their sisters and eventually several bystanders joined in the fray. The
unfortunate husband was beaten to within an inch of his life, losing an eye in
the fight.

1856 Twenty-seven-year-old James Hazard married at St Thomas's Church,
Bristol. However, he neglected to tell his new bride that he was already married.
Hazard's first wife, Ann, had become a lunatic shortly after their marriage and
had been confined to an asylum, considered incurable. However, in 1857 she
was discharged and naturally went looking for her husband.

Hazard was charged with bigamy and appeared at the Somerset Assizes in
March 1858. His second wife stated that she had asked Hazard to marry her
and he had done so to please her, although she was not aware that he already
had a wife living. Hazard was found guilty of bigamy and sentenced to four
months' imprisonment with hard labour.

1898 When Elizabeth Wood got home from work, her house at Weston-super-
Mare was locked up and there was no sign of her husband, William. Elizabeth
managed to get indoors and within thirty minutes her husband arrived.
As soon as he walked into the house, he began shouting and threatening
to turn everyone out. He threw a shovel at the couple's son Frederick and, when
his wife remonstrated with him, he seized a poker and threatened to hit her.

'You'd better not,' retorted Elizabeth, at which William dealt her a fearsome
blow, cutting her head open and leaving her with a scalp wound that poured
blood.

When Wood later appeared before magistrates at the police court at Weston-
super-Mare, charged with assaulting and beating his wife, he maintained that
Elizabeth's constant spending was running them into debt. He claimed that
Frederick had thrown the poker at him and, when he threw it back, it had
accidentally hit his wife. However, Frederick corroborated his mother's version
of events. William Wood had previously been imprisoned for a similar offence
and the magistrates sentenced him to six weeks' imprisonment with hard labour.

1830 Charles Capel Hardwick of Huish left Bristol market carrying about £450
in his pocket. At Newland's Hatch, midway between Bristol and Congresbury,
Hardwick passed a stranger on horseback and bade him 'Good night'. The man
asked Hardwick if he was going far, saying that he would be glad of the company
if Hardwick wished to ride with him. The two men rode through Congresbury
and beyond, to a rather desolate stretch of land known locally as 'The Heath'.

At that point, the stranger dropped back slightly, so that his horse's head was level with Hardwick's saddle. Suddenly, there was a loud bang. Hardwick felt a hard blow on his left shoulder and saw a flash of light out of the corner of his eye. Believing that his companion had fired a pistol at him, Hardwick shouted, 'Good God, what have you done?' The stranger turned his horse and galloped off. Hardwick chased him and eventually overtook him just past Congresbury. The man immediately began to rain blows on Hardwick with a bludgeon then galloped off again with Hardwick still in hot pursuit, shouting desperately to passers-by to help him.

Eventually, the two riders came across a cart in the road. The stranger attempted to turn his horse, which slipped and fell. Hardwick's horse also fell and, as soon as he had regained his feet, Hardwick seized his quarry and the two men grappled. In the course of the struggle, Hardwick was hit several times over the head and stabbed in his left side. With Hardwick stunned, the stranger mounted his horse but, before he could ride off again, Hardwick grabbed the bridle and hung on for dear life. Only then did someone come to his assistance and highwayman Richard Hewlett was captured.

Tried at the Somerset Assizes, he was found guilty of shooting at Hardwick and sentenced to death. He was hanged at Ilchester on 20 April 1831.

Hardwick had life-threatening injuries – a 7in-deep gunshot wound in his left shoulder and a stab wound that had penetrated his lungs. Whereas Hewlett was a strong, tall, muscular man, Hardwick was short, thin, rather puny and also unarmed and wounded. His fortitude and courage in capturing his attacker were highly praised by the judge.

22 OCTOBER **1853** A dreadful accident occurred on the road between Doulting and Chelynch, near to Shepton Mallet. A farmer named Davis sent three of his sons to milk his cows, together with two other men, Luff and Sparks. When the men were returning to the farm with the milk, Luff drove the cart. Unfortunately, he was not only driving too fast but he was also not holding the reins to steer the horse and, as a result, the cart was heading straight for a wagon from the Holcombe Brewery. Although the driver of the brewery wagon tried his hardest to turn his wagon out of the way, the cart driven by Luff was on the wrong side of the road and the two vehicles collided, throwing Luff, Sparks and the Davis boys onto the ground. The farm cart overturned, trapping Luff underneath, and he died almost instantly from a crushed chest. Sparks suffered a broken leg and other injuries, which it was believed would prevent him from ever walking again, while one of the Davis boys broke his back and died hours later. Fortunately, the two other Davis boys emerged from the collision relatively unscathed, although their mother was so affected by the tragedy that it was believed she would be 'deprived of her reason'.

At the subsequent inquest, the coroner remarked that he hoped the tragedy would serve as a warning to other carters to avoid the practice then common in Somerset of driving without reins.

1936 Twenty-year-old Kathleen Elsie Tolley walked into Shepton Mallet police station and told officers there, 'I have shot my mother. She has been using bad language to me again this morning.' Fifty-two-year-old Annie Elsie Tolley was found dead from shotgun wounds in the hall of Farcombe Farm, Doulton. Her daughter appeared at the Bristol Assizes in November of that year but was found to be unfit to plead and was ordered to be detained during His Majesty's pleasure.

23 OCTOBER

1878 Twenty-nine-year-old Charles Tyley was suffering from *delirium tremens*. The son of a prosperous farmer in Cheddar, he had inherited some property on his father's death and, according to the contemporary newspapers, had 'somewhat largely indulged in stimulants for a few days prior to his illness'. For his own safety, Tyley was placed in the care of his brother-in-law, Joseph Pavey, who maintained a constant watch on him, with the assistance of a friend, Charles Sergeant. However, at three o'clock in the morning, Tyley managed to escape. His body was found late the following afternoon in the garden of the Bath Arms Hotel in Cheddar.

24 OCTOBER

After his escape, Tyley apparently scaled the 8ft-high wall separating the hotel from the road but had fallen from the top, landing face down. When found, his nostrils were filled with earth; it was believed that he had stunned himself when he fell and was suffocated by the garden soil.

Cheddar, 1919. (Author's collection)

Old Cottages, Cheddar.

25 OCTOBER   **1838**   A petty squabble took place between two farm labourers at Milborne Port, which led to the death of one and the trial of the other at the Somerset Assizes for his wilful murder.

Foreman William Stacey was supervising a group of workmen who were mowing clover. During the day, each of the labourers drank about a gallon of beer and, as they were finishing work, James Osmond offered to match any man at mowing for a sovereign. When Stacey commented that it was the wrong time of year, Osmond threw his scythe over the hedge in a fit of pique. Having retrieved it, he then threw it into a brook and, taking another scythe, bent the blade until it broke. When Stacey called him a fool, Osmond challenged him to a fight.

It was obvious from the onset that Stacey was coming off worst in the tussle and he eventually said 'I am done' and fell to the ground. Although nobody had seen a knife in Osmond's hand, Stacey had a 6in gash in his stomach, through which his bowels protruded. A surgeon was summoned and Stacey was taken home, where he died the following day. He was found to have no less than eighteen wounds on his body, at least ten of which had been made by a knife.

Osmond had been seen with a knife earlier that day and a small penknife was found in the field near where the fight had taken place. Nevertheless, he vehemently denied having a knife in his hand at any time during the fight.

At his trial, the case hinged on whether Osmond had used the knife from the onset of the fight or whether he had resorted to using it after his blood had become 'heated'. The jury favoured the latter explanation and found Osmond guilty of manslaughter. He was sentenced to be transported for fourteen years.

26 OCTOBER   **1928**   A man walked into Paddington Green police station in London and told the duty officer, 'I have murdered my wife by hitting her over the head with an iron bar.' The man was William Bartlett, a one-legged shoemaker, and when the police checked his incredible story they found his wife, Marjorie, bludgeoned to death in the living quarters of the couple's sweet shop in Monmouth Street, Bath.

The Bartletts were both only twenty-three years old and had no business sense. Their little shop was making a loss and the couple were on the verge of financial ruin. On the day before her death, Marjorie had attempted to buy some time with their creditors by selling off some of the shop's fixtures and fittings. The £11 she received for the items was missing from the house.

Tried before Mr Justice Mackinnon at the Somerset Assizes for wilful murder, Bartlett professed to recall nothing after taking his wife an early morning cup of tea. Marjorie had made some 'sharp remarks' to him and a mist had descended before his eyes. The clang of a metal bar dropping from his hand to the floor brought him to his senses again and, when he saw Marjorie lying in their blood-soaked bed, Bartlett realised what he had done and fled in a panic.

The prosecution claimed that Bartlett had murdered Marjorie in order to steal the money she had recently received. However, his defence counsel, Mr J.D. Casswell, believed that Bartlett had killed his wife while in the throes of an epileptic fit. Casswell made a dramatic and emotive speech on behalf of his client that reduced most of the jury to tears. They found Bartlett guilty but insane and he was sent to Broadmoor Criminal Lunatic Asylum.

1868 The annual prize rifle shooting competition for the 3rd Somerset Battalion **27 OCTOBER** took place at the Mendip Butts near Shepton Mallet, and friends Mr Hale and Mr Dennis walked there together from Wells.

Hale was deployed as a marker for the third target, at a distance of 300 yards. The first of the forty-nine competitors had barely started shooting when it was noticed that there was a problem at the mantlet (bullet-proof shelter) occupied by Hale. The danger flags were raised and shooting immediately stopped. Two marksmen ran to check on Hale and found him lying dead next to the mantlet, shot through the heart.

At an inquest held by coroner Dr Wybrants, it was suggested that there had been a brief pause after the first volley of shots, during which Hale had emerged from the left-hand side of the mantlet, wrongly assuming that firing had ceased. The fatal shot was shown to have been fired by Hale's friend, Mr Dennis. Hale left a widow and six children and, according to Dennis, had been most reluctant to go to Shepton that morning, even though it was an occasion he normally relished. The inquest jury returned a verdict of 'accidental death' and stated that they attached no blame to Mr Dennis for his part in Hale's death.

1878 Seventy-year-old shepherd Jacob Short was returning from Warminster **28 OCTOBER** Fair to Frome with ninety sheep. He apparently stopped to take a drink from the river at Rodden, where he was later found drowned, his body on the bank and his head in the water. It was thought that he had either fainted or overbalanced as he leaned over the river, falling face first into the water. At the place where Short fell in, the river was only about 8in deep.

1926 The alertness of George Short, a night watchman at Middle Pit Colliery **29 OCTOBER** in the centre of Radstock, foiled an attempt to blow up two pits in the area.

Middle Pit and Norton Hill Colliery had both experienced problems with people pilfering coal, and consequently appointed night watchmen to try and catch the culprits red-handed. During the night of 29 October, Short spotted a man crouching near the colliery head gear. When Short shouted, the man ran away. The night watchman took off in hot pursuit but eventually lost his quarry to the dark, rainy night. Returning to the spot where he had first noticed the man, Short found two canisters, with fuses attached. Nearby lay a piece of sacking, in which was wrapped another larger canister. Short immediately informed the police and the pit manager of his discovery and, when the canisters were examined, they were found to contain highly explosive material, fixed with fuses and detonators ready for lighting. The larger canister was labelled 'Norton Hill Colliery', suggesting that it was intended for use there. Had the explosives been successfully detonated at Middle Pit, they would almost certainly have blown up the adjoining gasworks and devastated the town of Radstock.

30 OCTOBER   **1880**   Twenty-three-year-old bargeman Thomas Ames was tried before Mr Justice Denman at the Somerset Assizes for the wilful murder of nine-year-old Albert Edward Miles in Bath on 24 August.

Albert had climbed down the lock gates of the Kennet and Avon Canal to do some fishing. However, as he tried to climb back up again, his foot slipped and he fell into the lock. Ames stood at the canal side and watched as Albert, who couldn't swim, struggled to keep his head above water. Urged by bystanders to jump in, Ames replied, 'Let the little bastard get out the best way he can.'

Eventually, William Vowles, aged thirteen, and Francis Hillier, aged seventeen, stripped off their jackets and jumped in. They managed to grab Albert and, each holding one of his arms, they swam back towards the lock gates. They shouted for Ames to throw a pole down from the bank, but he ignored them, instead closing the gates on the boys, who were still clinging desperately to the bottom. Ames then took a winch and deliberately opened the hatches, flooding the lock with water. A woman begged him to stop, saying, 'For God's sake, don't you drown all three.' Ames just laughed at her and continued to open the hatches.

The resulting flood of water washed Albert from the hands of his rescuers and he drowned. Fortunately, Vowles and Hillier managed to save themselves and were later commended for their bravery, a collection being taken in court in appreciation of their valiant efforts. The judge told them that he intended to write to The Royal Humane Society in the hope that the boys would receive some official commendation. Ames was found guilty of manslaughter and sentenced to seven years' imprisonment.

31 OCTOBER   **1949**   Four people died when a Westland Wyvern prototype aircraft crashed into council houses at Yeovil, close to the Westland airfield. The plane spewed a trail of burning fuel behind it as it plunged to the ground. The dead were Michael Graves, the Westland Company's assistant chief test pilot; Ann Wilkins, a six-year-old girl who was riding her bicycle in the road; and Mrs Edith Brown, whose house was severely damaged. A neighbour, Edith Hockey, was badly burned and later died in hospital from her injuries.

The plane was on a routine test flight when its engines stopped and its undercarriage retracted. As soon as he realised that he was in difficulty, the pilot made a determined effort to reach the airfield rather than crashing into Yeovil town centre. However, he had little chance of controlling his stricken plane, which was then travelling at more than 200 miles an hour. Although the wreckage was thoroughly examined, no explanation could be found for the crash.

NOVEMBER

Ludlows Colliery, Radstock. (Author's collection)

1 NOVEMBER   **1880**   An inquest was held on the death of cattle and carcass butcher Harry Noad from Road. On 29 October, Noad set out for Bath market before dawn with a cartload of dead fat calves. He had not gone far when his horse took fright and bolted. The cart tipped over, spilling its load of calves into a ditch and Noad was completely buried. He lay for some time until after daybreak, when a relative happened along the road and spotted the overturned cart. At that time, Noad was still alive, imploring the passer-by, 'Get me out, or I shall soon die.' However, once Noad was extricated from beneath the dead calves, it was obvious that his back was broken and he died soon afterwards. The inquest jury returned a verdict of 'accidental death'.

2 NOVEMBER   **1884**   Borough coroner Mr P.O.H. Reed held an inquest on the death of Alice Tobin, aged three and a half. Alice lived with her grandmother, Mrs How, in Cannington, and on 1 November she suffered an attack of diarrhoea and complained of a stiff neck. Her grandmother gave her a tablespoon of brandy, leaving the bottle on a chair in the bedroom. At some time during that night, Alice got out of bed and drank almost half a pint of brandy. When Mrs How woke the following morning and noticed the empty bottle, she questioned Alice, who told her that she had felt thirsty. As the day progressed, Alice became very drowsy and her breathing grew laboured. By the time she was rushed to hospital that evening in a state of collapse, she was beyond assistance and died soon afterwards.

The inquest jury found that her death arose from purely accidental circumstances and absolved her grandmother of any blame in the tragedy.

3 NOVEMBER   **1938**   The quiet village of Hemington was disturbed by the sound of shots coming from the rear of the rectory. Seconds later, eighteen-year-old Gladys Freda Francis, who was employed as a housemaid, staggered into the rectory kitchen groaning and bleeding heavily from her mouth. The rector's wife, Mrs Jones, shouted to the gardener and parish gravedigger, Hugh Weaver, to fetch the girl's mother, before trying to give what first aid she could to the injured girl. However, her efforts were in vain, as Gladys died within minutes. Shortly afterwards, Weaver's dead body was found in the rectory garden with severe head injuries, a shotgun at his side.

Fifty-two-year-old Weaver lived in the village with his wife, two sons and a grown-up daughter. Eight years earlier, he had spent eight months as an in-patient at Wells Asylum, although since his release he had shown no further signs of mental illness. He was not known to have had any quarrel with Gladys, although the girl had complained to her mother in the past that Weaver sometimes 'looked at her funny' and she did not like it.

At the subsequent inquest, held at Radstock, the jury found that Weaver had shot Gladys and then shot himself, while his mind was unbalanced.

4 NOVEMBER   **1880**   An inquest was held at the Packet House Inn, Pill, by coroner Mr R. Biggs on the death of Thomas Neale.

After spending the evening of 11 October drinking, Neale was walking home with William Gidley when he suddenly needed to urinate. Asking Gidley to wait for him, he disappeared into the dark night. Gidley waited for about ten minutes before going to look for his companion and, not finding him, assumed that he must have continued on his way home. It wasn't until the next morning that he heard that Neale was missing. In spite of an extensive search, there was no trace of Neale until his body was pulled from the river Avon on 29 October, the front of his trousers open.

The coroner deduced that Neale had descended the steep bank to urinate in the river and had fallen in. The jury returned a verdict of 'found drowned'.

1826 Coroner Mr Caines held an inquest at Voale Farm, Mark, on the death of eighteen-year-old labourer Gabriel Chapple.

Driving some pigs out of an orchard on 30 October, Chapple tapped one large boar with a stick to urge it forward. The boar rounded on him and savagely attacked him, leaving him with punctured lungs, two broken ribs and several feet of intestines protruding from his body. In spite of the best attentions of surgeon Mr William, Chapple died from his injuries on 3 November. The inquest jury returned a verdict of 'died from a furious attack of a boar'.

1803 Thirty-six-year-old Mr Wheaton, from Honiton in Devon, was a guest at a shooting party in Henley, near Crewkerne. Wheaton fired several accurate shots and was teased by another member of the party that his good shooting was due to the quality of his gun rather than his skill. Wheaton offered to exchange guns and fired at a woodcock, which he missed. He climbed onto a tree stump and began reloading the gun but it slipped out of his hands and hit the ground, accidentally shooting him in the breast. Although mortally wounded, Wheaton insisted on being given a pencil and a piece of paper and wrote out his will, while lying bleeding on the ground. Only then did he allow himself to be taken to a surgeon. He died the following day.

1879 In the village of Templecombe, near Yeovil, ironmonger Mr Smith was tapping a cask of benzoline when it exploded. The room in which he was working was somewhat dark and he had taken in a candle to light his work. Although he suffered terrible burns to his arms, hands and thighs, miraculously, Smith was not killed.

The explosion was heard by PC Sharp, who was patrolling his beat nearby. Together with a young passer-by, he ran to Smith's shop, which was now ablaze, and began removing stock through the shattered window. Before long, the flames reached Smith's store of petroleum and gunpowder and there was a second explosion, even louder and more powerful than the first. Again, by a miracle, nobody was killed, although both PC Sharp and the young man suffered burns and the man was also cut by flying glass, a large piece of which lodged in his face. Several other bystanders had a narrow escape.

Fire engines arrived from Stalbridge and Henstridge and the blaze was finally extinguished, with the assistance of the villagers. However, by the time the fire was under control, Smith's shop had completely burned to the ground, as had the neighbouring property belonging to a Mr Goddard. A nearby stable was gutted and the house of the village butcher, Mr Barnett, was severely damaged by fire and water. Mr Goddard had no insurance and consequently lost everything he owned in the fire.

8 NOVEMBER   **1839**   At four o'clock in the morning, twelve miners assembled at the pit head at Wells Way Pit, Radstock, waiting to descend underground to commence their shift. Tragically, as the twelve were lowered, the rope bearing their weight suddenly snapped and all twelve plummeted more than 250 yards to the pit bottom. The men were literally smashed to pieces and only one was sufficiently intact to be recognisable.

Richard Langford (forty-four) died with his sons, Farnham (sixteen) and Alfred (thirteen). James Keevil (forty-one) also died with two sons, Mark (fifteen) and James (fourteen). The other fatalities were William Adam (nineteen), Leonard Dowling (twelve), William Summers (twenty-six), Amos Dando (thirteen), John Barnet (forty-one) and James Pearce (eighteen). Langford, Keevil and Barnet left widows and a total of fourteen children between them.

The nature of the tragedy was worsened by the fact that, on examination, it was obvious that the rope had been deliberately tampered with. Almost new, only the previous night it had borne a weight of 32cwt. 'Some diabolical malice caused this calamity wilfully and premediately' [*sic*], reported the *Bristol Mercury*. It appeared as if the rope had been partially cut through, its fibres weakened by a person or persons using a knife or chisel. Where the fibres had given way under the weight of the men, the edges were jagged and uneven, yet many of the fibres were cleanly cut and of regular appearance.

At an inquest before county coroner Mr R. Uphill, the jury returned a verdict of wilful murder against some person or persons unknown. Although a reward of £100 was offered, the murderer(s) remained undetected.

9 NOVEMBER   **1859**   Evan Scull and Mary Palmer, next-door neighbours from St George's, Bristol, got into an argument over the placement of pig dung in Mary's garden. Mary saw it as a useful fertiliser, whereas to Scull, it was a smelly, offensive nuisance. The argument ended when Scull hit Mary over the head and in the ribs with a shovel.

Scull was charged with assault and when he was brought before the Bench at the Lawford's Gate Petty Sessions to answer to the charge, his account of events differed greatly from Mary's. According to Mary, she had politely told Scull that she would be fertilising her garden, as usual, at which he threatened, 'If you do, I'll knock your ****** brains out,' and flew at her with his spade. She had been in constant pain ever since and suspected that her ribs were broken. Scull insisted that he had been quietly mending his hedge when Mary had called him a 'humped-backed, parish-bred bastard' and then attacked him, accidentally tripping and falling onto his spade.

The magistrates appealed to their better nature, asking them to sort the matter out between themselves as neighbours. However, Mary was adamant – she had 'come for law and would have law'. Magistrates finally fined Scull 6s plus costs, which he refused to pay. He was sent to Gloucester Prison for one week in default.

1928   The First World War took a dreadful toll on Stanley George Kingston. During his service on the front lines in France, he was blown up several times and saw many of his comrades killed and mutilated in battle. He returned to work on his father's farm in Hembridge a much changed man, suffering from shell shock and described by his family as 'a bundle of nerves'. He also developed a taste for alcohol.

In 1926, Stanley began courting Gladys, the eldest child of farm labourer Samuel Henry Martin. Stanley, who was twenty years older than Gladys, gradually became more and more abusive towards her, particularly when he had been drinking. By 1927, Samuel felt bound to intervene and, having heard that Stanley had shouted and sworn at Gladys, he confronted him and forbade him from contacting her again.

Prevented from seeing Gladys, Stanley resorted to stalking her. Once more, Gladys complained to her father and, on Friday 9 November 1928, Samuel witnessed Stanley's abusive behaviour for himself. Standing at the door of his cottage with Gladys, Samuel heard Kingston swearing at his daughter. On that occasion, he chose to ignore Kingston and simply went inside and shut the cottage door.

Early the following morning, Gladys's mother was walking downstairs when Stanley Kingston burst in and charged towards her, brushing aside her attempts to grab him and heading for the bedroom where Gladys was still asleep. To her horror, Mrs Martin saw that he was carrying a double-barrelled shotgun. She called out a warning to her daughter, telling her to jump out of the bedroom window as Stanley was going to shoot her but, for some reason, Gladys chose to try and escape down the stairs. She ran past Kingston, who immediately turned, aimed the gun and fired twice. Satisfied that Gladys was now dead, Kingston abruptly left and went to an empty cottage, where he shot himself, crawling from there to his own home to die.

'I never thought he would ever use the gun,' said Stanley's father, George Kingston, when the coroner at the inquest asked him 'Did you think he was dangerous?'

The coroner told the inquest jury that Kingston was more or less demented as a result of his wartime experiences and was totally incapable of accepting the rejection of his advances by Gladys Martin, spending much of his time brooding over her. The inquest jury returned the only possible verdict – that Stanley Kingston had murdered Gladys Martin then died from a self-inflicted gunshot wound.

11 NOVEMBER   **1927**   When smoke was seen coming from the windows of a house in Lark Street, Yeovil, it was discovered that the kitchen was on fire. Neighbours tried desperately to rescue three children from the house but the blaze was too intense. Eventually, having formed a bucket chain in an effort to douse the flames, one man managed to crawl into the house and the three children were brought out. Tragically Doreen Rood (four) and her siblings Kenneth (two) and Iris Dorothy (seven weeks) did not survive.

12 NOVEMBER   **1898**   Sixty-three-year-old blacksmith Edmund Pope set out to walk from Norton Fitzwarren to Bishops Hull. His body was found several days later, floating in the river Tone. It was surmised that he had missed a narrow footbridge in the dark and instead walked straight into the river. Pope left a widow and several children. The jury at his inquest returned a verdict of death by misadventure and suggested that something should be done about the dangerous state of the river at Bishops Hull.

13 NOVEMBER   **1858**   Fifteen-year-old Thomas Andrews was arrested in connection with the burning of a hay rick belonging to farmer Mr Worthy of Templecombe on 10 November.

The fire, which destroyed more than thirty tons of hay, had obviously been deliberately started and, when police began their investigations, they were told that James Hyde had been seen near the ricks about ten minutes before the fire was discovered. James, aged eight and a half, was employed by Mr Worthy but, when questioned, he denied all knowledge of the fire.

It was then discovered that Thomas Andrews had left Mr Worthy's employ on the Saturday before the fire, when a shilling was stopped from his wages for damaging a wall. Yet Andrews had a cast-iron alibi for the time of the fire. The police went back to James Hyde and asked him if he had anything to do with Andrews and, after a slight delay, Hyde admitted that Andrews had given him some matches and told him to fire the rick.

Brought before magistrates, both boys were committed for trial at the Somerset Assizes and both were sent to Shepton Mallet Prison to await the start of the proceedings. (It was reported that Hyde was only committed to gaol to prevent him from being 'tampered with'.) At their trial in December 1858, Hyde appeared only as a prosecution witness to the charge of arson against Thomas Andrews, who was found guilty and sentenced to be transported for five years.

1843 John Walter broke into the home of Thomas Lucas at Kingston, near Yeovil and stole two cheeses. He was later tried for the burglary at the Somerset Assizes, along with Jonas Palmer, who was charged with receiving the stolen cheeses. Since Walter had made a written confession to the theft, and one of the cheeses was found in Palmer's possession, it was an open and shut case and the jury found both men guilty as charged. Palmer was sentenced to eight months' imprisonment, with hard labour, but Walter, who had a previous conviction, was sentenced to be transported for fourteen years.

14 NOVEMBER

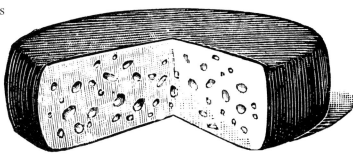

1821 At about nine o'clock at night, a fire broke out in Ilchester Gaol. In spite of the valiant efforts of the townspeople, the fire raged for more than two hours, sending up great clouds of smoke and ashes and lighting up the sky for miles around. The gaol's woollen factory and workshops were completely destroyed in the blaze. Fortunately, the prevailing wind was south-westerly – had it been in a more westerly direction, the whole gaol would probably have been consumed by the fire.

15 NOVEMBER

A plan of Ilchester Gaol.

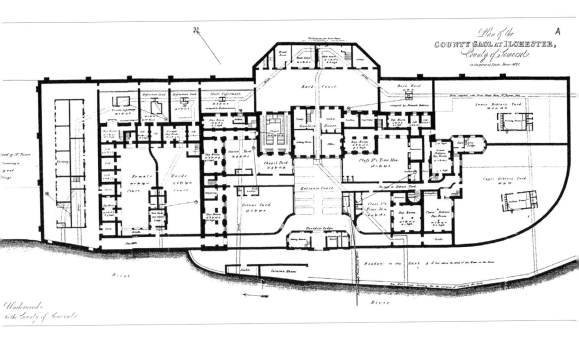

1858 Bootmaker Henry Rowe of Taunton secured his house before retiring for the night but, some hours later, he was awakened by noises downstairs. When he went to investigate, he found twenty-eight-year-old William Maclean wandering about in his stockinged feet. Leaving his shoes outside, Maclean had forced a window and was busy piling up articles with the obvious intention

16 NOVEMBER

of stealing them. When challenged, he claimed to be so drunk that he 'did not know what he was about'. He repeated this story at the Somerset Assizes, adding that, having enlisted in the 31st Foot Regiment earlier that day, he had celebrated too enthusiastically and was very tipsy. The jury found him guilty and he was sentenced to three years' penal servitude.

17 NOVEMBER   **1849** Twenty-year-old Elizabeth Hellier lived in extreme poverty in lodgings in St James's Court, Bath. Once a servant, her employment was abruptly terminated when it was discovered that she was pregnant; since that time she had been earning whatever money she could by taking in sewing. Her circumstances were worsened by her kind heart – she lent some of her clothes to a fellow lodger, who promptly pawned them and spent the money. Elizabeth applied to the Board of Guardians for assistance but was turned away. Thus she was completely destitute when she gave birth.

A weakly girl, Elizabeth had suffered throughout her pregnancy and was in the habit of retiring to bed in the early evenings. Hence, when she was heard walking about in her room late on 17 November, her fellow lodgers were concerned that she might be ill and went to check on her. They found her door locked. When she was finally persuaded to open it, it was immediately obvious that she was no longer pregnant, although she denied having given birth. Eventually, she asked all but one of her fellow lodgers to leave the room then revealed the dead body of a baby girl, which she had hidden under a petticoat in a locked box. The baby had marks around her neck, hence Elizabeth was charged with wilful murder and committed for trial at the next Somerset Assizes.

However, at her trial, the two doctors who had conducted a post-mortem examination on the baby gave conflicting evidence. Mr John Barrett believed that the baby had been born alive and stated that the marks around her neck were consistent with foul play. His colleague, Dr Tunstall, pointed out that the child's chest was much smaller than usual and he was only prepared to state that she might have cried or breathed. He believed that the injuries were caused when Elizabeth grasped her baby's lower jaw in an effort to assist nature and deliver her baby. In view of the contrary opinions of the medical witnesses, the jury acquitted Elizabeth Hellier on the charge of wilful murder but found her guilty of concealment of birth. She was sentenced to one year's imprisonment.

18 NOVEMBER   **1882** Crowds at the Yeovil Fair caught their first glimpse of a performing Zulu, which unaccountably sent them into a state of panic. Convinced that the man was going to run them through with his assegai – a traditional African spear – the crowd stampeded en masse for the exit. Several people were knocked over and trampled and the entire front of the show booth was demolished in the rush to escape.

19 NOVEMBER   **1891** George White arrived at his home in Kilmersdon so drunk that he fell over in the garden and went to sleep. With the assistance of a neighbour, his wife Eliza managed to carry him indoors. When she offered to make him a cup

of tea, George told her to get out of his house. Eliza went out into the garden but George followed and gave her a clip round the ear with his fist. He then seized her around the throat and dragged her back inside, where he proceeded to beat her with his fists and a poker. Eliza suffered a broken nose, several broken ribs, two black eyes and severe bruising. The couple's daughter ran to fetch her brother, who lived almost a mile away, and was returning to help her mother when she met her on the road, bloody and dazed.

White was picked up by the police the following morning but was still so drunk that they delayed charging him until the following day. He appeared at the Somerset Assizes the following March before Mr Justice Wills, charged with feloniously wounding Eliza with intent to kill and murder her. George White sobbed piteously throughout his trial, saying that he was very sorry for his actions and that he had been drunk and had never intended to murder his wife. He told the court that he wouldn't hurt her for the world, in spite of the fact that he had already served one prison sentence for assaulting her. Incredibly, Eliza White told the judge that she had no wish to press charges against her husband but simply didn't want to live with him any more.

'I do with you,' interjected George.

The judge told Eliza that it wasn't within his power to grant her a separation but he had no doubt that she would be able to obtain one under the circumstances. Once the jury had found George White guilty of wounding with intent to do grievous bodily harm, Mr Justice Wills sentenced him to five years' penal servitude.

1888   Acting Sergeant Francis Cook and PC William Bailey called at the home of John Lewis to talk to him about his behaviour on the previous evening, when he had walked the streets of Wrington claiming to be Jack the Ripper. When the policemen arrived, Mrs Lewis told them that her husband had threatened to stab her. Hearing this, Lewis ran upstairs. As Cook followed him, trying to calm him down, Lewis suddenly charged the police officer, brandishing a knife. He pushed Cook backwards until he came up against a child's crib, then began to saw at his throat. Bailey tried to intervene but was himself slashed and his hand badly cut. Only when another man came to the assistance of the police was Lewis subdued.

20 NOVEMBER

Lewis maintained that Cook had struck him with his staff and that he had only retaliated. He said that he was peacefully minding his own business in his own home and just happened to have a knife in his hand, insisting that the injuries to the policemen had occurred accidentally when they tried to take it away from him.

Lewis appeared at the Somerset Assizes, charged with assaulting Cook and Bailey while in the execution of their duty. It emerged that Cook had previously prosecuted Lewis on several different occasions, including once for attempted suicide, for which he was sentenced to six months' imprisonment but released after serving only three. Sentencing Lewis to twelve months' hard labour, the judge pointed out that he was extremely lucky not to be facing the death sentence for murder.

Wrington. (Author's collection)

21 NOVEMBER   **1891**   Tried at the Somerset Assizes before Mr Justice Cave, Dr James Caspar Clutterbuck pleaded guilty to fraudulently obtaining £16,500 by false pretences between December 1887 and October 1891. (Although only prosecuted for £16,500, the actual sum was nearer to £35,000.)

A Church of England Clergyman and one of Her Majesty's Inspectors of Workhouse Schools, Clutterbuck obtained money from various people under the pretence that he was investing it on their behalf. He then frittered away their life savings on his own reckless and mainly unsuccessful investments on the Stock Exchange and gambling on horse racing. One of his dupes, Mr Pearce, the master of the Dorchester Workhouse, was completely ruined. Clutterbuck was found guilty and sentenced to four years' penal servitude.

22 NOVEMBER   **1887**   At nine o'clock in the morning, Dr Hitchins of Weston-super-Mare heard the sound of shots from his daughter's bedroom. He rushed to investigate and, breaking down the locked door, found his twenty-five-year-old daughter Constance dead in bed, shot through the head. His son, Ernest, was also in the room, his face bleeding. As Dr Hitchins went to help Ernest, the young man pushed past him and flung himself down the stairs. When that didn't kill him, he dived headfirst onto the fire. When he was eventually subdued, a note was found in Ernest's coat pocket, part of which read:

Broadmoor Criminal Lunatic Asylum. (Author's collection)

I have been treated so badly by that beast of a sister Constance that I must put an end to her life by shooting and, knowing that I shall have to die for it, I'll also shoot myself. Goodbye all. I hope you will have a happy time of it.

Ernest's self-inflicted injuries proved not to be fatal and he lived to stand trial at the Somerset Assizes for wilful murder. Known to suffer from epilepsy, Hitchins was found guilty but insane and sent to Broadmoor Criminal Lunatic Asylum.

1829 Catherine Chappell (or Chapple) heard somebody open the door of the neighbouring room in her lodgings in Walcot, Bath, at about half-past five in the morning, followed by the sound of footsteps hurrying downstairs. Seconds later, she heard a strange gurgling sound and, thinking that her neighbour might be ill, she went to check. When she opened the door of the room occupied by James Beere (or Beare), his wife, Mary and the couple's infant son, Charles, she called out but received no reply. The room was pitch dark, so Catherine asked her husband to fetch a light. The Chappells found Mary and Charles dead in bed, their throats cut. James, a baker, was nowhere to be seen. Informed of the tragedy, police launched an immediate search for him and, a short while later, a bloodstained baker's jacket was found on a nearby river bank. When the river was dragged, Beere's body was retrieved. **23 NOVEMBER**

Beere was known as a loving husband and father and as a steady, reliable employee. Witnesses who had seen the family at home on the day before the murders described the Beeres as 'happy', 'comfortable' and 'completely normal'. Yet, at the inquest into their deaths, Mr Muckleway, a work colleague of Beere's, mentioned that he had twice recently complained of 'an illness in his head'. Even so, other than thinking that Beere seemed a bit 'low', Muckleway had noticed nothing unusual about his colleague's behaviour.

The inquest jury could find no motive for the deaths, recording verdicts of wilful murder against James Beere in respect of his wife and son, and *felo de se* in the case of Beere himself.

24 NOVEMBER **1863** William Rose went to visit his sister, Ellen Scammell, at her home in Broad Street, Bath. William was not a particularly welcome visitor and Ellen was later to complain that he had been at her house every day for almost a week, only returning home to his wife at nights.

William asked Ellen to lend him a shilling but Ellen told him she had no money to lend. Yet his lack of ready funds didn't prevent William from sending out for a half a gallon of beer, which he and Ellen's father began drinking. Exasperated, Ellen asked him to leave and, when he refused, she picked up a razor intending to frighten him and began to physically push him out of the door. Once in the courtyard, she stabbed William in his left shoulder with the razor then, as he turned to run away, she stabbed him again in the back.

Ellen was tried at the Somerset Assizes for maliciously cutting and wounding William Rose with intent to do him grievous bodily harm. Although she was not defended, the statement she had made to magistrates was read out in court: 'I have had a very shocking bad life for the last four years and a half through drink, owing to my father and brother.' Ellen insisted that she had picked up the razor to try and frighten her brother into leaving, never imagining that she was going to stab him.

The jury acquitted twenty-five-year-old Ellen of malicious wounding, finding her guilty of the lesser offence of unlawfully wounding, and she was sentenced to two months' imprisonment with hard labour.

25 NOVEMBER **1892** When the Bath branch of the National Society for the Prevention of Cruelty to Children were made aware of the shocking conditions in which fourteen-month-old Ada Bishop lived, they immediately sent a doctor to her home at Shepton Mallet. The doctor found Ada lying in a soap box in piles of her own excrement, covered only by dirty rags. Although Ada was surprisingly well-nourished, she had a gangrenous pressure sore on her buttocks measuring 2in by 3in. Ada was immediately removed from her home to the Shepton Mallet Hospital, where she died on 27 November.

Her parents John and Elizabeth were tried at the Somerset Assizes for her manslaughter. Although both were acquitted, Elizabeth was then indicted for wilfully neglecting Ada and found guilty. She was sentenced to three months' imprisonment with hard labour.

26 NOVEMBER **1822** Elizabeth 'Betty' Bryant of Wiveliscombe had two daughters, Elizabeth and Jane. Elizabeth was afflicted by fits and, when Betty consulted a conjurer, she was told that her daughter had been bewitched and that the only way to lift the curse on her was to draw blood from the witch. The Bryants accused sixty-eight-year-old Ann Burgess, who consequently went to their home on 26 November to refute the allegations against her.

Ann met Betty near her home. 'Betty Bryant, I come to ask you a civil question; whether I bewitched your daughter?' Betty insisted that she had, calling her a 'damned witch' and bemoaning the 10s she had spent on charms from the conjuror to try and rid Elizabeth of her fits. With that, she and her daughters attacked Ann Burgess, gouging her arm with a nail. Ann's cries of 'murder' attracted a large crowd of people, who watched the struggle without intervening on behalf of 'the witch'. Only one woman tried to help Ann, eventually pulling her free from her attackers' clutches.

All three Bryants stood trial at the Somerset Assizes. The Grand Jury ignored a bill for attempted murder, so they were charged with maliciously assaulting Ann Burgess in the belief that she was a witch. Found guilty, each was sentenced to four months' imprisonment.

1882 For two days, the occupants of Clevedon Court had noticed the acrid smell of smouldering wood in some rooms of the old manor house. Nobody was able to trace the source of the smell, even though the house was searched from top to bottom.

On the morning of 27 November, a housemaid lit the fire in the library. A little while later, she went to light the fire in the room situated directly above,

27 NOVEMBER

Clevedon Court.
(Author's collection)

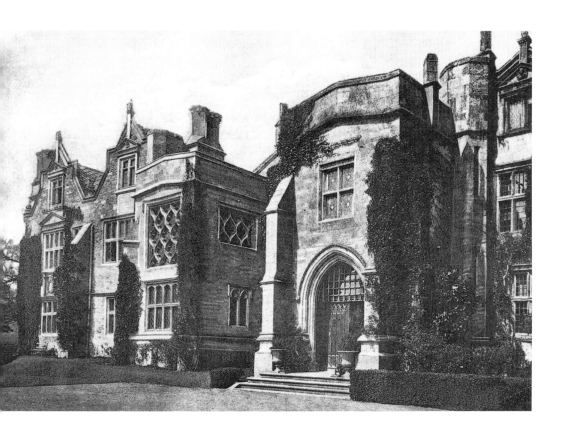

finding the room full of smoke. Bravely, she checked an adjoining room and discovered that it was in flames. The maid alerted Sir Arthur and Lady Elton, the only members of the family in residence at the time, and Sir Arthur sent a messenger to the Waterworks Company at nearby Clevedon, asking them to send their hose. Meanwhile, the other staff divided their efforts between dousing the flames with buckets of water and removing pictures and antiques from the house and placing them on the lawn. However, a strong wind fanned the flames and the fire soon spread.

The Bristol Fire Brigade arrived at ten o'clock and by two o'clock that afternoon the fire was extinguished. The south front and grand hall were saved but the more recently renovated apartments and the library, drawing room and dining room were completely gutted, as were several bedrooms. The total damage was estimated at £20,000, although fortunately the building was insured.

28 NOVEMBER   **1879**   A man named Hiscox stole a duck and a chicken at Shepton Mallet. He was seen by witnesses entering the premises from where the birds were stolen and was then seen going into a coach house, where the two dead birds were later found concealed. When his actions were reported to the police, Hiscox made no attempt to deny the theft, saying to the arresting officer, 'I hope you will forgive me and not have me locked up.'

Hiscox appeared at the Somerset Quarter Sessions, where the jury unaccountably found him not guilty. Thus the chairman, Mr T.E. Rogers, had no option but to dismiss the prisoner, although he was extremely scathing in his condemnation of the jury. He found it incomprehensible that Hiscox had been acquitted simply because nobody actually saw him steal the birds. He supposed the jury must think that, 'like the Babes in the Wood, the two birds simply placed themselves side by side in the coach house, covered themselves and then killed each other.' Rogers told Hiscox:

You are a lucky fellow. You were seen to go into the place from whence the duck and fowl were missed and from there to the stable where they were found. Besides, when charged, you admitted the offence. This intelligent jury obviously think that you are mistaken about your guilt and did not steal the poultry.

29 NOVEMBER   **1878**   Thirty-six-year-old cook Matilda Lock complained of feeling unwell and left her work in the kitchens of Clarke's Hotel, Taunton, retiring to her room. When the housemaid went to check on her, Matilda was writhing in agony on the floor. A doctor was called and, having examined Matilda, accused her of being pregnant. Although Matilda strongly denied this, she was dismissed from her job the next day.

Clarke's Hotel, Taunton. (Author's collection)

In January of the following year, a workman was called to deal with a blocked drain in the yard directly outside Matilda's room. The obstruction was revealed to be the body of a newly-born baby boy and, after a post-mortem examination, the surgeon estimated that the child had been in the drain for about five weeks. However, as the body had been partially consumed by rats, it was difficult to determine the cause of his death or to state conclusively that he was born alive.

Although the jury at the subsequent inquest returned an open verdict, Matilda Lock was arrested and charged with wilful murder. By the time she was tried at the Somerset Assizes in February 1879, the charge against her had been reduced to one of concealment of the birth of a child. The case against Matilda was purely circumstantial, with little evidence to prove that she had actually given birth or to indicate how or when the baby had died. Additionally, the yard was easily accessed by any passers-by. The jury were unable to agree on a verdict and Matilda was eventually discharged on her own recognisance to appear at the next assizes if called upon. There is no evidence to suggest that Matilda was ever recalled.

1909 A women's suffrage meeting at Yeovil was besieged by an angry mob. Although admittance to the meeting was strictly by ticket only, hundreds of people forced their way in. The speakers were pelted with stones and other missiles and one, Miss Naylor, was struck in the face. A man was injured as the platform was stormed, the protestors lashing out with sticks or their fists.

30 NOVEMBER

Scenes such as this, the arrest of suffragettes, were a common occurrence.

Chairs, windows and gas lamps were also smashed. The police eventually rescued the suffragettes and escorted them safely to their homes.

DECEMBER

Fore Street, Taunton. (Author's collection)

1 DECEMBER **1851** George Bush left his lodgings in Timsbury to attend an auction at Priston, after which he spent some time drinking in the Ring of Bells public house in the village. When he hadn't returned home the next morning, his landlady Ellen Flower sent her sons George and Isaac to Priston to try and find him. The boys found Bush's body lying in a field on his route home, his throat cut and the wound stuffed with grass.

Police initially arrested Ellen Flower, her daughter Harriet, her son-in-law Jacob Windmill and their friend Stephen Box. Bush had been robbed and Ellen Flower was aware that he had taken a considerable amount of cash to the auction with him. A few days later, a man named James Evans was also arrested, after police heard that he had argued with Bush at the pub on the night of his murder.

In July 1852, an Irish pedlar named Christopher Smith (aka John Hasley) was arrested in Dorset for vagrancy. In custody, Smith made a full confession to the murder of George Bush, saying that he wanted to clear his conscience and, brought back to Bath, he was tried at the next Somerset Assizes, where he pleaded guilty.

Judge Mr Baron Platt had his doubts and ordered Smith to be examined by doctors, who concluded that he was insane and therefore unfit to plead. He was sentenced to be detained during Her Majesty's pleasure but, as Smith had confessed to numerous other murders countrywide, it is highly unlikely that he actually killed Bush. Thus the real murderer(s) went unpunished.

2 DECEMBER **1808** Twenty-two-year-old Patrick Chastey, a drummer with the 19th Regiment of Foot, mysteriously disappeared after playing a game of cards with four residents of Taunton. Chastey, who had recently inherited some money, was on a winning streak and, at the end of the game, Anthony Jerrard, John Brooks, Charles Way and John Monckton (aka Monk) were all seriously out of pocket.

Nothing more was heard of Chastey until his body was found three weeks later, floating in the river at Creech St Michael. It was so putrefied that the surgeon who performed the post-mortem examination could not determine how he had died and, although there were strong suspicions that he had been robbed and murdered, the inquest returned a verdict of 'found drowned'.

Twenty-four years later, Jerrard, who was the landlord of the Black Boy public house in Taunton, happened to get drunk and blurted out that Brooks, Monckton and Way had murdered Chastey, stolen his money and thrown his body into the river. Jerrard's drunken admission was communicated to the police and he, John Monckton and John Brooks were arrested, (Charles Way had died some years earlier). They were tried at the Somerset Assizes in 1833, Brooks and Monckton charged with wilful murder and Jerrard with being an accessory after the fact. However, in view of the findings of the original inquest, it wasn't absolutely certain that a murder had even been committed, hence all three defendants were acquitted.

3 DECEMBER **1896** An inquest was held by coroner Mr B.H. Watts at the Guildhall in Bath on the death of sixteen-year-old labourer Charles Weston.

The Pump Room, Bath. (Author's collection)

The Pump Room in the city was being extended and Charles was working on scaffolding high above the ground. Whenever the workers needed fresh mortar, it was hauled up by rope and pulley. On 1 December, when the order was given to cease work, Charles exuberantly decided to descend from the scaffold on the rope used to raise the mortar. He obviously forgot that the rope wasn't secured and, as he seized it, it simply came off the pulley, sending him crashing to the ground. Charles died from a fractured skull and, after hearing that his employers provided ladders for ascent and descent, and had made it clear that anyone caught coming down by any other means would be dismissed, the inquest jury absolved them of all blame and recorded a verdict of 'accidental death'.

4 DECEMBER

1885 The inhabitants of the village of Wedmore were known as staunch supporters of the Conservative Party. However, during the election of 1885, a number of local tradesmen switched their political allegiance, stating that they would be voting for the Liberal candidate for the Wells division of Somerset, Mr J. Ralli, in preference to Tory candidate Colonel Paget.

Wedmore. (Author's collection)

In the afternoon of polling day, a group of Liberal supporters decided to steal a small blue flag which was flying in the garden of Mr Robert Redman, a friend and supporter of Colonel Paget. Triumphantly, they took the flag to the New Inn on the Wells Road. An enraged mob of several hundred Tory supporters laid siege to the pub and, even when the contentious flag was surrendered, they launched an attack on the premises, shattering

every single windowpane with stones. George Parker, the landlady's son, was severely injured by flying glass and narrowly escaped being stoned to death.

The rampaging Conservatives broke into the pub and proceeded to wreck the interior, smashing furniture and tearing down gas fittings with the promise that they would blow the place sky high. The rioters then turned their attention to the rear of the pub, shattering the windows and breaking down several fruit trees in the orchard. At one stage, shots were fired by a person within the pub whose political allegiance is not recorded and several people were peppered with lead shotgun pellets. Two men, William Hembury and Norman Day were severely wounded.

A total of 259 panes of glass were smashed at the New Inn before the rioters sought out the homes of other known Liberal supporters in the village and pelted them with stones. Numerous properties suffered broken windows, including those of Baptist minister Revd E. Edgington and Acting Police Sergeant Green, while Mrs Harvey suffered a cut face as stones were hurled at the house she shared with her Liberal husband. Acting Sergeant Green called to Axbridge for reinforcements to quell the riotous mob and order was eventually restored to the village just before midnight. Several private summonses taken out against the rioters were subsequently dismissed by local magistrates and, although seven men appeared at the Somerset Assizes charged with riotous assembly and disturbance of the public peace, all were discharged without penalty on their own recognisance to keep the peace in future.

5 DECEMBER   **1942**   The *Bristol Mercury* reported the inquest held on thirty-three-year-old Arthur William Grinter of Stoke-under-Ham. Having failed the army medical examination, Grinter joined the police force instead. However, an anonymous person or persons had taken exception to what they saw as Grinter's cowardice and had put up several posters in the area, some of which referred to him by name. One read: 'Stoke roll of honour. We shall remember them for their deeds.' Another read: 'Yellow. Avoiding his duty to his country by joining the police, while our husbands and sons are serving in the forces.' A third mocked: 'Joining the police force, dodging the Army. How brave they are!'

The implications preyed on Grinter's mind and he shot himself. Returning a verdict of suicide while the balance of mind was disturbed, coroner Mr C.J.P.C. Jowett stated, 'Who ever perpetrated these scurrilous rumours under the guise of anonymity will have the satisfaction of knowing – whatever they intended – that the result has been that this man took his own life.'

6 DECEMBER   **1873**   Reported in the *Guardian*, 16 December and 22 December. As ex-policeman Henry Cook and his wife walked home in the dark near Dundry, a horse ridden by farmer William Stallard accidentally brushed against Mrs Cook. Cook remonstrated with Stallard, threatening to knock him off his horse, and the two men exchanged a few cross words before Stallard rode off. When the Cooks reached the top of a hill, they found Stallard lying in wait for them. 'Come on, let's have a few rounds,' he challenged Cook, and before Cook could put down the basket of shopping he was carrying to defend himself, Stallard punched him, knocking him to the ground. As Cook struggled to his feet, Stallard hit him for a second time, before mounting his horse and riding off again.

Cook was carried home, where he died within forty-eight hours without regaining consciousness. A post-mortem examination revealed two fractures in his skull – one of which was 4in long – and determined that Cook had died from concussion of the brain. At the subsequent inquest, the coroner's jury returned a verdict of manslaughter against Stallard. However, magistrates later disagreed and committed him for wilful murder.

The Grand Jury ignored the bill for murder, so it was for manslaughter that Stallard stood trial on 20 December and very remorsefully pleaded guilty. As soon as he realised that Cook was badly injured, he had paid for a doctor to visit him and, after Cook's death, Stallard had paid his widow £250 compensation. He told the court that he had been a little drunk at the time of the assault and swore that he would never touch intoxicating liquor again. He was sentenced to six months' imprisonment with hard labour.

1841   Martha Walters, an inmate at the Yeovil Workhouse, lost her apron. She **7 DECEMBER** later found that another inmate, Mary Edgar, had taken it, and she snatched it back, hitting Mary several times on her head and back with her hand. Mary died from concussion of the brain about two weeks later and Martha was charged with her manslaughter.

She appeared at the Somerset Assizes in March 1842. It emerged in court that Mary was subject to fits and was frequently 'out of her senses'. Martha swore that she had ever intended to hurt Mary and several witnesses were called to testify that she was normally a good tempered woman. Nevertheless, the jury found her guilty and seventy-nine-year-old Martha was sentenced to one month's imprisonment with hard labour.

1873   At about four o'clock in the morning, the landlady of the Victoria Hotel **8 DECEMBER** in Bristol was woken by screaming and shouting, followed by the sound of a gunshot coming from one of the rooms. When Mrs Tongue went to investigate, she found that the occupants – a respectable married couple from Leeds – had jumped from the bedroom window into a courtyard 12ft below.

The couple ran to the railway station opposite the hotel and rushed into the office of the night superintendent, shouting 'Murder!' They told Mr Harker that they had just escaped a den of rogues and thieves and made him search the station to make sure that they hadn't been followed. Harker sent for the police and, when the couple were searched, Thomas Cumpston was found to be carrying a revolver and three knives, and said that he had been forced to defend himself 'against all sorts of strange things'. Charged at the Bristol Police Court with disorderly conduct and with letting off a firearm, both Thomas and his wife Ann insisted that they had heard terrible noises in the room, after which whatever they said to each other was repeated every time one of them spoke. The floor of their room had then begun to open up and Mr Cumpston had fallen into the crevasse, forcing his wife to pull him out. Ann had told her husband to fire his pistol to try and scare off whomever or whatever was besieging them and, when that hadn't worked, the Cumpstons had jumped out of the bedroom window and fled to the safety of the station.

With no satisfactory explanation for the Cumpstons' bizarre allegations, magistrates determined that they had suffered from a joint hallucination. They were discharged into the care of a Mr Butt, presumably a relative or a solicitor.

9 DECEMBER **1847** Sarah Seers of Bathwick realised that she had not seen her next-door neighbour, Jane Ridout, or Jane's four children all day. Knowing that Jane's husband William was working away, she decided to check on her. Although there was smoke coming from the chimney of Jane's house, Sarah could get no response to her knocks. Eventually, she looked through a window and saw Jane lying on the floor in a pool of blood. Sarah sent for help and, when Inspector Evans and Dr Baynton burst open the cottage door, they found Jane and her four children dead, their throats cut.

Jane was described as an industrious woman, of exemplary character. However, her eldest child had been born deaf and dumb, for which Jane blamed herself. Her guilt led to depression and, in recent weeks, her husband had become increasingly concerned about her mental state. She had previously taken the children to the canal, intending to drown them, but had been thwarted by passers-by. As a result, only a few days before her death, she had been officially certified insane.

Jane's husband was devoted to his wife and had baulked at the idea of confining her to a lunatic asylum. He had asked Jane's mother to move in while he was away, telling her to communicate with him immediately if she had any concerns. Jane's mother spent two days with her daughter and grandchildren, during which time Jane seemed relatively cheerful. Her mother decided to risk a short trip to see her landlord, intending to give him notice on her own cottage in order to move in with her daughter and son-in-law. During her absence, Jane seized the brief opportunity to end her life and those of her children, William John, Fanny, George and Mark, aged between nine months and six years old.

At an inquest held at the Crown Tavern in Bathwick, the jury returned verdicts of 'wilful murder' against Jane Ridout on the deaths of the children and 'suicide while temporarily insane' on Jane's own death. The coroner cited 'mistaken kindness' as the reason why she had been allowed to remain at liberty after her diagnosis of insanity, and hoped that the case would serve as a warning to those who neglected their duty towards their insane friends and relatives and induce them to take proper precautions against such tragedies.

10 DECEMBER **1896** Twenty-four-year-old boatman William Mees, from Bradford-on-Avon, drowned at Saltford. As his boat, *Curlew*, passed another boat, *Knot*, on the river Avon, Joseph Hewer, the captain of the *Knot*, saw Mees become entangled in a rope and fall into the river. Mees could not swim and neither could Hewer, hence he was unable to attempt to rescue Mees from the strong current. A third boatman, Joseph Haltham, who witnessed the incident from about fifty yards away, was also unable to swim, and watched helplessly as Mees sank. His body was found the next morning.

An inquest was held before coroner Mr Craddock at the Crown Inn, Saltford, at which the jury returned a verdict of 'accidental death'. They expressed indignation at the fact that men who could not swim were permitted to be employed on boats.

1844 Mary Ann Baker, a nursemaid at Langport, complained of feeling ill and was sent to see surgeon Mr Prankard. She returned with a powder, which she took upstairs. Housemaid Lucy Small went to check on her and found her in the under-nursemaid's bedroom. Lucy went to the nursery, where Mary Ann normally slept, and called Mary Ann to come into that room, since it was warmer. Mary Ann refused and, when Lucy went back to her, she had locked the bedroom door. Lucy then heard a baby crying. She fetched their employer, Mrs Rachel Badgett, who went upstairs and demanded to be let into the room. At first, Mary Ann refused, but when Mrs Badgett threatened to break the door down, she unbolted it.

Mary Ann denied the existence of a baby but, when Mrs Badgett searched the room, she found a baby boy wrapped in a parcel under the bed. The child was still alive and Mrs Badgett sent for Mr Prankard. The baby lived for two hours and, having noticed marks of violence on its body, Prankard conducted a post-mortem examination. He found that the baby had bruises and a broken leg, although the cause of his death was skull fractures – a sliver of broken skull bone had penetrated one of the baby's main arteries. Prankard concluded that the baby's head had made contact with something hard. Mary Ann insisted that she had accidentally dropped the child headfirst on the floor, although at her trial for wilful murder at the Somerset Assizes, the prosecution maintained that she had deliberately dashed his head against a hard surface. Prankard testified that either scenario was medically possible.

Mr Justice Wightman instructed the jury that if Mary Ann negligently struck the baby's head against a hard surface, without intending to murder him, then they should find her guilty of common assault. If they felt that the baby had accidentally been injured by suddenly falling on the ground, they should acquit her. After a few minutes' deliberation, the jury chose the latter option and Mary Ann Baker was discharged.

1896 Thirty-eight-year-old farmer Charles Candy Hodges of Doulting died after an accident.

While walking home at night two weeks earlier, Hodges fell 30ft into the Chelynch quarry. He broke several ribs and sustained internal injuries and, although he initially seemed to be making a good recovery, he later died from shock. At the inquest on his death, coroner Mr Louch severely reprimanded the manager of the stoneworks that owned the quarry, saying that leaving a quarry located so close to a footpath unfenced amounted to gross negligence and nearly deserved a verdict of manslaughter.

1900 An entire family from Sowton Oake was rushed to hospital in a critical condition, having apparently been poisoned. The first of the Maunder family to die was Lily, aged thirty months, who succumbed on 13 December. She was followed to the grave by her father, Eli Walter Maunder (thirty), and brother, Thomas (four), who both died on 17 December, while John (six) died three days later. Lily's mother, Emma, died soon afterwards, while three other children, James, Laura and an eight-month-old baby girl remained in hospital. James was described as 'dangerously ill', while Laura and the baby were 'progressing favourably'. All three eventually recovered.

Doctors suspected that the family had died from phosphorous poisoning. Yet, when Eli's stomach contents were analysed by county analyst H.J. Alford, he detected almost two grains of arsenic. Further analysis of the stomach contents of the children, conducted by Dr Stevenson, the pathologist at Guy's Hospital, found sufficient arsenic to account for their deaths, although Stevenson couldn't rule out the possibility that the family had also ingested phosphorous.

Mr T. Foster Barham, the coroner for West Somerset, described the case as the most incomprehensible he had ever come across. The Maunders' lodger had eaten exactly the same food as the rest of the family and been totally unaffected. Conversely, a neighbour who had helped nurse the family stated that she had eaten a piece of bread and butter and drunk a cup of tea at the house, which had made her violently sick. After exhaustive enquiries, the police were unable to determine where the arsenic came from or how, when and by whom it was administered. Thus the inquest jury returned an open verdict on all the deaths.

14 DECEMBER **1928** Inquests were held on the deaths of farmer Albert Richard Pearce (forty-two), his wife Beatrice May Pearce (thirty-eight), and their daughter, Vera May (nine), after all three were found shot at their farm at Redhill. The inquest jury recorded a verdict of murder and suicide during temporary insanity against Albert Pearce.

15 DECEMBER **1864** Two men were tried at the Somerset Assizes before Mr Baron Bramwell. The first, George Western, was found guilty of committing buggery with a donkey at Durston. The second, Charles Rawlings, was found guilty of the brutal rape of a fifty-four-year-old widow at Congresbury. Bramwell sentenced both men to penal servitude, Rawlings to five years and Western to ten.

16 DECEMBER **1843** Five-year-old George Parramore of Taunton died from severe burns two days after his linen clothes were set alight by a red-hot poker that fell from the fire in his home. At the subsequent inquest, the coroner remarked that rinsing linen clothes in alum water might prevent such tragedies occurring in future.

17 DECEMBER **1847** Brothers Charles, Anthony and Robert Manfield were seen walking towards Backwell, where labourer John Wall was at home cooking his dinner. Suddenly, Wall heard the crash of breaking glass and saw the muzzle of a gun poking through his window. Before Wall could react, the gun was fired, peppering his thigh with shot. The gun was then withdrawn and Wall saw a man peering through the broken window. Wall shouted and the man immediately ran away.

Several people had seen the Manfield brothers heading towards Backwell, and several more saw them running in the opposite direction and noted that sixteen-year-old Charles was carrying a gun. He was arrested at his home in Nailsea and John Wall positively identified him as the man who had peered through his window.

Initially, Wall's wounds were thought to be relatively minor. However, he died from lockjaw on 29 December and Charles Manfield was charged with his wilful murder, while Robert and Anthony were charged with aiding and abetting him. The boys were tried at the Somerset Assizes in April 1848 before Mr Justice Wightman, the *Bristol Mercury* describing Charles: 'A more hardened young scoundrel was never seen.'

No evidence was offered against Robert or Anthony, who were acquitted and called as witnesses. Charles insisted that he hadn't fired the gun, blaming his brother Robert. However, he failed to convince the jury of his innocence and was sentenced to death. His sentence was later commuted to one of transportation for life.

1854 Workmates William Lewis and Edmund Horner from Hinton-St-George fought at harvest time, when Horner gave Lewis two black eyes. On 17 December, the two men were drinking together at the George Inn in Merriott when their previous argument resurfaced and Horner threatened to give Lewis two more black eyes. The two men were still arguing when they left the pub at midnight and Horner took off his coat, ready to fight. He struck Lewis in the face, at which Lewis pulled out a knife and threatened to stab him if he hit him again. Unfortunately, Horner took no notice – he punched Lewis in the face and Lewis promptly ran his knife into Horner's belly. Horner died within minutes and Lewis was charged with his wilful murder. However, the jury at the Somerset Assizes considered that Horner had provoked Lewis by hitting him. He was found guilty of the lesser offence of manslaughter and sentenced to fifteen months' imprisonment.

18 DECEMBER

High Street, Hinton-St-George. (Author's collection)

High Street, Hinton St. George.

19 DECEMBER   **1792**   A fire broke out in a house at Preston, near Yeovil. High winds blew sparks in all directions, spreading the blaze until five separate areas of the village were alight. By the time the flames were brought under control, fourteen houses had completely burned to the ground and many more were severely damaged. Thus, at the height of winter, almost 100 people were left homeless.

20 DECEMBER   **1792**   Suffering from unexplained deafness, the wife of a publican from Bath was advised by a surgeon to pour some oil of almonds into her ears to try and soften a build-up of wax. By mistake, she applied oil of vitriol, otherwise known as sulphuric acid. She died in the greatest agony.

21 DECEMBER   **1931**   An inquest was held by coroner Mr C. Leslie Rutter on the body of an unidentified man found shot on the Channel Islands boat train near Yeovil on 17 December. The man was thought to be a foreigner, aged about thirty. He had constructed a homemade electric pistol from a copper tube, two dry cell batteries and a bell push, with which he had shot himself in the head. He left behind a fifty-seven page manuscript on the subject of life after death, along with a note signed 'Frank W. Bentron', part of which read: 'As before life, so after life, a return to the negative. The conditions of pre-life have become desirable, therefore I will commit suicide. I am an atheist therefore I desire no service.' The man also left five guineas to pay for his cremation.

The inquest recorded a verdict of 'suicide whilst insane', the coroner stating that it was possible that the man had committed suicide in order to justify his obsession that there was no life after death.

22 DECEMBER   **1901**   Sarah Melhuish took her son and his friend, Eric James, to see the ice on the frozen reservoir at Chard. Sarah's attention was momentarily distracted by the rare sight of a motor car and, as she watched it, her son rushed to tell her

Fore Street, Chard. (Author's collection)

that Eric had fallen through the ice. Eric's plunge into the freezing water had been witnessed by a skater, fifteen-year-old Lawrence Hussey. Hussey inched himself along the ice and reached out to grab Eric, but the ice gave way and he too went into the reservoir. Alfred Pearce, a Great Western Railway fireman, tried to rescue the boys. He saw both boys sinking but had to pull back when he too was in danger of falling through the fragile ice into the water. Eventually the boys' bodies were retrieved later that night. As a memorial to Lawrence's bravery, the townspeople of Chard purchased an inscribed drinking trough for the town.

1856 A runaway horse and cart stopped outside the cottage near Langley **23 DECEMBER** owned by Mr Hayes, who found a man in the cart, his throat cut. The man died before medical assistance arrived. He was quickly identified as John Aplin, who had been drinking in Wiveliscombe for most of that day with a man named Thomas Nation. Known to have had at least four sovereigns in his possession earlier that day, Aplin's pockets were empty and there was blood on the insides, suggesting that whoever had robbed him had bloody hands.

Thomas Nation was apprehended the next morning and was found to have four sovereigns in his possession, as well as a bloody knife. His hands were also covered with blood. Tried at the Somerset Assizes for Aplin's murder, Nation explained the blood on his hands and clothes by claiming to have had two teeth extracted on the day of the murder, and also to have skinned his knuckles. The blood on his knife had come from slicing raw beef and Aplin's father swore that he had given him the sovereigns earlier that day. Although the evidence against Aplin was entirely circumstantial, he was found guilty and executed on 21 April 1857.

1885 Ten-year-old Edward Light was found at Long Ashton, having been **24 DECEMBER** missing from home for six days. Edward told his rescuers, Mr Bryant and Mr Cook, that he had run away because he had spent his school money. Some boys had pushed him into a pool and he had taken his wet boots off, but his feet had swollen from the cold and he was unable to get them back on. Chilled to the bone, he had clambered inside a hollow tree on the Ashton Court Estate to try and get warm and got stuck. Although he could lie down inside the tree, he was unable to extricate himself. All he could do was put one hand through a hole in the trunk and wave it in the hope of attracting attention. On the first day, he had eaten some orange peel from his pocket but, since then, had eaten and drunk nothing. Every time a cart had passed on the nearby lane he had shouted for help, but nobody answered his desperate cries until 24 December, when some children playing on the lane finally heard his shouts.

Bright, who was 'reduced almost to a skeleton', was rushed to the hospital at the Bedminster Union Workhouse. He was given liquid food and then gradually weaned onto a light diet and, by the end of the first week in January 1886, was said to be well on the way to recovery. His legs were still swollen and his feet affected by frostbite, and doctors thought that it would be some time before he could walk again. His highly relieved parents were visiting him regularly.

25 DECEMBER   **1892**   Eighteen-year-old Mary Holloway, a servant at Old House Farm, Batheaston, died from serious burns received two days earlier. Farmer Charles Milsom Smith told a later inquest that he and his wife had heard a crash coming from the farm kitchen and found Mary enveloped in flames. Smith had rushed her outside and rolled her on a bed of turnip greens until the fire was fully extinguished. However, by then, Mary had received such terrible burns to the lower half of her body that she died in hospital on Christmas morning. It was thought that the paraffin in a lamp in the kitchen had become heated due to the wick being turned up too high, causing the lamp to explode.

26 DECEMBER   **1882**   Ann 'Nance' Rowsell was enjoying a quiet drink with friends in the Crown and Tower Inn in Taunton, when Frederick Ripley entered the pub and said, 'Nance, I want to speak with you.' The couple left together and, minutes later, Nance staggered back, bleeding from a single stab wound in her throat. A cab was summoned to take her to hospital but she bled to death shortly after her arrival.

 Nance and Ripley had been 'walking out' for four years but Nance had ended their relationship because of Ripley's jealousy. Arrested and charged with her murder, Ripley told the police, 'I done it.' Tried before Mr Justice Baggallay at the Somerset Assizes, Ripley insisted that he had been drinking at the time and had never intended to hurt his former girlfriend. In a written statement, he told the court that he was destitute, mainly because he had spent all his money on clothes for Ann, including the jacket that she was wearing when she died. Believing that Ann had ended their relationship because he had no money, he had asked her for the return of the jacket and, when she refused and slapped his face, he had tried to cut it off her, accidentally stabbing her in the throat as he did so.

 His defence counsel argued that Ripley was insane, due to the effects of drink, and that the offence was manslaughter rather than murder, since Ann had provoked him by slapping him. However, the jury disagreed, finding twenty-one-year-old Ripley guilty, although recommending mercy on the grounds of his youth and previous good character. Sentenced to death, Ripley was later reprieved and sent to Portland Prison in Dorset.

27 DECEMBER   **1663**   For several months, thirteen-year-old Elizabeth Hill from Stoke Trister had been subject to fits, which lasted anything up to four hours. During these fits, she alleged that a woman named Elizabeth Style (or Styles) appeared to her and tormented her. Eventually, the girl's father, Richard, challenged Style, telling her that he believed she had bewitched his daughter. He accused Style in front of witnesses, who urged him to make an official complaint to the authorities.

 On 27 December, Elizabeth's fits were worse than usual. Foaming at the mouth, she was seen by several witnesses, including the local vicar, to rise out of her chair and hover a few feet above it, and it took the combined strength of four or five people to hold her down. Thorns appeared spontaneously in her skin, leaving bleeding wounds when they were removed. When Elizabeth came round, she accused Elizabeth Style of pricking her.

A warrant was obtained for Style's arrest but when Richard Hill tried to serve it, his horse sat down on its haunches and refused to move. Eventually, Elizabeth Style was tried at the Somerset Assizes for witchcraft. She admitted selling her soul to the Devil for sixpence, since when she had the ability to summon a spirit named Abin, who would do harm on her behalf. Style confessed to regularly meeting the Devil on the common near Trister Gate, when she and two other women, Ann Bishop and Alice Duke, would stick thorns into wax models of people, saying, 'A plague on thee, I'll spite thee.' Style named a lengthy list of people who regularly joined her in worshipping the Devil, saying that she had caused Elizabeth Hill to be pricked because her father had once called her a witch.

Other villagers accused Style of causing them to be pricked and several women testified at her trial that they had seen a fly coming out of her head, which Style said was her 'familiar'. When her head was examined, there was a red, raw place where the fly had emerged, which healed within minutes. Elizabeth Style was eventually found guilty and sentenced to be burned to death. She died in prison before the time of her appointed execution.

28 DECEMBER **1876** After an argument with his wife Mary Ann, during which she threatened to leave him, Philip Hickman of Taunton cut first her throat and then his own. Fortunately both survived their injuries and Hickman was tried at the Somerset Assizes in March 1877 for attempted murder.

Hickman was an extremely jealous husband, who believed that his wife was being intimate with another man. Whenever he confronted Mary Ann about her supposed infidelities, she responded by telling him that he must be mad. Hickman interpreted this as a sign that she was scheming to get him locked away in a lunatic asylum, leaving the way clear for her supposed lover.

In his own defence, Hickman stated that he was drunk at the time of the incident and had injured his wife accidentally. The judge, Lord Chief Justice Cockburn, pointed out that even if his wife had been unfaithful to him, that was no excuse for attacking her with a weapon. However, Hickman was a large, powerful man and Cockburn seemed to believe that he could easily have murdered his wife, had he intended to. Thus, when the jury found Hickman guilty of unlawful wounding, Cockburn sentenced him fairly leniently to twelve months' imprisonment with hard labour, adding that if he couldn't treat his wife better, he should leave her.

29 DECEMBER **1886** At about one o'clock in the morning, Revd G.O.L. Thomson from King's College, Taunton, heard groans coming from a field behind the college. He and a porter went to investigate and found fifty-five-year-old John Trood lying in a ditch. Only his head was not covered by water. Thomson summoned assistance and Trood was extricated from the ditch and conveyed to Taunton Hospital but was pronounced dead on arrival. Almost-empty bottles of gin and brandy were taken from his pockets; it was thought that he had accidentally stumbled into the ditch and was too drunk to get out.

30 DECEMBER   **1857** Sarah Palmer of Stoke-sub-Hampden gave birth in July 1857, after which she complained of lowness of spirit and pains in her head. Surgeons Mr Walker and Mr Stuckey both prescribed medicines for her, but nothing seemed to help. In desperation, Sarah consulted a 'quack', Esther Peasdon. She gave Sarah some medicine, charging her 4s, but the concoction made Sarah sick. Sarah complained to Esther, who urged her to carry on taking it, saying that it would do her good. However, Sarah's condition worsened.

On 30 December, William Palmer called in Mr Walker. Walker found Sarah 'insensible' and prescribed medicine for her but she was too ill to take it. Two hours later, Walker visited her again, this time administering the medicine himself, but it was too late and Sarah died on 1 January 1858. Walker conducted a post-mortem and could find no explanation for her death. He sent the contents of her stomach and the remains of Esther's potion to analyst Mr Herepath, who identified mandrake in both.

Esther Peasdon was tried for Sarah's manslaughter at the Somerset Assizes, where prosecuting counsel Mr Edwards made a catastrophic error by neglecting to call surgeon Mr Stuckey as a witness. The judge pointed out that, without examining Stuckey, there was no way of knowing what his medicine contained, or of establishing that he hadn't mistakenly prescribed some dangerous drug, which had ultimately killed Sarah Palmer. The jury agreed and acquitted Esther Peasdon.

31 DECEMBER   **1898** Fishmonger William Rufus Crook rampaged around Bath in a drunken frenzy, assaulting Police Sergeant Bates, who attempted to place him under arrest. When he appeared before magistrates in Bath early in 1899, Crook was fined 20s for being drunk and disorderly and 40s for the assault on Bates. Magistrates warned Crook that, as this was his fifty-second appearance before them for similar offences, his next would result in a prison sentence.

BIBLIOGRAPHY

Aberdeen Journal
Bath Chronicle / Bath Weekly Chronicle
Bath Herald
Birmingham Post / Birmingham Daily Post
Bridgwater Mercury
The Bristol Mercury / Bristol Mercury and Daily Post
Bury and Norwich Post
The Daily Chronicle
The Era
Evening Standard
The Examiner
The Glasgow Herald
The Guardian / Manchester Guardian
Illustrated Police News
Leeds Mercury
Leicester Chronicle
Liverpool Mercury
Lloyd's Weekly Newspaper
The Morning Post
Reynolds's Newspaper
Sheffield and Rotherham Independent
Sherborne Journal
Taunton Courier
The Times
Trewman's Exeter Flying Post / Plymouth and Cornish Advertiser
Western Flying Post
Western Gazette and Flying Post
Western Mail

INDEX